D1500083

NIVERSITY OF WINNIPEG (LIBRARY) 515 Portage Avenue, Winnipeg, MB R3B 2E9 Canada

DISCARDED

AFRICA'S ELUSIVE QUEST FOR DEVELOPMENT

Africa's Elusive Quest For Development

Mathurin C. Houngnikpo

HC
79
E5 -
H67
2006

palgrave
macmillan

AFRICA'S ELUSIVE QUEST FOR DEVELOPMENT
© Mathurin C. Houngnikpo, 2006.

All rights reserved. No part of this book may be used or reproduced in any manner whatsoever without written permission except in the case of brief quotations embodied in critical articles or reviews.

First published in 2006 by
PALGRAVE MACMILLAN™
175 Fifth Avenue, New York, N.Y. 10010 and
Houndmills, Basingstoke, Hampshire, England RG21 6XS
Companies and representatives throughout the world.

PALGRAVE MACMILLAN is the global academic imprint of the Palgrave Macmillan division of St. Martin's Press, LLC and of Palgrave Macmillan Ltd. Macmillan® is a registered trademark in the United States, United Kingdom and other countries. Palgrave is a registered trademark in the European Union and other countries.

ISBN 1–4039–7124–2

Library of Congress Cataloging-in-Publication Data

Houngnikpo, Mathurin C.
    Africa's elusive quest for development / Mathurin C. Houngnikpo.
        p. cm.
    Includes bibliographical references and index.
    ISBN 1–4039–7124–2 (alk. paper)
        1. Sustainable development—Africa. I. Title.

HC79.E5H67 2006
338.96'07—dc22   2005057425

A catalogue record for this book is available from the British Library.

Design by Newgen Imaging Systems (P) Ltd., Chennai, India.

First edition: February 2006

10 9 8 7 6 5 4 3 2 1

Printed in the United States of America.

Transferred to digital printing in 2007.

To my mother
Maman AFIYÉYÉ ANDÉE COMBETHÉ
popularly known as
DO N'DÉ TÉ
whose audacity, hardwork, and outlook on life
remain my guiding principles.

Contents

List of Abbreviations

AIDS	Acquired Immune Deficiency Syndrome
ARVs	Antiretroviral Drugs
AU	African Union
COMESA	Common Market for Eastern and Southern Africa
ECA	Economic Commission for Africa
ECOWAS	Economic Community of West African States
ESAF	Enhanced Structural Adjustment Facility
FAR	Forces Armées Rwandanises (Rwandan Armed Forces)
FDI	Foreign Direct Investment
GDP	Gross Domestic Product
GNP	Gross National Product
HIV	Human Immunodeficiency Virus
IFI	International Financial Institution
IMF	International Monetary Fund
LPA	Lagos Plan of Action
NEPAD	New Partnership for Africa's Development
OAU	Organization of African Unity
OECD	Organization of Economic Cooperation and Development
PARMEHUTU	Party of the Movement for the Emancipation of Hutu/Bahutu
PTA	Preferential Trade Area for Eastern and Southern African States
REC	Regional Economic Commission
RPF	Rwandan Patriotic Front
SADC	Southern African Development Community
SAP	Structural Adjustment Program
TNC	Transnational Corporation

UN	United Nations
UNAIDS	Joint United Nations Programme on HIV/AIDS
UNAMIR	United Nations Assistance Mission in Rwanda
UNDP	United Nations Development Program
UNICEF	United Nations Children's Fund
WB	World Bank

Acknowledgments

This work grew out of the observation of numerous challenges encountered by the Africans since independence in state building, conflict prevention and resolution, and (re)democratization. Much to my frustration, the wealthiest continent, in terms of natural endowments, remains the poorest for lack of an effective leadership.

A number of colleagues and friends read parts of the manuscript at various stages and offered valuable criticism and suggestions. I owe a debt of gratitude to all of them. There is in particular one person to whom I literally owe this enterprise and who deserves special thanks: Amy E. Eckert of the Political Science Department at the Metropolitan State College of Denver. Her remarkable editorial talents enabled the final version of this book to take shape.

I would also like to thank the many individuals who helped bring this project to fruition. Besides anonymous reviewers, I wish to extend my heartfelt gratitude to Gabriella Pearce, Lynne Vande Stouwe, and the entire staff at Palgrave MacMillan.

While these people have been of tremendous help, they are not responsible for any errors of fact or interpretation. If I neglected to take some of their good counsel or heed some of their criticisms, that failure is mine alone.

Author's Biography

Mathurin C. Houngnikpo is Visiting Assistant Professor in the Program of International Studies at Miami University of Ohio, Oxford, OH (USA). He holds a PhD in Political Science from the University of Paris VIII, Saint-Denis, France, and a PhD in International Studies from the University of Denver (USA). Dr. Houngnikpo is the author of *Not Yet Democracy: West Africa's Slow Farewell to Authoritarianism* (with B. N'Diaye and A. Saine, 2005); *L'Illusion Démocratique en Afrique* (2004); *Des Mots pour les Maux de l'Afrique* (2004); *Determinants of Democratization in Africa* (2001), and other books and articles. His interests include democratization, security, civil-military relations, development, and conflict resolution in Africa.

Introduction

Africa lies low and is wretched. She is the maimed and crippled arm of humanity. Her great powers are wasted. Dislocation and anguish have reached every joint. Her condition in every point calls for succor—moral, social, domestic, political, commercial, and intellectual.

Alexander Crummell, *Africa and America.*

The end of the cold war has changed the nature of politics in Africa, prompting close observers of the African scene to speak of a new era for democracy and political reconciliation or even a second independence for the continent.[1] The scope and momentum of change everywhere points to the emergence of a safer, more democratic, and less violent Africa. To a great extent, support by great powers has vanished because of the continent's eroding strategic importance, forcing African leaders to face new realities. Indeed, by the 1980s, Africa was declining in importance as a site for superpower rivalry, and apart from some strategic minerals, there were few other economic interests at stake. Political demands that had fallen on deaf ears for decades resurfaced with more intensity and different results. The tsunami-like wave of democratization that began to lap the shores of the continent dictated new standards of behavior to African leaders. Even regimes desperately trying to push back the day of reckoning, hoping to weather a passing vogue for democracy through intimidation and patronage, have given in to demands for democratic reforms. In Decalo's words:

> While it is difficult to assess the *longrun* significance of what is currently transpiring in Africa, it is equally difficult to underestimate the magnitude of the change itself that is sweeping the continent. It is clear the pressures for democracy are continent-wide, and are irresistible. Even existing democracies have felt the heat, some moving to offer a more equitable share of social, economic and political power to opposition groups . . . in an effort to avoid the turmoil in neighboring countries.[2]

Internal and external pressures seem to have brought to a halt decades of Machiavellian personal rule marked by plots and faked coups, factionalisms, purges, rehabilitations, clientelism, corruption, and mismanagement. Anglin echoes the new optimism when he describes the end of

> the supremacy of the party over the government, the vanguard party concept, politicization of the public service and security services, monopoly of party power in perpetuity, subordination of mass organizations (such as trade unions, women's and youth groups), the media, etc., of party control, the cult of personality, abuses of power including corruption, permanent states of emergency.[3]

Against their will, African leaders had to introduce political and economic reforms in their countries. Unfortunately, real changes have yet to occur because African democracy, when it does happen, is far from being genuine and cannot by itself right several decades of wrongs. Several years later, the feeling that Africa might be heading for total insolvency remains palpable. According to Ottaway:

> Domestic pressure, coupled with foreign carrots and sticks, has brought about some remarkable changes. Political language in Africa in the 1990s has become virtually unrecognizable to those familiar with the rhetoric of the 1960s–1980s: at the center of the discourse are no longer the downtrodden popular masses in whose name governments long justified authoritarian rule, but the right of an organized civil society to demand transparency and accountability from the government. Political systems [began] to look different from the single-party model that dominated Africa for decades.[4]

Deaf to the paeans of donor countries that welcomed the advent of liberal democracies, celebrated the merits of good governance, praised the virtues of decentralized cooperation, and gave their blessing to an emerging African civil society, one scholar postulated that events on the continent more closely resembled "a return to the 'heart of darkness'" of senseless violence.[5] Unfortunately, inhuman conflicts in Africa only vindicate those who predict chaos and anarchy on the continent. Despite its wealth, Africa remains the poorest continent, lagging on all fronts. In spite of decades of economic assistance and foreign aid, Africa enters the twenty-first century containing many of the world's poorest countries.

Several decades after independence, much of Africa remains in a state of chaos, still equated with poor socioeconomic conditions, corruption, war, loss of political direction and legitimate leadership, widespread crime and unemployment, disintegration of the leaderless peasants and urban masses, and the continued plunder of Africa's wealth. For most Africans, independence has been more of a desperate struggle for survival rather than a steady path to development. In Cohen's words:

> Since the collapse of the European colonial system, Sub-Saharan Africa has sunk into a state of *de-development*. The world's poorest region, it is geographically atomized, torn by recurrent conflicts among and within its . . . national states. These states essentially follow the territorial frameworks that were established during the colonial period. There is growing consensus that these national frameworks are flawed because they have failed to account for many of the drives for territorial sovereignty of ethnic, tribal, and religious groups that are subsumed within them [emphasis added].[6]

Africa's participation in the world economy has declined alarmingly over the past fifty years in terms of Gross Domestic Product (GDP), exports, and foreign investment. Its share of global GDP in purchasing power parity terms fell by a third between 1950 and 2000 while its share of world exports shrank by two-thirds.[7] Meanwhile the continent's share of global population grew as its birthrate accelerated during the twentieth century. Unless production increases more rapidly than population, more food must be produced, more schools and housing built, more healthcare provided just to maintain the existing, quite low standard of living. All economic, political, and social indicators point to the sad reality that much of the continent is in a desperate plight. At both the 2002 Barcelona UNAIDS Conference and the 2003 International AIDS Conference held in Nairobi, Kenya, leading researchers depicted quite a bleak prognosis for the continent. Unless some dramatic actions are taken, Africa will lose millions of lives to HIV/AIDS.[8] Yet, African leaders remain almost oblivious to the impact of infectious disease on their nations' stability and prosperity. Judging by per capita income, economic growth, or foreign debt statistics,[9] Africa's deepening crisis is immediately apparent. Some believe that the continent is collapsing and turning into "a depository for the ills of humanity,"[10] a view sustained by apocalyptic images of "an impoverished Africa in a spiral of conflict."[11] It is quite hard, in the current state of Africa's politics and economy, to escape the image of a shipwrecked continent. Although a few nations have managed to make modest gains, every analysis of Africa's stalled development takes place within the bankruptcy paradigm, with focus on the blind alleys of "development." Ellis very eloquently stated that

> If there has been a key theme of the literature on modern Africa since
> 1945, it has been that of "development," a concept used to justify policies
> said to favour national political integration and economic growth, as
> well as the motive for massive transfers of funds and other forms of
> assistance from rich countries to Africa. In recent years there has been
> widespread agreement that Africa's development, however it is defined
> exactly, has run into serious problems.[12]

Either the theories of development were never meant to work in
Africa or Africa's political leaders never wanted development for their
continent. From the early days of independence, several scholars have
spent their lifetimes on economic development of "backward" continents in general, and of Africa in particular.[13] Unfortunately, their theories hardly changed the fate of Africa. Rather, there were periods of
cumulative crises that some attributed to a flaw in the development models and ideologies underlying African countries' policies and structures.[14]

Development means a capacity for self-sustaining growth. It means
that an economy must register advances that, in turn, promote further
progress. As such, development remains elusive on the continent. In
his evaluation of Africa's bleak picture, Samir Amin posits that "the
1960s were marked by the great hope that [Africans] were at the start
of an irreversible process of development throughout the third world,
and especially Africa. But [Africa's independence] has become the age
of disenchantment. Development is at a standstill, its theory is in
crisis, its ideologies in doubt. It is generally agreed that development
in Africa is bankrupt."[15] The dimensions of the African tragedy can be
described most accurately as a failure of development, making the
continent an abnormality. Since the end of World War II, former colonial powers have tried to help African countries attain higher standards
of living by providing foreign aid, investing in technology, fostering
education, controlling population growth, and both making and
forgiving loans on condition of institutional reforms. However, none
of these solutions has delivered as promised because African leaders
failed to apply economic principles to practical policies.

With extraordinary effort and innovation, a great deal of literature
has indeed tried to tackle Africa's elusive quest for economic development, suggesting remedies of all kinds. Scholars and analysts have
examined Africa's travails through different conceptual prisms, yielding
an assortment of prescriptions for policy and strategy. In recent years,
the World Bank, the Organization of Economic Cooperation and
Development (OECD), and the United Nations Development
Program (UNDP) have all produced important surveys and reports

on Africa that constitute an essential corpus of documentation. Some individuals have also produced general treatments of their own in the form of essays,[16] and the French government has commissioned a wide-ranging survey of African development with a focus on the French contribution.[17]

In their scrutiny of the diagnostic, analysts have correctly pointed to the harm wrought by European colonization.[18] Indeed, colonization created unfair and exploitative relationships that continue to affect Africa in a major way. Naively, African monarchs fell prey to European deception, thereby contributing, albeit unwillingly, to the destruction and cruel exploitation of their continent. The unflinching desire to provide European factories with raw materials made colonialism a harsh and unforgiving undertaking. Some determinist views even contend that the transfer of power in Africa never allowed a "thorough-going radical transformation through which descent into crisis might have been averted."[19] Without denying the impact of colonialism on Africa, any serious new analysis of the crisis on the continent should go beyond laying all the blame on Europe. Although the colonial legacy explains some of Africa's economic dependency, political disorder, and social decay, postcolonial African leaders have played a debilitating role in their continent's plight. Authoritarian rule and weak states combined with the international political environment to create deep disincentives to Africa's development. Consequently, the continent is marred with stagnant economies that yield meager financial returns that end up in private bank accounts in Europe.

At independence, the major tasks confronting Africa's new leaders consisted in constructing stable political regimes and raising the standard of living for their peoples. Owing to the European scramble for Africa, the nation-state became the chosen political model everywhere. The ideal of national unity informed postcolonial leaders' political speeches, but the diversity of their populations demanded guarantees of political pluralism. However, most African leaders quickly abandoned the partially democratic institutions adopted at independence. After liberation, these leaders placed the problems of political unification and economic development ahead of the creation of a fair multiparty system of government. Soon, power passed into the hands of a political elite made up of civilian politicians and ambitious military leaders. Authoritarian regimes set in, bringing instability and misrule.

African leaders sought ever-greater power by manipulating parliaments, extorting state funds for their personal enrichment, and creating mass parties designed to serve and glorify them. In Ake's words, "what was adopted was not so much an ideology of development as a strategy of power that merely capitalized on the objective need for development."[20] Little or no political freedom existed, and enemies, both real and imaginary, ended up imprisoned or assassinated. Lack of real political stability added to permanent power struggles and unprecedented civil and military violence. Consequently, Africa has been described by various scholars as a continent betrayed, in chaos, in self-destruction, in crisis, existing only in name, being predatory or kleptocratic, or having collapsed into anarchy and viciousness.[21] Although these images depict a sad picture of the continent, they largely seem accurate.

African leaders seem to lack the capacity and willingness to develop an institutional environment conducive to good governance, entrenchment of democracy, peace and security, growth and development, and poverty reduction. Although they seem very imaginative in generating their "wealth," African leaders have yet to lead their continent to higher grounds. Poverty, an offshoot of social injustice, became a tool used by the ruling elite to blackmail their cadres. Because of Africa's deep-seated belief in unity, geographic realities, economic interdependence, and cultural and political background, integration became the natural policy choice for dealing with the challenges of security and welfare. Yet, effective regional political and economic integration has eluded the continent for decades. Although such global factors as the North/South divide and globalization do impact negatively on Africa, perennial domestic calculations and short-sightedness are the true culprits responsible for defeating integration on the continent.

Many saw a new dawn in the end of colonialism. However nominal or "flag" independence failed to bring true freedom. While old-style colonialism has gone away, neo-colonialism moved in to recreate the economic interests of colonial rule. In Ama Ata Aidoo's words:

> On a continent whose natural resources continue to be plundered for the benefit of outsiders, where "development" is made according to the terms of foreign debt servicing, and in which social cohesion is undermined by geopolitical agendas set above or beyond the peoples of Africa, the *post* of postcolonial is not only a fiction but "pernicious."[22]

Africans are learning that the colonial idea does not end with independence, national flags, or even indigenous leaders at the helm of their countries. While necessary, formal independence is not sufficient to take the continent out of its misery. Besides the competitive global environment, several key obstacles make the journey to prosperity in Africa difficult. The search for economic development is thwarted by high levels of inefficiency and corruption due to the lack of a *res publica*, that is a Weberian state able to fairly allocate resources. Rather, the workings of the political economy are complicated or disrupted because those in public and private organizations cannot assume predictable behavior and observation of rules. In recent years, a number of economists and political scientists have come to identify the quality of public institutions and the civic culture that underpins them as vital factors determining the development of states and nations. At the root of the culture deemed required for economic growth are social attitudes developed over long periods of time.[23]

Although corruption goes as far back as human existence, in Africa it is especially pervasive, demoralizing the population, and draining the productive energy. Reliance on exporting primary commodities while importing most manufactured goods and advanced services from developed countries turned out to be a misguided strategy. The euphoria of the early days of independence was marked by the belief that liberation would bring not only political freedom but also the economic prosperity that colonialism withheld. However, events on the continent have proved otherwise. Instead of being transferred from European minorities to the African majority, wealth either remains in the hands of non-Africans or is controlled by the political elite.

While one cannot downplay the colonial legacy and its consequences on Africa, the real locus of Africa's current crises lies rather in African leaders' behavior. In a candid acknowledgment of the problem, the "civilized military" President Obasanjo who has yet to take Nigeria out of its socioeconomic problems, maintains:

> The main causes of Africa's economic and other problems were political and stemmed from a failure to establish democratic practices in African countries. The lack of democratic institutions led to a failure to "stimulate the spring sources of creativity in our people." Oppressive regimes led to uproar and internal crisis. Between the beginning of the 1960s and the end of 1980s, Africa experienced some sixty coups d'état and countless other coup attempts. Internal conflicts displaced masses of people, both within their countries of origin and across international borders. The outflow of refugees often resulted in the destabilization of neighboring countries and even of entire regions.[24]

Ellis concurs that while

> some scholars have attributed a part of the explanation for the widespread problems encountered by many African countries to the state system which they inherited at independence, for over a decade now some of the most thoughtful African writers have declared categorically that at least some African countries suffer from "simply and squarely a failure of leadership."[25]

African leaders, though aware of their continent's economic marginalization, failed to take appropriate measures to stop Africa's degradation. With huge debt, increasing dependence on foreign aid, and desperate need for foreign investment, Africa became vulnerable to outside states' policies. Although African leaders had repeatedly evoked the urgency of regional and, ultimately, continental unification, they have done little to achieve this unity. Regionalism, Ahmad Aly argues persuasively, is the most appropriate strategy for the achievement of autonomous, self-sustained development in Africa. Tracing the causes of failed attempts at economic cooperation in the continent, he cites in particular the adoption of inappropriate integration schemes, the multiplicity of overlapping arrangements, the dominance of politics, and, most fundamentally, the widening gap between aspirations and reality.[26]

A survey of regional organizations in Africa displays a whole array of institutions, huge bureaucracies, most of which overlap one another. At its inception in 1963, the Organization of African Unity (OAU) was established mainly to accelerate the recovery of Africa's economy. But it failed due in part to the lack of political will, and has been replaced by the African Union (AU). Other such regional institutions as the Economic Community of West African States (ECOWAS) set up in 1975, the Preferential Trade Area for Eastern and Southern African States (PTA) founded in 1981 and replaced in 1993 by the Common Market for Eastern and Southern Africa (COMESA), or the Southern African Development Community (SADC), to name but a few, remain mostly huge bureaucracies without hardly any real achievements. Alarmed by the economic nightmare of their continent, African leaders met in Lagos, Nigeria, in 1980. The Lagos Plan of Action (LPA) was therefore designed to tackle the economic difficulties facing Africa. However, more than two decades later, the ambitious plan has not been implemented. Recently, a new scheme was designed once again to try to right several decades of development failure: the New Partnership for Africa's Development (NEPAD). Whether the AU or NEPAD will succeed where the OAU and the LPA have failed depends, once again, on African leaders.

The early 1990s brought high hopes about the prospects of Africa, but, a decade later the balance sheet remains almost depressing. Once again African leaders have displayed their inability to grasp the opportunities that presented themselves, leaving the impression that Africa is politically immature. With the end of the cold war and consequent disappearance of superpower conflict from the African political and security equations, there was a belief, now shown to have been overoptimistic and naïve, that a major and malignant influence had been removed from the continent. This was seen as a golden opportunity for Africa to make a new start politically and to achieve a greater level of continental, regional, national, and human security than it had previously enjoyed. Unfortunately, this opportunity seems to have been missed and Africa has descended once again into anarchy.[27] Although African leaders are lip-synching the democratic tune, they do not mean to see profound political reforms on the continent because of the stakes and implications of such changes. Amid a great deal of rhetoric, there is very little genuine alteration of behavior as demonstrated by several attempts, some successful, to amend constitutions in order to keep power.

Even those believed to be "dynamic and assertive," the best representatives of Africa's "new leaders," and the epitome of a new generation of statesmen,[28] have yet to show a serious alternative to the failed policies of their predecessors. There is a crisis of expectations arising from the belief that change in itself would be automatically positive and that the very existence of a plurality of parties would mean more accountable and efficient government. Although democracy seems to be the current catchword, strong, centralized, and autocratic incumbent leaders are bent on clinging onto power and will not allow opposition parties to fare well in elections. It is clear that African leaders, civilian as well as "civilianized military" are still dragging their feet, or strenuously haggling with pro-democracy movements, aware that they are unlikely to remain in power in any new political order. Despite civil society's vibrancy, "some die-hard authoritarian regimes refuse to accept the message that the old political ways of post-independence Africa are no longer acceptable."[29]

Africans will have to put pressure on their leaders to operate within open legal frameworks that promote democracy. African governments will remain disguised autocracy as long as the effective power of elected officials is limited, or political party competition is restricted, or the freedom and fairness of elections is compromised and economic, civil, and political liberties are limited. Until recently, widespread social disaffection, declining regime legitimacy, and weakening state capacity have been marked politics in Africa.[30] Taking advantage of this second chance, Africans must strive to fundamentally alter both politics and economy on the continent.

The lack of improvement in living standards brought about the end of African citizens' acquiescence. Of course, the democratically elected governments in Africa have no greater chance of healing their chronically sick economies because democracy, by itself, is not a panacea. However, governmental accountability may lead to reduced corruption and increased efficiency. At the end of the twentieth century, the mood on the continent has come full circle, repeating the euphoria of independence in a joyful optimism about the dawn of an African renaissance, but this time around there is the sobering experience of more than four decades of difficulties in confronting the complex issues inherent in the creation of new independent states, and of the obstacles in the way of establishing continental unity, which remains an unfulfilled dream.[31]

Although Africa's political new dawn is exciting, democracy needs to be molded within a strong set of rules to allow Africans to truly enjoy the rights they are entitled to, but also encourage them to fulfill their duties as citizens. Former UN Secretary-General Boutros Boutros-Ghali did not exaggerate when he characterized democracy as "essential to the protection of human rights."[32] Democratic government should create a political atmosphere in which none of the major political actors can consider an alternative to democratic processes, and in which no institution or group can veto the action of democratically elected decision makers.[33] Africans need, among other things, a new framework that allows a clear separation of powers among the executive, legislative, and judiciary branches, *habeas corpus*, respect for the rights of minorities, press freedom, and a nonpolitical professional army. Besides competition, inclusiveness, and civil liberties,[34] Africa's emerging democracies must create a socioeconomic environment capable of sustaining political stability on the continent. The charge against the current wave of democratization in Africa is that, in most cases, it has not performed its most basic function of protecting the ruled from the ruler.[35] Unless the rule of law prevails, and the socioeconomic conditions improve, Africa's political and economic "renaissance" might prove illusory.

Having acknowledged that Africa's problems are primarily the result of underdevelopment and abject poverty, Deng draws a painful picture of the continent:

> Africa's list of problems calling for urgent attention must place internal conflicts highest in the order of priorities, followed by human rights violations, dictatorial or authoritarian regimes, and flawed economic policies, all of which are closely interconnected in a chain of cause and effect. A correlative list of solutions would include conflict resolution, human rights protection, democracy, and sustainable development.[36]

At independence, Africans were tacitly asked to abandon their traditional communitarian security for an individualistic society created elsewhere and under totally different circumstances. It is not surprising then that its attractions only lasted a few years, once Africans realized that their votes did nothing to free them from the oppression of hunger, poverty, and disease. Changing the course of Africa's nightmare requires excellent governance with responsibility, accountability, and active participation on the part of the citizens, and transparency and creative vision on the part of honest, passionate, inspired, and enlightened leaders. Without improved governance in Africa, sustained growth will not occur, because behind problems of economic mismanagement and corruption are political problems of leadership, interest group pressures, patronage politics, a lack of transparency and probity in government decision making, and an absence of public accountability. Although blame for the bleak current state of affairs in Africa can, to some extent, be leveled against the burden of colonialism and contemporary international political and economic circumstances, the bulk of the responsibility rests squarely on the shoulders of the African political elite.

Structure of the Book

This book investigates African political, economic, and social crises from a perspective other than the oft-told tale of colonialism and the cold war as the main cause of Africa's problems. Instead, European colonization is considered a given, in an attempt to define the unknown quantity of the equation. The first chapter provides a brief historical overview of Africa's current predicament. After acknowledging the damage done by colonialism, the crux of the continent's misfortune—its leadership—is evaluated. Until recently, much of postindependence Africa was marred by weak authoritarian regimes. Despite the variety of leadership forms, ideologies, and political institutions, politics was restrictive and autocratic. African leaders have exercised considerable leeway in the use of power, with catastrophic consequences. The second chapter takes issue with the nature of the ongoing democratization on the continent. After the early euphoria it generated, democratic transition seems to be running out of steam in Africa, raising important questions about the willingness of the leadership and its outside supporters to see a genuine new dawn on the continent. A decade after transitions from authoritarianism burst onto the African scene, several countries that have undergone democratic reform are now experiencing immense struggles to institutionalize democracy. Disillusionment has set in as the monotony of single-party dominance has been replaced by hybrid regimes that also fall short of the democratic ideal. The stakes seem too high for both incumbent power holders and their "patrons" to afford the establishment of true accountable regimes in Africa.

The third chapter looks at the root cause of Africa's debacle—the African state. The very nature of the African state permits the kind of personal rule exhibited on the continent. Postindependence leaders were not adequately trained to operate a government system on a national scale. Although they inherited the essential machinery of government, they failed to adapt to their own purposes the structures of power established within the former colonial state, putting in place a state that served the few as opposed to the majority. The lack of a Weberian state capable of pulling all the national resources toward economic development and social progress explains, to a great deal, why rich Africa lags behind every other continent. The fourth chapter examines one of Africa's debilitating diseases, corruption, which allows the position of power to be used toward generating personal wealth. Through a deliberate blurring of public and private spheres of the state, politicians and civil servants of all ranks engage in bribery, corruption, and sheer looting. Because of the weakness of civil and political institutions, and the very nature of the state in Africa, corruption is widespread. With prominent political leaders indulging in corrupt practices, lesser civil servants follow suit in behaving as if they were also granted a "license to steal."[37]

The fifth chapter explores Africa at its lowest point in history by describing why and how the continent has been marginalized, and by comparing and contrasting the early hopes and expectations of postindependence Africa with subsequent disappointment. Particular attention is given to conflicts, the Rwandan tragedy, and the scourge of HIV/AIDS because of its current and future impact on the continent. The "lost decade" of the 1980s, offered very little hope to the African population, a condition that remained in place until the early 1990s. The sixth chapter explains the need for a paradigm shift in light of changing perspectives on development and new assessments of governance. While the violence and determination of the independence struggle presaged a similar dedication to economic, political, and social development, the state of the continent is far below expectations. In face of that painful reality, a new map is required to chart a different course of action. In a Kuhnian sense,[38] a paradigm shift is necessary if Africa is to fare better in an age of globalization.

The last chapter elucidates the components of the Herculean task ahead for Africans if their continent is to come out of its current predicament. A genuine new dawn requires truly giving power to the people, a vigilant civil society, a patriotic and professional military, a transformed citizenry, and a new breed of leaders.

Admittedly, Reno's description of warlord politics is not encouraging:

> Rulers reject the pursuit of a broader project of creating a state that serves a collective good or even of creating institutions that are capable of developing independent perspectives and acting on behalf of interests distinct from the rulers' personal exercise of power. Economic development is abjured when it threatens to put resources into the hands of those who might use them to challenge the rulers' position. Consequently, anxious rulers contract a wide array of economic roles to outsiders, in part to deny resources to internal rivals and to use outsiders' skills and connections to gather as much wealth as possible. Rulers then convert wealth into political resources, buying the loyalty of some and buying weapons to coerce others and thus gather more resources and so on.[39]

Before such a bewildering scenario of wars, conflicts, economic stagnation, political instability, poverty, and underdevelopment, one can still see a tiny ray of hope. However, tackling Africa's huge problems will take more than new acronyms and institutions. For African countries to turn the tide, they will have to meet the challenge of building the three pillars of sustainable growth—capital accumulation, productivity gains, and institutional reforms—in order to combat long-term abject poverty. Besides obvious economic indicators, elements of genuine change in Africa must also include measures of governance, efficiency and democracy of institutions, and an appropriate climate for business. A reversal of the political, economic, and social plight of Africa lies in better policies, good governance, and, more importantly, a new type of African—leader and citizen.

Chapter 1

A Synopsis of Africa's Plight

Some people will blame our colonial oppressors. Well in some cases part of it is true but a whole lot of the blame should be put squarely on our own shoulders . . . Independence was thought to be the beginning of the golden era where political freedom and expression, freedom of association, free enterprise, economic prosperity, less ethnocentrism, responsibility and accountability of each and every one prevailed. These lofty ideals never happened because we replaced white imperialism with the black one.

Ghana Drum, March 12, 1992.

In the name of their *mission civilisatrice* (civilizing mission),[1] of taming the "savages," Europeans returned to Africa and despoiled the continent of material and human resources.[2] They left no stone unturned in their search for wealth, and Carter and O'Meara maintain rightly that "Africa has suffered the rape of its people through the slave trade . . . and the exploitation of its natural resources."[3] After realizing the true goal of European presence on their continent, Africans started fighting back. More than a century after they reappeared on the continent, Europeans faced a continent-wide liberation struggle. Whether through peaceful negotiation or armed struggle, most African countries were granted their independence in the 1960s.[4] Unfortunately, African leaders' eagerness to become free prevented them from catching Europeans' subterfuge. To quench their thirst for independence, they accepted a hollow victory. Most anticolonial nationalists had been too busy organizing the campaign against colonial rule to give much thought to the future of their countries postindependence. Their most crucial weakness was blindness to the foresight of imperial designs and goals in Africa.

European powers tactfully designed a flawed political arrangement and handed to African leaders, a "dependent" independence that could not allow the continent to function on its own. Through various schemes, agreements and *accords de coopération*, European powers made sure they still held a grip on their former colonies. In reality, independence and the cooperation agreements were interwoven. The acceptance of the latter by African states was a precondition for the attainment of the former. Although the post–cold war environment allows some scholars to maintain that "the post-colonial era in Africa is now, and only now, coming to an end,"[5] such an assertion seems overly optimistic, in light of the fact that African leadership continues to display neither vision, nor compass in its search for solutions to the continent's problems.

The Colonial Legacy

While contacts among nations or continents could, in theory, enhance cooperation and trade, it is hard to credit Europeans' arrival in Africa with such intent, given the harm that European colonialism inflicted upon the continent.[6] Although early explorations seem to have been motivated by genuine curiosity to discover the "dark" continent, and to spread the gospel, European powers quickly seized the opportunity to use the explorers for their own political and economic ends. Before they realized it, fake explorers and missionaries were working hand in hand with the more sincere, traveling to the most remote corners of the continent, taking the Bible to the doorsteps of villagers, often, beyond evangelical mission. Europeans took it upon themselves to enlighten Africa, the "dark" continent. Under the cover of "civilization" then, Europeans exploited the continent to the fullest extent.

Any assessment of Africa's present development plight should take into account colonization and its legacy. The undeniable truth is that colonization did harm Africa through its unfair and violent practices. Through the burning of villages, destruction of crops, the killing of women and children, and the execution of "stubborn" leaders, colonialism showed the extent of its resolve. Barbaric punitive expeditions and atrocities were frequently used to "quell" revolts or uprisings. Behind the official veil of civilization, the true purpose of European colonialism lay in the search for raw materials and new markets. By empowering Europeans to dominate native peoples, creating arbitrary units without any regard to existing identifications and loyalties, and establishing exploitative and brutal rule, colonialism left on Africa severe wounds that continue to haunt the continent today. Elaborating on how traumatic colonization was on Africans, Hatch posits that:

> The effects of sudden change always tend to be destructive of social and
> personal security. Africans have been subjected to more catastrophic

changes than most of mankind. Many African societies were uprooted or dislocated by three centuries of the slave trade. Then virtually the whole continent found itself under European rule. But it was the impact of European technology and social manners rather than of alien government which had the most catastrophic effect on the way of life of the majority of Africans.[7]

Although other parts of the world experienced some form of colonialism, the Americas and Asia for example, Africa's was the most vicious and merciless. The Africans naively welcomed the Europeans as fellow human beings, albeit with a different skin color, not realizing that their intentions were malicious. Before Africans became aware of the true intent, the harm had been already inflicted. The aftermath of the encounter between Europe and Africa continues to hurt. Their experience with other peoples forced Europeans to rationalize their colonization in Africa. The resentment they faced elsewhere required a new strategy. Their contact with Africa would be justified by the need to "civilize" Africans who would otherwise become extinct according to the Europeans' Darwinist argument. The reality is that Europe's rapid economic expansion needed new markets.

Mission of Civilization

Although Europeans were present in Africa well before the nineteenth century, including Plato, Aristotle, and Herodotus who studied in Egypt, it never occurred to them that the continent needed enlightening. Despite the fact that African societies flourished before the advent of civilization in much of Europe, Europeans eventually reached the conclusion that Africans needed to be "civilized." The French concept of "*mission civilisatrice*" or the British version of "white man's burden" became the main justifications for contacting and enlightening the "dark continent." While they claimed to respect traditional cultures, Europeans simply discarded habits and customs "offensive" to European sensibilities or "in opposition" to European interests. Traditional chiefs who refused to "cooperate" were frequently replaced with friendlier chiefs, even if their authority was challenged. According to Europeans, Africa needed to be brought to the modern world by any means necessary. Such an attitude combined arrogance and ignorance. While it is true that by the nineteenth century, Europe, as compared to other continents, had made tremendous progress thanks to new technological discoveries, it is also true that several brilliant civilizations existed before Europe's rise.

One aspect of the arrogant side of Europeans' attitude lies in Darwinism. By the late 1880s, Charles Darwin had come up with theories and laws on the struggle for survival among plant and animal species. Darwinism allowed some scientists to derive that *homo sapiens* were not immune to the struggle for survival. These social Darwinists believed that European human species and their institutions had evolved into a position of superiority vis-à-vis non-Europeans. Consequently, to prevent the latter from extinction, the former took on themselves the duty to "civilize" the rest of the world, including Africans. European imperialism implied the right of Europeans to dominate and instruct the conquered "savages," and to force them to absorb European institutions and values based on universal, natural, and immutable laws.[8] Such a mission helped justify the brutal conquest and exploitation of Africa. Africa was viewed as a "dark" continent without history and lit only by the flashes of foreign penetration.

Europeans' belief and behavior could also be explained by their limited knowledge of the world. It has been well documented that the "dark" continent had at different times in history great civilizations comparable to those of Europe. Even Western scholars refuse to acknowledge the civilizations of Egypt, Axum, Meroe, and Kush, communities within *Sudan* (from Arabic *Bilal as-Sudan*: Land of the Negroes) formed such powerful states as ancient Ghana, Mali, the Songhai Empire, Kanem-Bornu, the Hausa Kingdoms, Danhomê, Benin, Oyo, Zimbabwe, and others.

Such important centers as Awdaghost, Gao, Djenne, Timbuktu, to name but a few, are indisputable testimonies to the rich civilization in Africa before Europeans set foot on the continent. Modern archaeology has indeed confirmed that Benin City was extant by the thirteenth century, and that the urban culture of Ife goes back to at least the eleventh century. There was a network of trade routes and regular markets arranged daily to avoid competition among neighboring markets. Another example of how advanced some African civilizations were resides in the Dogon cosmogony in Mali. Modern astronomy and astrology pay tribute to the important role of the sun, the moon, and the stars in Dogon universe. In fact, these natural elements allowed Africans to navigate to China and India in search of spices that ended up in Europe through Ottoman merchants.

Renowned scientists and researchers have uncovered facts that belie the notion that Africa was a jungle filled with primates, bound to extinction if it were not for European civilization. It remains true that at a time when Africa had powerful kingdoms, geology made Europe inhospitable for human life. According to Palmer and Colton,

Europeans were by no means the pioneers of human civilization. Half of man's recorded history had passed before anyone in Europe could read or write. The priests of Egypt began to keep written records between 4000 and 3000 B.C., but more than two thousand years later the poems of Homer were still being circulated in the Greek city-states by word of mouth. Shortly after 3000 B.C., while the pharaohs were building the first pyramids, Europeans were creating nothing more distinguished than huge garbage heaps . . . At the time when the Babylonian King Hammurabi, about 2000 B.C., caused the laws of a complex society to be carved on stone, the most advanced Europeans were peoples like the Swiss Lake Dwellers, simple agriculturists who lived in shelters built over the water to protect themselves from beasts and men. In a word, until after 2000 B.C., Europe was in the Neolithic or New Stone Age.[9]

A closer look at the social organization of these empires and kingdoms shows that they had very little reason to envy their contemporary European counterparts. Buttressing that point, Falola maintains that:

Africa has been inhabited for more than three million years. By the first century A.D., many states had evolved; some were large and many were small. The state system continued to change until the nineteenth century, either by way of expansion or contraction. Political, social and economic institutions were adjusted to suit various times and needs, to adapt to the environment, and to respond creatively to new ideas from within and abroad.[10]

As a matter of fact, the difficulties encountered by Europeans in bringing their so-called civilization on the continent attest to the strength of these institutions. Europeans met unexpected harsh resistance all over the African continent. Despite their technological superiority, Europeans' attempt to implement the Berlin Conference decisions proved difficult. Although they first welcomed the Europeans, Africans organized to oppose European domination and conquest after the real purpose of their penetration became evident. Although bringing civilization was the official motive of European contact with Africa, that version of history lost any credibility when the actual goals of European colonialism, the search for new markets required by the expansion of trade became obvious.

Expansion of Trade

In the expanding global economy of the eighteenth century, each continent played its special part. To finance the swelling demand for Asian products it was necessary for European nations to constantly replenish their stocks of gold. The British found an important new supply in Africa in the Gold Coast (present day Ghana). In a few decades a new economic system arose based on "plantation." A plantation was an economic unit consisting of a vast land, a sizable investment of capital, often owned by absentee Europeans, and a force of impressed labor, supplied by African slaves. Sugar, was one of the new crops produced with cheap labor at low cost that proved to have an inexhaustible market. The wealth accumulated along the Atlantic seaboard of Europe was by no means produced by the efforts of western Europeans. The entire world contributed to its formation. The natural resources of the Americas, the resources and skills of Asia, the gold and manpower of Africa, all went into producing the vastly increased volume of goods moving in world commerce.

The origins and impact of colonial policy and rule in Africa, raise a question: why was it, if European colonialism was an extension of European capitalism or civilization, that colonial policy was overtly hostile to the hallmarks of capitalist political economy such as the creation of private property in land, a wage-labor force, the accumulation of capital? In her book, *The Enigma of Colonialism*, Phillips argues that while colonial policy makers wished to, and to some extent did, create a new African political economy, they were unable to do so under conditions of their own choosing. Indeed, as she convincingly demonstrates, the first generation of imperial rulers sought to create institutional features of capitalism but found themselves confronted by an African social and political reality which brooked their every move. In the face of that reality, they retreated in close order not just to an acceptance of what they could not consciously change but to a positive celebration of what came to be seen as African precapitalist life replete with a sense of wholesome community to remain unsullied and undisturbed by capitalist intrusions.[11]

Through unfair trading practices, Europeans sought to spread capitalism, but also to lead in technology. Unlike other continents, Europe understood early on that technological breakthroughs were the key to economic growth and development, and spared nothing to reach that goal. Resources were therefore invested in discovering new methods to improve standards of living and master the universe. With new technological achievements, industrialization took off for new heights. Thanks to new technology, Europe's capacity to produce exceeded its capacity to consume. Each European country was therefore faced with the need to sell its goods beyond its borders. Unfortunately, customs barriers were erected, making intra-Europe trade very difficult. The only alternative left to Europeans was the search for new markets outside their continent.

Search for New Markets

Although Europeans powers ended up annexing or conquering territories outside Europe, the first contacts, from the fifteenth century
onward, seem to have been dictated foremost by economic calculations.
Europeans believed that

> they must have new markets for their growing manufactures, they must
> have new outlets for the investment of their surplus capital and for the
> energies of the adventurous surplus of their population: such expansion
> is a necessity of life to a nation with great and growing powers of
> production.[12]

The Monroe Doctrine closed markets in the Americas to Europeans,
and the search for new export opportunities had to be redirected
toward other continents. Africa was not the first choice. The harsh
climatic conditions made going to Africa a risky business. Europeans
targeted then Asia and the Pacific Islands. While Russia's intention to
conquer Siberia and China became obvious, Great Britain aimed at consolidating its gains in India and moving into China, Burma, and
Malaysia. French explorers made their presence felt in Indochina. The
French Navy settled in Tahiti in 1842, and in New Caledonia in 1853.
   For several years, France and Britain concentrated their efforts
toward the Far East and the Pacific. In the meantime, bolder
Europeans were trying to make contact with Africa on behalf of their
governments. Despite the risks involved, Portugal, Holland, and
Denmark sent envoys to explore the coasts of Africa. Several kingdoms and empires saw in the contacts with the Europeans a genuine
opportunity to exchange goods. Trade agreements were sealed and
markets for European products were established. But when the
French and British agents joined the exploration, their aggressiveness
altered the rules of the game.
   Based on their experience in the Far East and in the Pacific, France
and Britain took the conquest for new territories beyond just the
establishment of new markets. Instead of making fair deals with local
chiefs and kings, Europeans used force to impose their will upon
Africans. The acquisition or annexation of territories became the vein
of Europe's economic expansion. From then on, the economic necessity
to find new markets for European goods gave way to political imperialism. The diplomacy and the armies of European nations compelled
African institutions to deal with Europe.
   However costly and perilous imperialism was, it had to continue,
for without it Europe might face a difficult future. With such a new
understanding of the role and importance of territories or colonies for

European economies, the race was on for more and more land. Economic imperialism rendered colonizing Africa a necessity. The conquest of the continent got a privileged place on the agendas of European nations. Old rivalries resurfaced, manifesting themselves in their desperate attempts to send colonial expeditions to the most remote areas of Africa to secure colonies. The competition became so intense that the Berlin Congress was convened to determine the cardinal principles of imperialism and to carve up the continent.

Because colonialism involves the acquisition, often by force, of foreign territories, the maintenance of rule over a subordinate population, and the separation of the ruling group from the subject population, the relationship between the "mother country" and the colony is necessarily exploitive. Characteristic features of colonialism include political and legal domination by an alien minority, economic exploitation and dependency, and racial and cultural inequality. Colonialism has been a major force in shaping the political and economic character of the modern world. It was seen as an inevitable consequence of great power politics. In Wunsch's words,

> colonialism must be seen as an epochal event in Africa's history. In many powerful respects it worked to prepare and incline the path of post-independence politics toward Hobbesian theories of sovereignty, to depreciation of the value of indigenous and decentralized social infrastructure, and to reliance on centralized, hierarchical mechanisms to order human relationships.[13]

According to Stewart Easton, the deeper causes of colonial policy may be found in the industrial revolution, in strategic motives, and in national prestige. He saw imperialism only as an urge for expansion and conquest, a "sickness" from which all "nations of western civilisation" have suffered.[14]

While very little of Africa was known to the outside world at the beginning of the nineteenth century, hardly anything remained unexplored by 1890. To fully understand the European need to tame the "barbarous tribes," one has to remember European view of Africa, summarized by Sir Harry Hamilton Johnston when he said of Africans that:

> The Negro, more than any other human type, has been marked out by his mental and physical characteristics as the servant of other races . . . in a primitive state [he] is a born slave. He is possessed of great physical strength, docility, cheerfulness of disposition, a short memory for sorrows and cruelties, and an easily aroused gratitude for kindness and just dealing. He does not suffer from home-sickness to

the over-bearing extent that afflicts other peoples torn from their homes, and, provided he is well-fed, he is easily made happy. Above all, he can toil hard under the hot sun and in the unhealthy climates of the Torrid Zone. He has little or no race-fellowship—that is to say, he has no sympathy for other negroes; he recognizes, follows, and imitates his master independently of any race affinities.[15]

Johnston's views reflect the prevailing opinion of the era. Europeans believed that because they were physically and mentally superior to Africans they should conquer them to civilize the continent. Europe was at a stage where industrialization and imperialism allowed the thought of a "natural and necessary polarization of the rulers and the ruled, the bearers and the receivers of culture."[16]

Although European states were politically divided, they shared a similar way of life and outlook. Europe and its offshoots such as the United States, Australia, and New Zealand constituted the "civilized world." Other regions, including Africa, were said to be "backward." Europeans were extremely conscious and inordinately proud of their civilization, which they believed to be the well-deserved outcome of centuries of progress. Feeling themselves to be the most advanced in the important areas of human endeavor, they assumed that all peoples should respect the same social ideals. Inasmuch as other peoples were unwilling or unable to adopt these ideals those were backward. There was no doubt that Europeans had, and still have, a higher standard of living. But it is also true that the "civilized" world attained this standard of living by exploiting the "backward" world.

In his explanation of Europeans' use of history to deny Africa a past, Markovitz eloquently states that:

The denial of an African past was part of an effort at dehumanization. Colonialism turned people into objects in order to facilitate their manipulation. Colonialism sought to eliminate that inner tension of men possessed of a critical intelligence by denying them their ability, and their "right," to question. All repressive systems use ideology and psychological coercion in addition to physical violence to buttress their rule. All governments, regardless of their ideological content, seek to convince their subjects that the state has the *right* to command and the people are morally *obligated* to obey. The state, they maintain, fulfills suprahuman tasks necessary for the common good. History is a weapon for these purposes.[17]

Africa's place in European history is well known albeit downplayed. In fact, Bloch bluntly posits that "without the grain of Africa, the existence of Imperial Rome is as little conceivable as Catholic theology without the African Augustine."[18]

Because of the industrial revolution and the mastery of technology, European civilization sped ahead of that of Africa. Consequently, the Caucasoid type was perceived as the ruler and the bearer of culture while the Negroid type was viewed as the ruled and the receiver. Under those circumstances, colonization was not only good but also indispensable, if "historyless" Africa were to survive. Europeans were, in their view, saving Africa and its populations by sharing their knowledge. In contrast to such a Eurocentric view, according to which nothing of value originates from Africa, some believe that Europeans' contacts with Africa, instead of helping the continent made *things fall apart*, in the words of Chinua Achebe.[19] The Ghanaian historian Adu Boahen's view is very much in agreement with Chinua Achebe's when he said:

> By its disruption of the existing political organization and its creation of the present independent states, by its generation of the new classes of Africans, by its introduction of cash-economy and above all by its spread of education and the Western way of life, colonialism has launched Africa on a course of development that is fundamentally different from its earlier patterns.[20]

In the same vein, Anice believes that European penetration in Africa brought "conquest, exploitation, brutalization, dehumanization, westernization, expropriation, subjugation, dislocation, and final integration into the imperial, global, capitalist economy."[21]

Through conquest and trade in people and commodities, colonialism incorporated Africans into a wider global economy. Colonial powers mapped out their territories and subordinated diverse African polities to their rule. They redefined state forms, social identities, gender relations, religious beliefs, and class relations. Colonial transport networks reorientated the relations of African producers and economies to changing international economic networks. Colonialism subordinated African producers to the needs of new, and often coercive, labor regimes and patterns of cultivation, to meet the requirements of railways, mines, plantations, and revenues. Prior to colonial rule, Africans defined their identities primarily by their allegiance to a ruler or their status within a political community. Polities had interests in incorporating settlers and acquiring slaves to strengthen their productive and military capacities. Under colonial regimes, political communities were defined according to administrative, religious, and linguistic demarcations without reference to political allegiance. With colonialism, Africans had to fight to exclude outsiders from access to their resources.[22]

Although colonialism did have some positive impact on Africa, mainly the building of modern infrastructures, its negative consequences were so severe that the continent still continues to suffer. According to Falola, "colonialism was exploitative, taking as much as possible away from the people, orienting their economy to serve external interests, and manipulating their labour for selfish ends."[23] Colonialism left as its legacy a trend toward impoverishment that cannot easily be reversed. However, more than colonialism, neocolonialism dealt a harsher blow to the continent. After several years of resistance and struggle by Africans, Europeans loosened their grip on the continent. The year 1960 virtually ended an era that began with the "scramble for Africa" in the last part of the nineteenth century. That year saw most African nations become independent. Although only a few of these new states had been able to adapt to the world, most were convinced that they had secured in the form of the signs, symbols, and trappings, the substance of political sovereignty. Political sovereignty and the mystique of independence obscured the fact that the road ahead would be very difficult. Against their will, European powers relinquished their political control of their former colonies. However, their departure was only replaced with two successive generations of leaders. The very first generation of postindependence African leaders was too concerned with self-determination or independence to realize the type of freedom it was being given.

African nationalists who took over sought state power as a means of transferring control of political office and economic resources from foreigners to Africans. Political independence was seen as a major remedy for the scourge of the "unholy trinity of poverty, ignorance and disease."[24] Following Nkrumah's famous exhortation to "Seek political freedom first and the rest shall follow,"[25] African leaders bet on independence to solve their continent's problems. In their eyes, the postcolonial state should take responsibility for bringing development to their continent. Consequently, they mobilized political support to establish their claims as the authentic representatives of the people. Control of the state conferred authority to rule its subjects, to exact taxes and rents from imports and exports, to receive aid and contract "sovereign" debts, and to allocate public resources. The state was central to achieving the goals of nationalism and development. At the same time it became the object of the struggle for power and the key instrument in keeping power.[26] In most African countries, first-generation postindependence leaders were charismatic figures, with a few lieutenants, wielding extensive power and making most policy decisions. The personal nature of power and the arbitrariness and insecurity accompanying it are significant characteristics of early African leadership.[27] By force or through negotiation, institutions of rule have been recast after independence. However, while first-generation African governments inherited the institutions through which, and the boundaries within which, they exercised state authority, poor performance led their respective regimes to bankruptcy.

Enter the second generation that condemned the behavior and meager achievements of their predecessors. Unfortunately, civilian and military leaders who replaced the nationalists became preoccupied with self-aggrandizement. Having denounced, rightly sometimes, the fathers of independence for dismal performance, they took over only to destroy the continent. Several years of political and economic decay left the continent with most Africans caught in a net of poverty, ignorance, and disease.

African Leadership on Trial

According to neorealism, the structure of the international system constrains the unitary state and its leader.[28] The fact of the matter is that the primary actors in that arena, the states, are led by human beings whose actions or decisions shape the system. Although Aron, Morgenthau, and other classical realists have understood and explained international behavior through the actions and interactions of the states and their leaders, Waltz and other neorealists believe that the anarchic international system and the distribution of power dictate state's behavior.[29]

Unfortunately, power remains very elusive in Africa. Through coercion or benevolence, more powerful nations impose their will on African leaders who acquiesce. According to Ikenberry and Kupchan, "acquiescence is the result of the socialization of leaders in secondary nations. Élites in secondary states buy into and internalize norms that are articulated by the hegemon and therefore pursue policies consistent with the hegemon's notion of international order."[30] Through coercion and material inducement,[31] the hegemon structures the international system and socialize weaker states to accept its principles and beliefs. Through what Nye describes as "cooptive power,"[32] some nations manage to dictate the rules of the game. Nevertheless, even among those who had to comply, some have handled the constraints and hurdles better than others, which suggests that leadership does matter. In essence, effective individual leadership enhances the opportunities for emerging nations to circumvent the structural handicaps of the international system.

Without downplaying the importance of the international system or its structure, leaders' behavior can make a difference, even if their behavior reflects what the system allows them to do. The international system does not dictate a single course of behavior, but presents a set of options from which leaders choose well or poorly. Monte Palmer has amply demonstrated the importance of good leadership in a country's fate in *Human Factor in Political Development*. He credits the effectiveness of any state's political system to, among other variables, the skills, attitudes, and behavior of those individuals charged with running the system.[33] In Tucker's words, "politics in essence is leadership or attempted leadership of whatever is the prevailing form of political community."[34] In other words, actions or behavior of decision makers at crucial moments can help shape the range of choices as well as the risks facing the leaders and their successors. The average citizen can ill afford to be unconcerned with the judgment, character, experience, and abilities of those seeking or occupying positions of political leadership.

A quick overview of contemporary Africa reveals a whole range of painful problems attributable to ineffective leadership. Instead of exceptional individuals displaying overriding concern for the public good and providing crucial leadership that makes an important difference for the well-being of society, Africa was, and still is to some extent, littered with ruthless and opportunistic rulers.[35] Military dictators turned out to be worse than corrupt civilian leaders, and Falola is right in his evaluation of the military brutality in Africa:

> Military leadership is above reproach: alternative opinions are discouraged or punished, the press is restrained in most countries under military rule, and real opposition is not tolerated. A culture of silence is enforced, to allow arrogant dictators to govern as they wish. Critics are known to have been killed or jailed, and the lucky ones live in exile outside their countries. Some African rulers struggled for many years to retain power at any cost, and they denied civil liberties. Even peasants, without voice or power, are suppressed and destroyed, to prevent their being mobilized to demand reforms.[36]

More than four decades of independence seem to have brought more negative than positive returns to the continent, and although it is more convenient to blame Africa's ills on colonialism, the sad reality remains that Africans, especially their postindependence leaders, are the main root of their malaise. After all, Africa is not the only continent that has experienced imperialism and colonialism, even if African colonialism is more severe because of slavery and its impacts. Given the performance of ex-colonies on other continents, the reason for the execrable result of African economies and polities has to lie in sources other than colonialism and its legacy.

The new states emerged from colonial independence as replicas of their former masters. They all began "with a system of government which was a minor image of that of the former metropolitan power."[37] The manner of handing power was itself hazardous, because power was simply presented to those nationalists who had been most vociferous in their call for the end of colonialism. In short, power was given to an elite composed primarily of Westernized Africans. However, once independence was granted, the new leaders were ill-equipped to face the new pressures from below. Because these charismatic leaders could not satisfy expectations, they were eventually replaced by rivals within or outside the main party, or by soldiers who had discovered a taste for political power. Having rested Africa's problems on colonialism, independent leaders were faced with delivering the goods as soon as possible without taking into account the structure of international economy. Although European powers left the continent, they maintained a hold over their former colonies. Such an unfavorable environment, coupled with lack of vision and political will, stalled economic and social development in Africa.[38]

Despite its overwhelming wealth in natural and human resources, Africa remains crippled by mass poverty and deprivation because of the African leadership's handling of the main challenges facing the continent. Echoing the views of several writers, African and non-African alike, Anice states that "it is the failure of African rulers, African governments, African governance institutions that account for the emergence of first, political decay, then sociopolitical instability, followed by social fragmentation, and finally political disorders in contemporary Africa."[39] The behavior of African leaders vindicates those who opposed decolonization and predicted that Africans would never command the wisdom and moral maturity to govern themselves in peace and progress. In Anice's words,

> Africa's descent into decay is due to the tragic failure of African leadership in the social, political and economic arenas, the personalization of rulership, the expropriation of societal resources by the kleptocracy of the ruling classes in a patron-clientelist, autocratic, coercive and dangerously intrusive state.[40]

Contrary to expectations, independence did very little, if anything, to resolve Africa's basic problems. Although the first decade of liberation could be considered the starting point for analyzing the role of African leaders, a critical book by Leonard Barnes in 1971 should have sent out a warning signal. Already, Barnes observed a false euphoria in postindependent Africa. His contention was that the greatest obstacle to the social and economic progress of the continent was Africans themselves. He noted that leaders had exercised poor judgment by avoiding closer political and economic associations, which he saw as the only guarantee to breaking the endless round of poverty.[41] There were also several pessimistic signs to force a French sociologist René Dumont to write his famous *L'Afrique Noire est Mal Partie* (False Start in Africa) in which he depicts why Africa was bound for failure.[42] In his eyes, the kind of independence granted to the continent and the type of leaders at the helm of the continent did not augur well for Africa.

The second decade signaled the beginning of a long crisis. The 1970s saw the decline of the initial optimism toward political independence and the concomitant acceptance of the ideology of development by African populations. At roughly the same time, the hope that modern economic thinking, through development plans funded by former colonial powers, should transform nascent African economies, vanished. The continent was already facing such severe problems that a French political scientist, Gonidec, observed in 1978 in his *Les Systèmes Politiques Africains* that: "whether the 'capitalist' path or 'third path' of 'socialism' has been chosen, the post-independence period manifests a constant policy which, by its vacillation, tends to maintain the African populations in a situation hardly different from the colonial one."[43]

The 1980s were characterized as the "lost decade" because, contrary to expectations, Africa's problems grew deeper. Although countless studies are keen to lay blame for Africa's deepening crisis at the feet of multilateral lending agencies such as the International Monetary Fund (IMF) and the World Bank (WB), the locus of the problem should be in the roots of the crisis, that is, the reasons why these economies requested the lending institutions' prescription in the first place. According to Aderanti Adepoju, "much of the blame rests with the economic crises that preceded structural adjustment, but clearly the adjustment measures themselves contributed significantly to this decline."[44] This view is widely shared and one can understand Africans' frustration. But, at this stage, it might be too late to complain since Structural Adjustment Programs (SAP) have become a fact of life on the continent. What is important is to figure out how to alleviate the severe problems created on the continent before and after involvement of the IMF and the WB.

According to the Ghanaian scholar, Ayittey, true freedom and development never came to much of Africa.[45] In a similar vein, Claude Ake believes that development has never been on the agenda of African leaders.[46] Axelle Kabou developed the same argument in her book *Et si l'Afrique Refusait le Développement* (What If Africa Said No to Development).[47] Kofi Hadjor also condemned African leaders when he said that "with every year that passed, Africa proved less capable of realizing the most elementary aspirations of its people."[48]

The hope that the first generation of postindependence African leaders ignited got shattered, leaving the image of the continent battered. The leaders just could not deliver their promise. Acknowledging their responsibility in Africa's maldevelopment, the late President Julius Nyerere of Tanzania gave a candid response when asked why the project for an East African Federation came to grief:

> It was our fault, the fault of the leaders. We are guilty men—in the East as in every other part of Africa. It was we who refused to carry our people towards unity. The masses are too rational to turn away from unity on their own. The leaders merely mutter "What would happen to me? Who would come out on top?" The masses don't ask that sort of question. But leaders in office simply will not run any risk of losing it.[49]

Although African leaders were aware of the urgent need to improve economic and social conditions of postcolonial Africa, they chose to defend their personal interests. Ethnicity became an outward symptom of a deeper malaise, deriving its salience from the willingness of African politicians to play the tribal card. As Diamond suggests the "political class" in each region fought so hard to establish a monopoly of political power precisely because exclusion from public office simultaneously implied the loss of a class base:

> Because state office or patronage was virtually the only means to attain a position in the emergent dominant class, and yet state resources were too limited to satisfy all comers, competition for state control was inevitable—and inevitably tense. No candidate or party could afford to lose an election, for that would mean exclusion from the resources of class formation. Having triumphed initially, none could afford to risk defeat, for that would mean losing the means with which to consolidate the structure of class dominance, and one's own position in it.[50]

Besides ethnicity and its corollary, clientelism, Joseph maintains that "prebendal politics" also contributes seriously to the zero-sum struggle for the control of power and state in Africa. In Joseph's view,

> the mere existence of a patronage system, even one based on clientelistic ties of significant duration, should not warrant the application of the term "prebendalism." To preserve the analytical sharpness of this formulation, a prebendal system will be seen not only as one in which the offices of state are allocated and then exploited as benefices by the

office-holders, but also as one where such a practice is legitimated by a set of political norms according to which the appropriation of such offices is not just as act of individual greed or ambition but concurrently the satisfaction of the short-term objectives of a sub-set of the general population.[51]

Political power in Africa is built on the resources of extroversion, and rulers draw the bulk of their economic resources from the control of foreign trade, from the diversion of food aid, from the preferential allocation of import licenses, and from smuggling. Looking at Africa's current level of poverty and income maldistribution, it is clear that African leaders failed to provide their populations with appropriate means and mechanisms to alleviate misery on the continent. After decades of independence, several continental gatherings resulted in deadlocks, early institutions could not function, and conflicts continued unabated because of faulty leadership.

From the early days of independence to today, African leaders continue to display very little knowledge of international politics. Though mostly unwritten, there are laws that govern international behavior. The evidence is overwhelming that, out of necessity or *raison d'état*, powerful states will act according to their national interest regardless of the impact of their action upon other players of the system.[52] Until African leaders take heed of that basic premise as they develop their policies, chances are they will make wrong assumptions with dire consequences, resulting in the betrayal of their continent.

These leaders have demonstrated ingenuity in domestic politics by clinging to power for decades, often against the will of their people. They have succeeded in creating strong patron–client relationships, permitting all kinds of political gymnastics for the survival of their regimes. It is, however, difficult to assert that they have ever been concerned with the well-being of their people. Through an unfortunate system of privatization of the public sphere, they see themselves as "owning" their respective countries.[53] With no distinction between the public and the private spheres, mismanagement and embezzlement have been rampant at all levels. Corruption has reached such an alarming level that Olivier de Sardan believes that corruption became "socially embedded in 'logics' of negotiation, gift-giving, solidarity, predatory authority and redistributive accumulation."[54] At the same time, most citizens have gone without food, education, healthcare, clothing, and shelter, demonstrating African leaders' myopic policies. However, the domestic political skills of these leaders suggest that their ignorance of the international system might be willful. In this day and age where autarky is practically impossible, given how interconnected the world has become, grasping the basics of international conduct is the key to any country's good performance on the world scene.

Although contemporary African leaders would like to believe in an altruistic international system, in reality states act according to their interests as determined by their leaders. Although states may act on altruistic or humanitarian grounds, such action is the exception, rather than the rule, in international relations. Looking back at the very reasons that forced Europeans to invade, occupy, and colonize Africa, as well as European resistance to decolonization, it is still a mystery why African leaders continue to expect their former "masters" to become altruistic partners in their quest for African development. Of course, the needs that required foreign lands and markets have diminished, but the desire to remain ahead in the game is still alive.

Some level of economic progress would serve the developed world's interests by allowing poorer states to buy their exports and repay their debt, but any country's development strategy should be first endogenous, primarily based on its leaders' creativity and ingenuity. Therein lies African leaders' deficiency, because of their inability to understand how the world operates. Today's international relations could be likened to a rigged soccer game. The game has rules that are, in this instance, defined by the more powerful, with might being the real referee. Without a clear understanding of these rules, a weaker country can never win, despite its efforts. By the time a small weak country is about to score, the more powerful country moves the goal posts farther away. Unfortunately, African leaders show no dexterity in mastering international politics, displaying, instead, an astonishing naiveté.

Conclusion

After decades of independence, a glance at the continent reveals a land of degradation and humiliation and a betrayal of the sense of pride that came with decolonization. Now, this sense of pride has vanished, and Africans must account for decades of political, economic, and social failure. The last decade of the twentieth century opened up with a great deal of relief and hope. The end of the cold war and political events in Eastern Europe hastened the democratization process on the continent.[55] A rekindling of civil society and the military's positive contribution brought democracy back to Africa. After the successful national conference that triggered a peaceful political transition in Benin, several other African countries followed suit with more or less success. Although the initial enthusiasm and euphoria about the transition from authoritarianism or totalitarianism toward multiparty politics have now given way to more nuanced assessments, the hope is that the worst is over, and democracy will allow Africans to finally live their overdue dream of having a decent life. Given the millions of Africans still affected by dire poverty, unemployment, malnutrition, illnesses, and inadequate education, the cry for freedom from want should be much louder.

Chapter 2

Democracy's Travails in Africa

There is no effective way of changing regimes. Rulers refuse to relinquish power and the military uses violence to perpetuate itself. Political coercion and repression replace democracy. Life presidents have emerged, with a notion that a leader should "possess" a state and government.
                                      Toyin Falola, "Africa in Perspective."

While African politics remains volatile and complex, the thaw of the cold war ushered in a new era marked by the collapse of authoritarian regimes and democratization. There was a hope that the new political systems would institute legal and political accountability. However, the early euphoria gave way to bitter disappointment after incumbent regimes refused to relinquish power. It then became obvious that democracy's fate on the continent was in doubt at best. Concern over their own fate led some dictators to hold onto their power. Clearly, the international community seems to be pleased, genuinely in some instances, with Africa's nascent democracies, under the assumption that a new democratic dawn will take the continent out of despair and poverty. However, if Africa's past is any guide, democracy's road will be long and painful. Although there is room for cautious optimism, the realities of Africa's political conundrum and economic plight, coupled with foreign powers' interests on the continent, might undermine democratic efforts in Africa.

After several decades of mismanagement, corruption, and a leadership lacking both vision and compass, Africa finally embarked on a democratic path in the late 1980s and early 1990s. Thanks to civil society's resilience, but most importantly to the military's cooperation, one-party regimes had to relax their grip on power. Unfortunately, early hope has been tempered, not only by the military's quick return or obstinate refusal to cede power in such countries as Togo, the Gambia, Guinea Republic, the Congo, and Mauritania, but also by the stagnant or even regressing economic conditions of Africans. Africans took to the street to demand a more peaceful and account-able political setting that they believed would trigger a fundamental change in their living conditions. But, unless persistent autocratic rule and declining social conditions are dealt with, the ongoing democratization process on the continent will fall short, failing to contribute to either economic development or peace and stability on the continent.

This chapter probes democracy's journey in Africa. The first section explores *demos'* painful pilgrimage to *kratia*. The second section uncovers the roles played by civil society and the military in the democratization process. In the face of efforts by Western nations to promote democracy as conducive to economic development and peace, the third section disentangles the complex relationship among democracy, economic development, and peace. The next section exposes the Achilles' heel of the democratization process in Africa by depicting the impact of lingering sufferings of African populations, while the last section tackles one of the keys to democracy's success in Africa: trusting civil–military relations.

Democracy's New Dawn in Africa

Right after the first elections, the African masses found themselves increasingly excluded from real involvement in political life. In contrast to pre-independence rhetoric, the promise of democracy remained unrealized, and the people remained an object, rather than an agent, of government. Constraints on popular participation in the political process blunted the momentum of popular struggle and consciousness aroused during the struggle for liberation. The failure to democratize the overall development process has undermined the mass participa-tion of the region's most important resource, its people. Demands for greater democratization in the postcolonial period smacked of disloy-alty to the newly independent states, meaning that opponents had to articulate their demands carefully or be considered traitors.[1]

Evidently, disaffection with colonial regimes did not generate coherent social forces capable of maintaining and developing a sus-tainable effective opposition. New leaders managed to highjack the political process, by altering the terrain of political struggle to their advantage. Despite the existence of conventional political parties, elections, parliaments, and other paraphernalia of participatory democracy, the few maintained a tight control over the political process. Dissenters who wished to press beyond token gains had to learn to cope with the new reality. Unable to develop a new strategy and adequate tactics, opponents of neocolonialism lost ground and became marginalized until the wave of democratization.

According to Held, "democracy seems to have scored an historic victory over alternative forms of governance."[2] The collapse of communism has indeed left the world political scene without a serious ideological competitor. Though flawed, democracy's flexibility, its built-in commitment to equality of representation, and its recognition of the legitimacy of opposition politics make it an appealing proposition. Praising democracy's value, Shapiro and Hacker-Gordon state that:

> Democrats expect much of democracy. They expect to participate in making the collective decisions that govern them. They expect these decisions to be informed by extensive public deliberation. They expect those who hold lead public discussion and implement the collective will to be held accountable for their actions by the electorate. Democrats also expect democracy to help make the world a better place. They believe it will diminish injustice and oppression, and bring reason to bear on the organization of collective life . . . Democracy is often touted as diminishing the likelihood of war, protecting human freedom, and facilitating economic growth. It might be going too far to say democracy is all things to all people, but it is fair to say that there is a strong propensity to associate democracy with a wide array of activities and outcomes that people value.[3]

The spread of democracy has been one of the most heartening trends of recent years. Democracy can ensure that a country's political and economic affairs are conducted in ways compatible with the interests and wishes of the people. Democracy provides the environment within which fundamental rights are protected. Although democratic regimes may not always be virtuous, autocratic governments can never be trusted with the citizens' welfare. In Anyang's view, the built-in accountability of democracy can lead to more responsible use of public resources and hence, high levels of development.[4] Africa needs democracy not only because democracy is desirable in itself, but also because it will greatly facilitate development.[5] Whether it is due to the strong belief that democracies do not fight each other,[6] or to a correlation between democracy and development,[7] Western countries believe that spreading democracies might sometimes serve their interests.

When the third wave of democratization[8] sent ripples to every corner of the planet, there was a sense that "democratic peace"[9] could finally take hold. Although neorealists dispute the Kantian proposition, arguing that the evidence is not compelling, Western nations have embarked on democracy promotion worldwide based, in part, on the belief that democracies do not fight one another. However, whether what is being promoted is a genuine democracy or national interest wrapped in democracy remains controversial. Like the missionaries who "enlightened" the Third World with civilization through Christianity, democracy seems like the new gospel.[10] Both donor and recipient countries appeal to democracy, hoping that democratization will reverse several decades of misfortune. In Fieldhouse's words, "economic and social development came to be seen as a moral obligation on the West, very much as the dissemination of Christianity had appeared a century earlier."[11] By adopting the refrain of democracy as a prerequisite for their help or assistance to Third World countries, both donor nations and multilateral financial institutions seek better control over political and economic systems of the so-called developing nations. In several instances, when their national interests contradict democratization, Western nations have always chosen to defend their interests.

In Africa, democracy was dubbed the "second liberation." When massive demonstrations first called for a new political order, some scholars gave democracy no chance on the continent. Concurring with the idea that "outside the core [industrialized nations] democracy is a rarity . . . [and] with a few exceptions, the limits of democratic development in the world may well have been reached."[12] However, Africans beat the odds, as authoritarian governments gave way to democratic regimes with legitimacy and a mandate to attempt to right so many years of wrongs in Africa. After decades, many variants of one-party rule degenerated into a form of oligarchic patrimonialism unknown in precolonial Africa. Frustrated by declining economies and degrading standards of living, Africans demanded an end to corrupt and misguided rule. In Decalo's words,

> the continent was ripe for a massive populist upheaval, and a number of internal and external factors played a role in leading the democratic pressures to fruition. Among the internal variables was the fact that much of Africa was not only at a political dead-end, but economically bankrupt to boot.[13]

All over the continent, the advent of democracy brought a genuine sense of relief and hope. However, the initial sense of elation was crushed when some leaders simply "re-arranged" their authoritarian regimes to accommodate democratic demands.

Within a few months, the "People's Republics" were truly given back to the people, market economies introduced or re-introduced in many countries, and single party and military rule was dismantled. However, democracy's ongoing journey is proving treacherous.

Several countries, originally on a democratic path are now back in the hands of "born again" military democrats. Several African countries still struggle to democratize, with the chances of success seeming more and more remote in other countries. Because of disunity among the opposition, the skills of incumbent leaders, and outside support from allies, democracy's travails continue unabated. The stakes are such that old regimes cling to power with unexpected resolve. Regardless of conjecture about an ideal sequence of economic and political liberalization, many African countries face concurrent political and economic reform. If political liberalization enables a departure from the practices and institutions associated with neo-patrimonial rule, then democratization in African states can also begin to shift the terms of economic governance. There is, however, a possibility that traditional politics may persist, although perhaps in a different guise. Civil society's resilience after decades in a coma, and the military's willingness to see democratic change, delineate the path to genuine political and economic reform.

Civil Society's Resilience and the Military's Cooperation

In most African countries, political transition has involved a reconfiguration of political, economic, and military elites, rather than an opening up of the political system and broadening of participation. In such cases, the *status quo* is likely to be maintained until countervailing state and civil society institutions develop to pressure both the political system and the military. Many African military establishments need to be more representative of society's ethnic and religious composition if they are to contribute to the process of democratization. The importance of the military's cooperation in democratic transition has become clear with democracy's travails on the continent.

The battles waged against unpopular African regimes in the 1980s by Africans reflected a new intensity. Africans have long taken to the streets to demand more freedom and flexibility in choosing their leaders. A few years after independence, Africans started challenging their leaders. After the heady days of anticolonial mobilization, demonstrations and demands, Africans expected *uhuru*[14] to deliver democracy, prosperity, and self-rule. The expectation of a new virtuous African leader, committed to collective betterment failed to materialize. However, the resentment of postindependence autocratic and corrupt regimes took a milder form, with the hope that the tendency to seek consensus a prevalent feature in African societies, would help open a dialogue. Unfortunately, their complaints and demands fell on deaf ears. Having inherited power from the colonizers, the new leaders became determined to remain the sole decision-makers. Their absolute power corrupted them absolutely, and they led the continent to a *cul-de-sac*. Faced with such a situation, civil society, the private sphere that challenges state behavior,[15] started searching for ways to be heard, but its lack of organization and resolve thwarted its chance to change the course of events. Civil society's failure to influence new leaders opened up the door to "military" society. On behalf of their postindependence constitutional duty as the guarantor of the nation, the military moved in with both messianic rhetoric and a political program.

Early coups d'état were welcomed, even praised, by Africans fed up with the deplorable political, economic, and social conditions of their continent. Wunsch and Olowu maintain that by 1990:

> Of Africa's 54 independent states, *only* [emphasis in original] 18 have avoided successful military coups. Of these 18, at least 6 have experienced serious coups attempts, military revolts, or sustained civil conflicts. Coups by generals have given way to coups by colonels, captains, flight lieutenants and, finally, sergeants and corporals. A weary sameness sets in: each regime denounces the previous one and promises an early return to civilian government after it "cleans up" and "reforms" the government. Too often the military regime has indeed "cleaned up," but not in the way it promised.[16]

Unfortunately, the similarity between corrupt civilian leaders and military dictators soon became apparent. Ultimately, the military leadership turned out to be worse, since the legitimate use and control of weapons gave it a *carte blanche* for any action. Hit with this ugly reality, civil society resumed its struggle, but from a different perspective. Because such basic freedoms as free association, free speech, and free press had been taken away, and opposition had to be clandestine, underground organizations became the only vehicles for the struggle against incompetent military dictators. In countries where corrupt civilian leaders were still in charge with no legitimacy, civil society took a harder stance. However, neither open nor underground activities had any serious impact on African governments until the wave of political transition from Eastern Europe tolled the knell of the autocrats' power. In his accurate assessment of the military's adventure into politics in Africa, Falola posits that:

> The major bloc to democracy has been the military. Usually self-motivated and greedy, the military has justified itself by accusing civilians of corruption and inability to manage the state. By 1970, half of the continent was governed by the military, a tradition that is currently sustained. Now totally discredited in many countries, the military [rode]

into power by offering a better government and an improved economy. The military [has been], however, no different from the rest, and its performance [has been] shoddy and unimpressive, to say the least. With the control of the means of violence, it violate[d] human rights, spen[t] a huge proportion of national revenues on arms, destroy[ed] democratic institutions, and promote[d] an anti-intellectual culture.[17]

Whereas before corrupt and inept governments have always turned a deaf ear to civil society's demands, this time they could no longer ignore the people's request for freedom and reform of the structure of governance.[18] Indeed, the sharp deterioration in living conditions, the worsening economic crisis, and the blatant corruption of politicians combined with political repression and disrespect for human rights to cause social explosion in many countries on the continent.[19] As Legum eloquently states:

Signs of mounting discontent across the entire African continent are reminiscent of the anti-colonial storm that gathered after World War II and bear some resemblance to the current movement of dissent in Eastern Europe. Whereas the anti-colonial movement spearheaded a revolt against alien rule, the present targets are the post-independence African ruling classes and, especially, the political systems they built and now defend.[20]

In the hope of nipping these movements in the bud, several governments instituted hasty but superficial political reforms. However, civil society's determination forced incumbent leaders to realize that Africans demanded more than cosmetic changes. They wanted genuine political reforms and economic liberalization. Their obstinacy and resilience paid off, and new methods of governance were introduced. Many observers credited civil society for internal struggles, which had been incubating for several decades.[21] Consequently, recent scholarship has focused on the role of political leaders and strategic elites.[22]

In his praise for civil society in the third wave of global democratization, Diamond, acknowledged that the overthrow of authoritarian regimes through popularly based and massively mobilized democratic opposition has not been the norm. He nevertheless states that:

Even in . . . negotiated and controlled transitions, the stimulus for democratization, and particularly the pressure to complete the process, have typically come from the "resurrection of civil society," the restructuring of public space, and the mobilization of all manner of independent groups and grassroots movements.[23]

In all fairness, the African masses deserve a great deal of credit for their impact on the democratic transition in Africa. Although popular unrest had long been an intermittent feature of African politics, the intensity of recent popular demands was unprecedented.[24] Often equated with the emergence of new patterns of political participation outside of formal state structures and one-party systems,[25] civil society is a necessary condition for the persistence of modern democracies. It has always determined the birth and growth of any democracy since time immemorial.[26]

Most scholars saw civil society in Africans' successful struggle against despotic rulers, repressive regimes, and governments that violated both their individual and their collective rights. According to Baker "an autonomous civil society is seen as a necessary bulwark against undemocratic state power, whether potential or actual."[27] Alluding to the importance of civil society in democratization, Woods states that:

> The relationship between civil society and democracy is a complicated one. The emergence of a civil society does not guarantee the development of democracy; however, it is highly unlikely that a viable democracy can survive without a civil society. Civil society is a necessary foundation for democracy . . . It is within civil society that public opinion is formed and it is through independent associations that individuals can have some influence on government decision-making.[28]

While an inactive civil society leads to unresponsive states, a politically self-conscious civil society forces the state to remain within its boundaries. In Habermas's words, "the legitimacy of a state lasts as long as the 'political public' accepts the boundaries prescribed by the state."[29] Any transgression or redrawing of these boundaries alters previous arrangements and can lead to a rupture of the political discourse.[30] However, one needs to measure praise of civil society so as not to overemphasize its role, particularly at the expense of other key actors. If the masses were the only trigger of democracy in Africa, there should be no military leaders left in power, given the amount of political protest leveled against them.[31]

Whether the military has intervened in African politics because of internal institutional characteristics of the military, like its size, cohesion, hierarchical command, and corporate interests,[32] or because of societal conditions such as low economic development, social cleavages, and low political culture and institutionalization,[33] the military has ruled most of Africa most of the time. Such a usurpation of African politics and government prevents an acknowledgement of the military for allowing, either actively or passively, the democratization process to succeed. Given the track records of both the military and civil society in African politics,[34] it is indeed malapropos to even think of the military as a force that might subscribe to democratization, albeit out of self-interest. As Luckham and White contend, "the military and repressive apparatuses of the state may not seem the best vantage point from which to study democratization."[35] The military, whether colonial or postcolonial, has always been heavily involved in politics on the continent, most of the time at the expense of the population. The force at the disposal of the African military became its main weapon of oppression.

Against this background, the reluctance to credit the military with any contribution to democratization is understandable. The military and democracy seem to be in diametrical opposition. The military is a taut chain of command while democracy is an egalitarian framework of rules intended to promote pluralism. Democracy presupposes human sociability whereas the military presupposes its total absence to prepare soldiers for the inhuman extremity of killing the opposition. The military demands submission, where democracy enjoins participation. One is a tool of violence, the other a means of consensus building for peaceful coexistence. These views expressed by the late Nigerian scholar Ake,[36] reflect the military's behavior on the continent, and underscore the reluctance of African armed forces to subordinate their interests to those of society at large.

However, several facts seem to weaken the theory of civil society as the real source of democratization in Africa. Expressing doubt about African civil society's capabilities, Lemarchand posits that "the nature of African civil society is . . . highly contradictory and that this makes the institutionalization of democratic governance very problematic because the structures of accountability are segmented, syncretistic and fluid."[37] Press' views also remind us of the complexity of African democratization:

> Some of the old-guard incumbents got wise to the new democratic movement. Having seen electoral defeats of incumbents in other parts of Africa, they learned quickly how to adapt, how to make just enough political concessions to take the heat off for a while, how to tamper with the electoral machinery just enough to win again. Some heads of state used outright force or had the potential to do so, which is why there were few pro-democratic victories against military regimes. Most civilian authoritarian regimes were more subtle, calling elections quickly, before opponents could get organized, or not allowing potentially broad-based parties to run for various reasons, or passing laws designed to prevent particular strong potential candidates from running.[38]

The persistence of such military leaders as Lansana Conté of Guinea, Maaouya Ould Sid'Ahmed Taya of Mauritania, and Yahya

Jammeh of the Gambia who remain in power, in defiance of civil society, the military interruption of the democratic experiment in the Congo Republic,[39] armed rebellions against a democratically elected government in Côte d'Ivoire, General Bozizé's March 2003 coup in the Central African Republic, the July 2003 military intermission in Sao Tomé and Príncipe, the September 2003 military takeover in Guinea-Bissau, and the February 2005 military show of might in Togo demonstrate that democratic transition in Africa does not lie solely in the vibrancy and strength of civil society.[40] The truth remains that smooth democratic transitions, although short-lived in most cases, have occurred only in countries where the military leadership has initially supported democracy. So far no successful democratization has occurred over the military's opposition, making the armed forces a serious potential hurdle on the path to a democratic Africa.

Democracy, Economic Development, and Peace: A Complex Relationship

Despite the elation generated by the new wave of democratization, there is little agreement on what democracy entails. Democracy has, since an early stage, been subject to some controversy. Even from the introduction of *demokratia* around the fifth century BC in several Greek city-states, disagreement surrounded the essential elements of democracy. The fact that slaves and women were not allowed to vote in ancient Greece raised a fundamental question about who "the people" were. Only with several centuries of social movements did suffrage become universal in the twentieth century.[41] Here, democracy is defined not only as a system of government that allows *demos* (the people) to decide its own fate through free, fair, and periodic multiparty elections, but also as a political system that facilitates economic redistribution and peace. Economic development entails a process through which the real *per capita* income of a country rises over a long time period. Peace is the sustained stable environment without which neither democracy nor economic development can prevail.[42]

Africa's political instability has been a major concern to Africans as well as the world community because of its negative impact on the continent's development. African economies have experienced neither economic growth nor reduced inequality since independence and most will probably not enjoy any such progress in the near future while underlying social cleavages remain constant. Unfortunately, colonialism failed to create genuine conditions for sustainable development. According to Naidu, the sequel of colonialism is either underdevelopment, meaning "development that is fragmented, lopsided, uncoordinated and limited both vertically and horizontally," or misdevelopment, which is "ill-conceived, ill-timed, ill-executed, mistaken and misdirected development."[43] Due to a false start,[44] and decades of economic and political decay, Africa plunged into misery, chaos, and dictatorship. Consequently, Africans welcomed the new wave of democratization as the beginning of the end of their nightmare.

The strong belief that democracies do not go to war with each other also contributes to the euphoria surrounding democratization.[45] Since time immemorial, humanity has grappled with the problem of war and peace, and the search for more stable relations among groups of hunters, city-states, empires, and nations. After the reign of force and sheer might, imperial conquest is one manner through which international order has been imposed. Before the difficulties and shortcomings of imperial peace, a state-based balance-of-power system has become the surest means of maintaining peace and harmony among nations. Unfortunately, competition, diffidence and glory[46] have proven the balance-of-power system incapable of sustaining eternal peace, resulting in two costly international "hot" wars. At this so-called end of history,[47] many "peace-loving" nations of the North seized the opportunity, pretending to be planting the seeds of perpetual peace in humankind through the spread of democracy in the South. However, early hopes are waning because deteriorating economic conditions continue to threaten stability and peace. For democracy to be an alternative to war,[48] it needs to provide overall peace and economic and social well-being to citizens. The lack of war does not necessarily satisfy other fundamental needs such as food, shelter, clothing, and health care. Besides the absence of war, peace should allow the "presence of opportunities for human happiness."[49]

In addition to the democratic peace hypothesis, connections between democracy and prosperity fuel enthusiasm about democratic governance as a panacea, especially in Africa. A few years after independence, many African countries found themselves caught in a debt trap, unable to maintain interest payments, let alone repay debt to international financial institutions (IFIs) and private lenders. Investment and imports were curtailed, exacerbating the difficulties of growing out of debt. Economic growth and per capita income fell. As a result, Africans are poorer today than they were at independence, leading many to place their faith in democratization as the solution to their economic problems. Although not a panacea, democracy is sometimes treated as a precondition for economic development, which in turn sustains democratic governance. Starting with Adam Smith, who identified economic development with material progress,[50] the neoclassical or "trickle-down" paradigm was equated with maximization of growth through an efficient allocation of resources. Kuznets predicted that, after an initial exacerbation of inequality, growth would make the poor richer.[51] However, empirical evidence belies the "trickle-down" paradigm in developing economies, and economic development became gradually linked to a reduction of poverty, income inequality, and unemployment.[52] Economic development, defined as income redistribution and the satisfaction of basic needs, is viewed as an important engine of democracy.

The other, and more crucial, obstacle to democratization in Africa lies in the economic hardship that Africans continue to experience. Since independence, several scholars have linked economic development to a strong democracy.[53] Although the association between democracy and growth has some merit, economic development alone does not produce democracy. National idiosyncrasies, historical, cultural, and political forces, as well as leaders' behavior, may advance or prevent democracy.[54] Although evidence as to whether democracy fosters or hinders development is inconclusive, ardent proponents of democracy would like to believe that democracy is not merely an inherent good, but is also instrumental in enhancing the process of development. However, because of the positive correlation between economic development and political democracy, the common perception among many Third World countries is that democracy should improve living conditions.

The advent of democracy in Africa raised similar expectations. African populations had a great deal of hope that the democratization process would not only allow them political expression but also improve their standard of living. African masses were willing to put their lives on the line because of the sharp deterioration in living conditions, the intensification of the economic crisis and the blatant corruption of politicians. Economic grievances lay at the root of initial protests. Repeated economic failures fuelled political discontent.[55] Although African populations were unhappy with their corrupt leaders, the harshness of the repression forced civil society into hibernation. Civil society only woke up once citizens' basic needs went unmet while leaders had several palaces and well-endowed bank accounts in Europe.

The gap between leaders and followers widened at an alarming rate. In several cases, specific economic problems sparked demands for political change. In Zambia, the price of maize, a staple food, doubled because of subsidy cuts demanded by the structural adjustment programs (SAPs). The price increase triggered riots in the mid-1980s. In Côte d'Ivoire, a "solidarity tax" linked to an austerity program, and frequent electricity cuts on campus, fuelled the pro-democracy movement in 1990. In Benin, civil servants, teachers, and students went on strike in 1989 when their emoluments, scholarships, and stipends were delayed for several months.[56] African states have been unable to realize and sustain the delivery of development, while serving the immediate interests of those in power, and exacerbating inequalities to power and material resources.

African masses equated democracy with better standards of living, believing that by attaining democracy, a society could resolve all of its political, economic, and social problems. Democracy can, undoubtedly, help economic development through its openness. An honest and fair set of rules could entice foreign investments that might create jobs and improve conditions of living. Inherited and reformed institutions have proved ineffective in achieving many of the objectives for which they were created and the hope was now in democracy. However, much to Africans' disgust, democracy alone cannot change a continent lagging on all fronts. Contrary to expectations, democracy has not delivered the goods for Africa, and the chances of improving African masses' lives seem to be waning.

The harsh conditions imposed by the WB and the IMF do not permit new democratic leaders to ameliorate the economic conditions of their compatriots. In their attempt to stop the downward spiral of economic and quality of life indicators, new "democrats" have to address some fundamental economic imbalances through a bitter pill of SAPs prescribed by IFIs. Structural and sectoral adjustment loans entail a number of policy conditions including removing import quotas, cutting tariffs, reducing interest rate controls, devaluating currencies, eliminating state marketing boards, eliminating restrictions on industry, privatizing and restructuring state-owned enterprises, and removing price control on food, energy, and agriculture. In theory, those programs are probably efficient given the reportedly positive economic growth in such African countries as Benin and Ghana. However, their constraints corrode democratic practices and value, and achieve economic success at a high social cost. As Clapham argues, "the critical point about structural adjustment was the challenge that international institutions posed to control by African states and rulers over their domestic economies."[57] However, African leaders have not always been powerless in the face of SAP constraints, and, whenever and wherever possible, they have tried to maintain some control over resource allocation and the process of economic development. By the second half of the 1990s it was very widely accepted that structural adjustment and stabilization packages had failed to work wonders in Africa. Consequently, the WB has now embraced such concepts as "social capital" and has acknowledged the pervasiveness of market failures and the need for effective public intervention. The IMF has also come as close as ever to admitting failure even if it was forced to design an Enhanced Structural Adjustment Facility (ESAF) to alter shortcomings in earlier programs. Although some have tried desperately to vindicate the IMF by putting a positive spin on SAPs in Africa,[58] most respected scholars tend to associate these programs more closely with harm than relief. In his *cri de cœur*, a former WB Vice-President, Edward Jaycox laments:

> After 30 years of technical assistance, and so much money spent, Africa's weak institutions, lack of expertise, and current need for more—rather than more—assistance tell us we have failed badly in our efforts . . . The donors have done a disservice to Africa, and many African governments have participated blindly.[59]

At the very moment when African governments need a stronger state to tackle the Herculean tasks, the WB and the IMF recommend a leaner one. Although some contend that the Western developmental models are neither applicable nor desirable for the Third World,[60] most African leaders have yet to design their own development path, leaving their countries still stuck at the "initial development" stage[61] of the Western model. Although some suggest that "a new generation of enlightened African leaders has now decided to stake Africa's claim to the twenty-first century,"[62] a careful look at the "ship" supposed to take the continent out of its crisis reveals that it is sinking in dock. The novel framework for renewal, the NEPAD, may be a perfect tool for alms begging, but has little chance of improving living conditions on the continent.

With growing unhappiness among the populations, democracy might lose *demos*, the people, and prompt another round of military takeovers. As Aristotle pointed out, "a society divided between a large impoverished mass and a small favored elite will become either an oligarchy, in which a few rule dictatorially, or a tyranny, a popular-based dictatorship."[63] Despite the debate over democracy's contribution to economic development, Africa will need a tremendous amount of support to maintain its democratization process. As Brown aptly put it, "[e]xternal donors need to continue pressure for institutional reform, but in their push for liberalization need to be more conscious of the economic impacts and the consequences they may have for peace."[64] Concurring with Brown, Cornwell maintains that:

> Structural adjustment programmes involve a sharp decline in living standards for most and a steep rise in the price of food and social services . . . [They] tend to aggravate social welfare problems, diminishing the

capacity of governments to cope with political demands. So there is an apparent contradiction between the imperatives of democratization and structural adjustment: just as the former stimulates the popular demand for better social and welfare services, the latter requires that this be denied.[65]

While democracy might be worth fighting for, the welfare of those fighting for it also deserves serious attention. Empty stomachs cannot sustain their struggle for democracy in face of enduring economic hardship.

Civil–Military Relations and Sustainable Democracy

Although most African countries are in the process of political transition, the diverse nature of the transitions defies generalizations. However, in all transitions, whether from single-party politics to more pluralistic systems, from military to civilian government, or from war to peace, the military seems the most important variable. The military has influenced, dominated, or participated in politics to varying degrees in African countries, and this legacy in part affects the role played by the military in the ongoing processes of political transition. Other potentially determining factors include the nature of politics in individual countries, how political power is perceived and obtained, the interface between political institutions, prevailing civil–military relations, and how new political leaders develop relations with military establishments.

While much of the current literature tends to give full credit to civil society, the reality is that peaceful democratic transition occurred only in countries where the military has consented to democratization. Although the military's record in African politics is not exemplary, the military did play an important role in peaceful political transition in such countries as Benin, Mali, and Niger. Even in states such as the Congo or Madagascar, the military leadership did contribute to the initial democratization process before nullifying its achievement by taking back power through force. Recent coups d'état in Africa prove that until the military is brought under civilian control at a later stage of democratic consolidation, the military leadership needs to be given political incentives to play a positive role in democratization.

Because the merits of civil society include political participation, state accountability, and publicity of politics, civil society has the potential to interrogate the state.[66] As an ideal site for the production of a critical rational discourse to challenge the state, democratic theory privileges civil society as a vital, though not a sufficient, precondition for the existence of democracy.[67] Whether the state can be made accountable to its citizens depends greatly upon the self-consciousness, vibrancy, and political vision of civil society.[68] Contrary to conventional wisdom on democratic transition in Africa, civil society alone does not trigger democratization. The military's weight in African politics and history makes the armed forces and their leaders' attitudes and positions a requirement for embarking on a democratic path.

By late 1950s and early 1960s, when most African countries became independent, the struggle to transfer the bureaucracy into African hands intensified. Because of Europeans' evident reluctance to pass the baton to Africans, especially in the domain of security, their last minute plans to create an African officer corps did not include clear policies and institutions to exercise political control over the new national armies. Given the colonial army's behavior in Africa, "apolitism" was a foreign concept to African armies.[69] The clear separation between civilian and military authorities found in Europe did not exist in independent Africa. In Hatch's words:

> At the time of independence [the] colonial armies were handed over to African governments. Usually the white officers recognized a duty to obey the new government's orders, but the African soldiers felt but scant allegiance to those who had led the anti-colonial campaign and now occupied the seats of office. Sometimes they came from different, often rival, communities, especially when, as was common, soldiers were recruited from particular tribal groupings. Some politicians were less well educated than new appointed African officers. They certainly did not share the esprit de corps which characterized the military community.[70]

The legacy of colonial armies spawned several coups d'état in the first decade of African independence.[71] By the twilight of Europe's scramble for Africa, the military had gained ascendancy over civilian leaders in many indigenous governments. According to Hull, "the great leaders of Africa were no longer men of peace and statesmanship, but of war."[72] At independence, government in Africa was almost equivalent to the military. During colonial times, African armies had, in defense of European interests, taken security measures against the nationalists who inherited power at independence. Having experienced the use of colonial armies for civil repression, tax collection, and conquest functions, new leaders were perplexed about the role the military should play in the overdue development process.[73]

While African leaders still wondered about the proper avenue for a rapid political and economic transformation of their continent, policy-makers and scholars in the West encouraged military participation in Third World politics. As early as 1962, Lucien Pye favored the military's involvement in governmental affairs when he praised military leaders for being more pro-Western than their civilian counterparts.[74] In other words, the West valued a friendly Third World government over a competent or democratic regime. Even Edward Shils,[75] who had praised earlier the intellectuals as the creators of political life in their new countries, later divided them into two categories: the politicized intellectuals (civilians) and technical-executive intellectuals (military). In Shils's view only the latter could allow the emergence of a stable and progressive civil society. Similarly, Gaile argues that because the military often exhibited greater leadership and organizational skills than civilian politicians, it could more effectively pursue the goal of national integration in the developing world.[76]

Following that line of thinking, many theories and hypotheses on the role of the military in the development process evolved. Many other scholars shared Shils's and Gaile's views that the military ought to play an extensive role in political life.[77] There was an implicit notion that

> with its administration and managerial skills, the military's involvement in the politics of new nations is likely to result in favourable consequences as these skills are transferred from the sole administration of military affairs to those of the general society.[78]

Their view rested on the core assumption that the Western type of army organization, which the new African states copied, had a hierarchic structure that emphasized discipline and unity of command. On this assumption, the military, imbued with the spirit of rigor and hard work, should help African military leaders adapt more easily to the problems of modernization.

For Ergas, the armed forces may be able to play the function "of educator, of guardian of the secular character of the state, and guarantor of political stability and honesty in government."[79] Unfortunately, the first wave of military coups and interventions disappointed the proponents of military rule. Once in office, the military's performance did not differ from the civilian governments, belying the prognostications of the organizational model. Consequently, another generation of studies arose to explain the military's behavior in Africa.[80] While many of these studies produced good profiles of the military establishment in particular countries, and in the process challenged previous assumptions, they failed to agree on the main cause of military's intervention in African politics.[81] According to the literature, two main theories attempted to explain the military's involvement. These centered on military professionalism and the causes of coups.[82] In his 1957 seminal work, *The Soldier and the State*, Samuel Huntington compared the professionalism of the Western military with the nonprofessionalism of Third World military, and attributed military intervention in politics to the lack of professionalism.

As a general proposition, the military intervenes in countries without adequate institutional frameworks. In societies with relatively well-developed institutions of state coercion, but with poorly rearranged institutions for popular participation, the military's involvement in politics arises from the failure of the political system to effectively handle increased demand for popular participation. Civilian regimes' failure to address citizens' concerns led the military into politics and their disengagement will have to be negotiated. Out of this debate, it appeared that military's intervention was a direct function of the level and degree of a country's political development. Civil–military relations hold the key to sustainable democracy in Africa.

Welch sounded quite optimistic in equating, too precipitously it turned out, the decline of military rule with democracy:

> The rule of the "man on the horseback" is declining, as a consequence of the global political and ideological changes . . . Civil–military relations are changing dramatically with the spread of the call for democracy around the world. Although armed forces remain primary political actors in most states, their direct political roles have been reduced in recent years. The result, to overstate the case, is fundamental transformation and nowhere is it more marked than in developing countries. The Third World is now witnessing the slow, difficult, but significant consolidation of civilian governments after, in many cases, several decades of military rule.[83]

Contrary to Welch's anticipation, democratic transition and economic liberalization did not materialize. Given the military's endemic involvement in African politics, it is difficult to bestow any scholarly praise on that institution for its contribution to the new dawn on the continent. It is, however, important to assess the military's behavior vis-à-vis democratization in certain countries.[84] Because of the complex civil–military *problématique* in Africa, both civilian leaders and military officers need to reevaluate their relations for a brighter democratic prospect on the continent.

After many decades of mistrust, the military and civilian politicians need to redesign their relationships in order to facilitate a smooth political transition of their country. Diamond and Plattner make a good case for a badly needed new civil–military relationship in Africa:

> Sound civil–military relations are the product of longstanding national tradition and a complex set of formal and informal measures that affect

the government, civil society, and the military itself. If civil–military relations are to be given an ideal framework, it is vital that the state clearly demarcate the limits of the military's role and that both the broad public and the military feel that a role is legitimate. This requires that civilian leaders take the lead in defining the military's overall strategy and defense planning, in laying out the armed forces' roles and missions, and in regulating the military's budget, recruiting and training practices, force structure, and level of armaments.[85]

Civil control of the military is managed and maintained through the sharing of control between civilian leaders and military officers. This theory of shared responsibility, suggested by Bland, rests on two assumptions. First, the term "civil control" means that the sole legitimate source for the directions and actions of the military is derived from civilians outside the military establishment. Second, civil control is a dynamic process susceptible to changing ideas, values, circumstances, issues, and personalities, and to the stresses of crises and war.[86] Ideally, a professional military should hold the defense of state security as paramount and foster values of order and hierarchy internally to support that goal.[87] However, military intervention in politics has made the division between the armed forces as an institution and the military as government a critical issue in African politics.

In a democracy the challenge of civil–military relations is to "reconcile a military strong enough to do anything the civilians ask them to with a military subordinate enough to do only what civilian authorize them to do" and the civilian problem has centered around the question of "how to ensure that your agent is doing your will, especially when your agent has guns and so may enjoy more coercive power than you do."[88] On the other hand, the military's challenge is either to embrace the whims of society, which threaten to blunt the capability of the armed forces, or to risk alienation from the very people it purports to defend if it impedes social change. Although popular wisdom on the topic of civilian control of the military would deny any political role to the military, as evidenced in the concept of "apolitical" armed forces, the African army has been so politicized it has a direct stake in politics. Only a redefinition of boundaries and more astute management by civilians will, hopefully, prevent the military from intervening continuously in the political process.

Because of the complex civil–military *problématique* in Africa, both civilian leaders and military officers need to reevaluate their relations in order to protect democracy on the continent. The major problem of civil–military relations is the "praetorian problem . . . the need to curb the political power of the military establishment and to make the armed forces into a professional body committed to providing for the external security of the country."[89] While liberal democracies and emerging democracies must guard against the ancient and persistent problem, they more usually need to concentrate on how to manage civil–military relations after the power of the military has been curbed.[90]

According to Burk, the extensive empirical domain of civil–military includes:

> direct and indirect dealings that ordinary people and institutions have with the military, legislative haggling over the funding, regulation, and use of the military, and complex bargaining between civilian and military elites to define and implement national security policy. Moreover, each of these relations varies in form and consequence depending on whether they are found in strong democratic or weak authoritarian states, in economically developed or impoverished states, in states at war or states at peace.[91]

From a normative perspective, civilian political control over the military is preferable to military confiscation of the state, and democratization, at least at its early stage, should seek to establish and maintain civilian or democratic control over the military. Instead of being thought of as a struggle for power between irreconcilable enemies, civil–military relations should be reconceived of as exchanges between "friendly adversaries,"[92] in order to prevent African democratization from ending up as a mere fleeting vogue. Given the range of experiences and historical legacies on the continent, there is no consensus among participants as to how and when the military should be involved in politics. Some are of the opinion that the military is a political institution, and should be regarded as such, whereas others considered that the military should be essentially apolitical. The main challenge is, however, how to find agreement on certain basic principles of the relationship between the military and politics. These include the need for the military to respect the process of democratic transition, support democratically elected governments, and reject the taking of political power by force or extra-constitutional means.

While democracy has a new chance on the continent, African leaders, both political and military, need to reach a *modus vivendi* capable of creating and expanding democracy's longevity in Africa. The historical role of the military clearly affects civil–military relations and the way the military is viewed by society. Considerable differences exist throughout Africa, but generally those countries characterized by greater direct military influence over politics also have more fragile civil–military relations. As a result of past experiences, civil–military relations in most African countries are characterized by mistrust, misunderstanding, and misconceptions. The military is frequently seen, and indeed sees itself, as a society apart. Civilians often assume that the military enjoys a higher standard of living and greater privileges than they actually do. Improving civil–military relations is a key challenge for most African countries. A more complete integration of the military into civilian life, along with enhanced civilian understanding of the role and function of the military and of defense and security issues, is in the interests of both the military, and the democratic process.

The debate on whether or not the military should be political seems moot, given historical realities. At the early stage of democratization, the military might be granted a political status, in order to come to the negotiation to lend its crucial contribution. Until then, the process of democratization remains fragile, vulnerable, and susceptible to military reversal.

Conclusion

Since colonial rulers transferred power to their African successors, these new leaders have recast political institutions by force or negotiation. Political, social and economic arrangements have continued to be reproduced in new guises through periods of dramatic change. African nationalists sought state power as a means of designing a new state capable of bringing development to their continent. However, power in postcolonial Africa became an effective tool that both civilian and military autocrats use to their own advantage. What some described as the "vampire state," and characterized by "dishonesty, thievery and speculation"[93] only widened the gap between modern and traditional Africa, paving the way for continued violence and instability. During the past decade and beyond, Africa has been described by various scholars as a continent betrayed, in self-destruction, in crisis, existing in name only, being predatory or kleptocratic, or collapsed into anarchy and viciousness.[94] At the center of African states' failure to chart viable paths for domestic accumulation of wealth lies the problem of accountability that the new wave of democracy is hoping to correct. According to new Western orthodoxy, Third World countries must democratize if they are to develop, and aid is increasingly conditional on political reforms. However, the birth, life, and sustainability of democracy in Africa depend on several variables that need to be addressed by Africans and donor countries.

Decades of rhetoric on democracy's potential economic achievements render improving standards of living an understandable expectation. Ironically, the movement toward democracy might allow the return of the military if the suffering becomes unbearable. Any credible foreign policy using democratization as a new tool to generate brighter prospects in Africa should be aware of the potential backlash against a democracy without bread. Unless democratization is a hidden agenda to promote capitalism in Africa, the priorities need to be reassessed. Both bilateral and multilateral programs as well as IFIs' targets should be, at this stage at least, the improvement of living conditions, in order to keep the transition process from backsliding. Although many African countries appear to be on a path of political reforms, democratic practices are yet to be rooted in the political culture of the continent. Despite early elation, the new wave of democratization has yet to produce any consolidated democracy. Rather, there seems to be a revival of the "cult of the military," incumbent military leaders using constitutional means to strengthen their position. Whenever the military has tasted the forbidden political fruit, it has usually been a challenging task persuading it to return to and stay in the barracks. The challenge is not only to foster new civil–military relations conducive to a genuine democratic dawn in Africa, but also, and more importantly, to reform the nature of the African state.

Chapter 3

The Contemporary African State: *Res Publica* or *Res Privata*?

African states may vary in terms of their ideology, economic development, style of leadership, nature of the regime in power, size of population and fertility of soil, but they all have to a significant extent, a patrimonial core.
                                        Zaki Ergas, "Introduction."

Though several African states possessed democratic governments at independence, these democratic governments contained the seeds of their own destruction. Having destroyed precolonial democratic structures on the continent, Europeans never intended to replace them with functioning European-style democracies. During the colonial era, democracy was dualistic, selective, and necessarily oppressive. The elite white settler saw democracy as perfectly functional, whereas the colonized viewed African democracy as an irrationality laced with contradictions.[1] According to European colonizers, democratic institutions constituted an appropriate response to a particular set of political circumstances in which the colonial rulers ceded power to a new set of nationalist politicians.[2]

In many cases, the multiparty elections that preceded independence enabled qualified citizens to choose their new postcolonial leaders through the ballot box. Whatever the circumstances at its inception, democracy managed to survive in Africa, for varying periods of time, in a small number of states, and in the aspirations of many Africans. Ultimately, one of the major obstacles to sustainable democracy in Africa lay in the profound *statism* of African political systems. African leaders, at independence, inherited states rather than nations. As a consequence of this situation, the new leaders found themselves saddled with the difficult task of forging nations.[3] The vast majority of African states lacked consensus on any domestic values capable of maintaining support for democracy.

Despite reforms, traditional politics of self-interest persist because of the very nature of the African state. According to Aron,

> the state in Africa in the past has presented an odd dichotomy between a strong state and a weak one: at once authoritarian with enormous power often concentrated in the person of the president, and yet weak in institutional and administrative capacity, with limited material means, indebted, and with little control over peripheral regions in some cases.[4]

While colonialism endured, European powers hijacked the state mechanism to serve their own private interests rather than the public good of those living in these territories. With such a legacy, postindependence states understandably lacked the capacity to sustain a common good for their citizens. Until the nature of the African state has been transformed, democratic reforms stand little hope of success.

In the face of current excitement about democratic reforms in Africa, this chapter looks at a crucial variable of reform on the African continent: the African state and its shape and form. After a review of the literature on the state, the concept of *res publica* or the "ideal" state is explored in the first section. The second evaluates the behavior of the political entity of precolonial Africa. The third section dissects the colonial state. The fourth examines the *res privata* or the "privatized" state of independent Africa. The final part of this chapter describes the linkages between contemporary African states and the political, economic, and social nightmare the continent has experienced since independence.

The State in Theory

The state remains central concern to political science, as evidenced by various attempts to grasp its meaning.[5] Indeed, many political theorists consider the study of the state to be the *raison d'être* of their subject.[6] Because of its exceptional impact on society, theorizing about any social phenomenon without reference to the state's role becomes impossible. Several scholars have attempted to capture the ever-changing nature of the state. Some of these definitions draw on Max Weber's notion that the modern state is a compulsory organization, which organizes domination and monopolizes the legitimate use of physical force as a means of domination within a territory.[7] Much of the literature on the state emphasizes its institutional character as an organization or set of organizations, its rule-making attributes, and its recourse to coercion. At the core of the definitions lie questions of authority in the state's claimed territory, and legitimacy of the state, which compels voluntary compliance.

In the 1960s, Nettl expressed concern about the lack of any valid notion of the state. In his view, the concept ought to be treated as a reflection of the varying empirical reality with which social science concerns itself. Insofar as social science aims to separate all epiphenomenal or occasional factors from exigencies, fundamentals, and invariants, the concept of state is at risk. Besides providing a central administration of society, the institutionalization of sovereignty, and law enforcement, the state sets and attains social goals. Theorists differ on the importance of the concept. While Easton[8] downplays the importance of the state, suggesting that any conceptualization of the state leads to futile debates and a conceptual morass, Hoffman[9] argues for the centrality of the state in any theory of politics.

Nnoli distinguishes among three definitions of the state: legal, philosophical, and political. The legal definition of the state consists of an entity with a population, a government, a territory, and the monopoly of force. This conception of the state originates in the Treaty of Westphalia of 1648 that altered the hierarchical structure of society and ended the sacred–temporal dichotomy in Europe.[10] The philosophical conception tackles the characteristics of the ideal state. It includes three main schools of thought: first, the state is designed to harmonize the various parts of society, as explored in the writings of Plato, Aristotle, Aquinas, Augustine, and Cicero; second, the state has come about as an expression of a "social contract," as described by Rousseau, Locke, Machiavelli, and Hobbes; and third, the state as a result of the struggle between conflicting social forces in the world, as an organ of class rule, and of the oppression of one class by another, a view proposed by Hegel and Marx. Politically, the state is the product of the struggle for dominance among classes in society, and at the same time an instrument in the struggle.[11]

Classical political theory placed justice, good life, social welfare, and human dignity at the fore of institutional arrangements. However, the state plays a paradoxical role in the life of individuals and collectivities. On the one hand it is a coercive institution; on the other, it provides certain benefits and protections to its members. While the state represents the interests of the dominant classes, it is also the political space in which the community can formulate a common good for all citizens. Further, the state establishes the legal, political, and coercive framework within which society exits, establishing a sense of belonging to a wider political community. And, if it is an instrument that maintains law and order, it is equally an institution that dispenses justice.[12]

Despite the intense debate surrounding the state as a theoretical object, nearly all agree that some kind of state is needed. Even libertarians such as Hayek, who resent the welfare state as inimical to freedom, still argue for a minimal state with regulatory power. Similarly, scholars concerned about the oppressive power of the state agree that only real political power can adequately protect their citizens.

> Political power can significantly disrupt patriarchal and class . . . power. It holds the potential, at least, for disrupting the patriarchal/economic oppression of those in the lower reaches of class, sex, and race hierarchies. It is indisputable that, in the nineteenth and twentieth centuries, it has been the political power of states that has confronted the massive economic power privately constructed out of industrial processes and has imposed obligations on employers for the welfare of workers as well as providing additional social supports for the population at large.[13]

Conceptualizations of the state almost always criticize existing states. Despite such criticism, the state remains indispensable as the main mechanism for economic redistribution. The scale of such transfers remains quite high, even in *laissez-faire* governments such as Britain. Unlike other traditional functions of a state that can be easily carried out by private agencies or the market, the redistributive function can only be performed by the state.[14]

The relationship between the state and economic development is the most fundamental in society. Because the solution of many economic problems, including the country's economic development, depends on the correlation of class forces and political interaction, the state becomes the dominant class' tool to advance its interests. Although questions regarding the limits of state influence on economic processes, the effectiveness of state control over economic life, and the identification of key state tasks in the economy vary from one end of the ideological spectrum to the other, economists of all persuasions agree on the crucial role of the state.

In a capitalist economy, individual self-interest drives the economy. The "invisible hand" of supply and demand, rather than state intervention assures the efficient functioning of the market.[15] In a socialist economy, the state intervenes in many, if not all, areas of economic activity. In order to create the ideal socialist society, the vanguard leaders used state power to abolish capitalism and to take control of the economy away from anarchic market forces. A plan reflecting the prospects of development in all basic fields of society's activities underlies management of social and economic development.[16]

In a recent debate, the state was viewed as a tool of the bourgeoisie that occupied a distinct and irreducible place in society. Concepts such as "relative autonomy," "intermediate classes," "bureaucratic bourgeoisie," "political-administrative class," "state capitalism," among others were coined to describe the overwhelming power of the state.[17] This debate elucidated the specificity of structures and political power arrangements by putting into perspective the state–civil society *problématique*. After several decades of subordinating politics and political contestation to the power of the state, scholars became disillusioned with the state-centric theory of power. The almost obsessive preoccupation with the omnipotence of the state had led to the neglect of the mutually constitutive relationship of the state with civil society.

In marginalizing the phenomena of political contestation, the state-centric theory fails to take into account the various ways in which people have managed to interact with the state, sometimes disrupting its power. According to some academics, the state cannot be abstracted from civil society, its zone of engagement. The nature of the state cannot be explained without reference to developments outside the strict boundaries of the state. While the debate confers on the state certain coherence, a purpose, a direction, a vision, and a capacity for actually carrying out its political projects, recent social movements demonstrated that state power is more than often subjected to contestation. In other words, the substance and the boundaries of state power are contingent upon, and determined by, struggles in civil society.[18]

Although governments cannot successfully establish new social orders or carry out reforms for which the economic conditions have not ripened, they do possess significant power to direct and reform society and the economy. When used appropriately, the state can play a vital role in launching a new country or strengthening an old one. The utility of state power, whether for good or evil, renders the state an object of struggle, the actual control of which may intoxicate politicians. The ideal *res publica*, a public thing at the service of an entire people, has not been present everywhere. Third World countries in general, and Africa in particular, remain notorious for states that literally serve selfish interests of a few.

The contemporary state system is relatively new in Africa. Colonial powers did not extend the Westphalian concept of the state, with its attendant rights and duties, to African political entities that existed prior to colonization. European powers characterized precolonial African governments either nonexistent or despotic and unjust. European colonialists characterized them as such, in part, because they were interpreting those political authorities through lenses of self-interest and self-justification. This view gave colonizers a license to destroy the political entities that existed prior to their arrival. Before considering what replaced these traditional political structures, let us examine the social and political structures that existed prior to colonization.

The "State" in Precolonial Africa

Pierre Legendre reminds us that as a normative structure, the modern state preceded the naissance of capitalism.[19] The state's origins lie thirteenth century in Western Europe, when Christianity took over the historical legacy of the Roman law, which was five hundred years old. The state played a key role ever since as the center of society. It is the State that made mercantilism possible. The state became a major historical player when Machiavelli underscored the importance of state cause or *raison d'état*. However, that conception of the state did not exist in Africa in the sixteenth century.

Although precolonial Africans may have found the Westphalian state an alien concept, it is clear that precolonial Africa had functional equivalents to the modern state. The behavior of different monarchs demonstrates their need to impose power or authority on their subjects. The expansion of relatively homogeneous kingdoms into empires, and embracing peoples of different cultural traditions, religious beliefs, and ethnic backgrounds, required a more powerful authority. However, the symbiotic relationships between the leaders and their followers demanded some accountability and responsibility that no monarch could ignore. In the absence of written records, the richness and multiplicity of precolonial African political systems remains unappreciated.

The multifaceted history of precolonial Africa offers a vivid portrait of diversity and political choice. Constant modification of societies through migration led to ongoing alteration of societal values and political forms. African peoples developed their political systems to fit their particular political philosophies. Based on the assumptions that Africans made about the nature of human collectivities, social interaction, and relationship between power and authority, they designed political means to achieve certain shared purposes. The process through which societies "invented" their pattern of authority constantly reminded the leader of his or her role as a fair enforcer of community rules and preserver of the pluralism inherent in African political philosophy. Ideally, the monarch also effectively monitored the constant tension between centralization and diffusion of political power, and exercised political power in a manner cognizant of the quasi-constitutional limits.[20]

Some societies in Africa based political power on kinship, incorporating the notion that authority should be inherited. Others insisted that power should be earned. Still others maintained that various interest groups within society should share political power. Other political systems in precolonial Africa granted power to a specific class, organization, or racial caste. While some systems placed great reliance on religious authority to guide the destiny of the political ruler and society, others were more secular. Despite such a wide range of political systems, they all shared a belief in pluralism.[21]

Recent studies dispel the myth of African political systems as unorganized, citing evidence of well-developed and complex political and social organizations with procedures and processes deeply rooted in tradition and customs.[22] The monarch at the apex of the social pyramid spoke on behalf of society and wielded judicial, administrative, and legislative authority over the subjects. In theory, the monarch's power was absolute but, in practice he or she operated within defined limits and sought advice from the council of elders whose recommendations framed any political decision.

Although there still is debate about the extent to which precolonial Africa was democratic, given the existence of slavery and discrimination, ancient African communities had several ingredients of democracy.[23] Clearly, not all traditional African societies were democratic. Despotic and vicious kings ruled several of these precolonial societies. Nevertheless, some of them engaged in relatively democratic practices. Corroborating democratic practices in Ashanti societies in Ghana, Busia contends that:

> The Ashantis of Ghana have one of the large kingdoms in Africa, and yet there were various elements of democracy in their government. The powers of the *Asantehene* were not absolute, because he had to abide by the custom and advice of a representative council. If an *Asantehene* decided to ignore these checks on his power, he could be deposed [destooled]. Though the throne of *Asantehene* was hereditary, the electors had a choice of replacement from other members of the same lineage.[24]

Concurring with Busia, Kunz found in African political culture a tradition of checks and balances stating that:

> [This] tradition [exhibits a] rich body of varied constitutional practices in African societies long pre-dating the colonial period, a set of "leadership norms" often enshrined in oaths, song and drum texts, maxims/proverbs, prayers on ceremonial occasions. Cumulatively, they gave shape to the rival "principle of equality" or equal potentiality to authority ("the king in every man") and they constituted what Maxwell Owusu has referred to as "fiduciary obligations of trusteeship," subordinating the wielders of political power to "constitutional law." Conversely, they established the "right" and duty of the subjects to disobey and even kill an autocratic or tyrannical ruler.[25]

With all the imperfections of traditional political systems, the monarch enjoyed primarily adjudicative power to interpret and apply customs and laws. These norms, passed down from generation to generation without question, enjoyed great respect and the ruler disregarded them at their peril. Although the monarch may not have been democratically elected, the norms that the monarch enforced represented the consensus of the community. Because chiefs were considered custodians of tradition and customs, their selection followed specific rules designed by society. Abuse of power could result in "de-stooling" proceedings that forced leaders to maintain popular approval and confidence.

Colonization disrupted this system of political representation. European invaders used the concept of "civilization" to disguise their predatory interests.[26] Concerned about France's policies vis-à-vis African democracy, Martial Merlin, French General Governor (1919–1923) observed that the "fierce struggle against chiefs" had been a misguided crusade inspired by the newly triumphant bourgeoisie's republican ideology.[27] By the time Europeans left the continent, they had destroyed or diluted any democratic practices in African societies.[28] Rupert Emerson even predicted that "democracy in Africa, as in Asia, would bleed and die on the altars of national consolidation and social reconstruction."[29] Alluding to the history of the state and of democracy in Africa, Pfaff maintained that:

> it seems fair to say that when Europeans first came to Africa there were coherent, functioning societies of varying degrees of sophistication, some of great political subtlety and artistic accomplishment, others simple hunting and gathering communities, some extremely cruel in their practices, but all possessing their own integrity and integrated into the natural environment of the continent. This was destroyed by colonialism.[30]

Contrary to the nineteenth century view of pre-European Africa as a vast anarchic wasteland, Africa's well-organized political institutions rivaled European states. Although some lived in stateless societies organized around the family, kinship groups, and clans, most precolonial Africans resided within powerful empires and kingdoms respectful of their subjects.

The State in Colonial Africa

Western political thinkers regard constitutional checks and balances and formal institutionalization of a separation of powers as prerequisites for effective restraints on governmental power, believing that these restraints prevent, or at least mitigate, the abuse of power. In African societies, checks on the use of political power were unwritten and informal but no less real, functioning effectively in virtually every African political system. However, colonialism administered a severe blow to traditional political systems. The arrival of European traders, missionaries, settlers, and colonial civil servants brought traditional African systems into contact with new cultures and political structures. The impact of Western civilization shook the foundations of the traditional African political systems.

The search for raw materials and new markets as well as the power struggle among European powers, drove Europeans' entry into Africa. European colonial powers disregarded traditional African political systems. Colonial powers governed their newly acquired colonies without regard to the consequences for the societies they ruled.[31] The colonial states, characterized by ambiguous borders coupled with trans-state population structures, were initially designed to fulfill the requirements of "effective occupation" and "pacification" imposed by the Berlin Conference. Subsequently, they evolved to facilitate the extraction of resources. As Young rightly states:

> The colonial state in general while insisting upon the ascendancy of its law, did not (and could not) enforce a comprehensive legal monopoly. The colonial legal order confined its demands for exclusivity to economic and social spheres covering the activity of the external estate of Europeans and other immigrants, as well as criminal offenses which were deemed, directly or indirectly, to affect the colonial peace.[32]

While a few colonial governments retained some indigenous social institutions and redefined others, most imposed a new administrative structure on existing social and political orders. Given the nature of the competition among European nations, boundaries took on new meaning in Africa. In this respect, colonial powers redefined the communities themselves in addition to reshaping the institutions that governed them. Because they wanted to operate within newly delineated boundaries, Europeans imposed physical definitions of frontiers on indigenous populations who saw boundaries as a belt of separation between social units.[33]

European powers adopted various systems of colonial administration. The British Empire administered its colonies by means of "indirect rule," meaning that British officers governed through the traditional chiefs. The British sought to preserve as far as possible the power and prestige of those leaders while adapting the customary methods of rule to meet the needs of modern society. By doing so, the British hoped to ease the impact of transition from traditional to modern government. By the late 1930s, however, the British Empire became dissatisfied with "indirect rule," since the chiefs could not adapt to new ways, and the system left no place for the young, educated elites to share in local administration.

In contrast to the British system of indirect rule, France pursued a policy of assimilation and "direct rule" in its African colonies. France intended to acquaint its African subjects as fully as possible with French institutions, language, and culture, the ultimate goal being complete assimilation of the colonies to the *métropole* (France). Consequently, France expended very little effort in creating representative political institutions or maintaining the traditional authorities, which were subordinated to the French administration. Most Africans were unwilling to give up their traditional culture in favor of *francisation*.

Portuguese policy embraced assimilation to a greater extent than France, making the colonies sheer overseas provinces of Portugal. Abuse of authority, a low level of education, and severe limitations on economic development characterized Portuguese rule. In the Belgian Congo, the colonial power pursued a policy of strong paternalism. While Congolese received primary education for technical positions, Belgium made virtually no attempt to prepare a potential transfer of power, leaving the colony unprepared for self-rule. When Belgium finally relinquished power chaos ensued. Whether it is Britain's "indirect rule," France's "direct rule," Spain's "unstructured paternalism," Portugal's "centralism," or Belgium's "paternalism," they were all designed to control Africans.[34] Europeans designed a "Native Authority" system based on principles opposed to the African system it displaced, including the belief that nothing would guide the chiefs and remove abuses but the way of enlightenment. Then, having cleaned and polished their instruments, they would turn them to constructive use.[35]

Colonial states created an administrative hierarchy by concentrating political and administrative functions in the hands of the colonial service. The task of governance, including such responsibilities as revenue collection, public order, education, social services, infrastructures, adjudication, were given to a representative local body, even if broad or important decisions were made in the *métropole*. The essential feature of the colonial state was a lack of distinction between decision-making and implementation roles. As "the organized aggregate of relatively permanent institutions of governance,"[36] the colonial state was more an exploitation machine than anything else.

To assist in these exploitative functions, a well-developed coercive apparatus supported the colonial state. Police forces in each territory ostensibly maintained order but also to ensure compliance with specific dictates. The colonial government relied on a strong security service composed of troops from either the *métropole* or other colonies to quell expressions of resentment. In Schraeder's assessment, "a coercive apparatus of police and military was . . . created in every colony with the intention of ensuring local compliance with colonial rules and regulations."[37] Despite measures to "pacify" their colonies, European powers realized that pockets of resistance remained, making the colonial state essentially a military-administrative tool of exploitation. The goal of exploitation pursued through policies of coercion and force diverted the state's resources from the common good of the colonized to the private gain of the colonizers.

To fulfill such a mission, the colonial state needed to be undemocratic and authoritarian. The urge to despoil Africa of its human and material resources prevented European powers from investing time in improving Africans' standards of living. Authoritarian in both form and substance, the colonial state made decisions with no feedback from the subjects. Unlike precolonial Africa, political patterns within the colonial state were overwhelming hierarchical, and Africans were systematically excluded from decision-making roles. Even colonial powers such as France, which pretended to give Africans access to the political process through representation, designed these mechanisms not out of genuine sympathy for Africans' concerns but rather out of a desire to delay independence movements.

In addition to authoritarianism, all colonial systems displayed a great deal of racism in declaring their values superior to those held by Africans. Ironically, that ideology of racial and cultural superiority had an enormous psychological impact on postindependence leaders. Unable to truly decolonize themselves, the new leaders failed to create the ideal state that could take their continent to higher ground.

The Postcolonial State in Africa

At independence, new governments embarked on welding together people who were divided along ethnic and cultural lines. As Africa achieved independence under majority rule, a number of common problems stood out. Colonial boundaries, though artificial, generally survived as national borders. Within them, however, national integration proved difficult. Because few African countries had ethnically homogeneous populations, political conflict among ethnic or kinship groups—often complicated by religious differences—became common. Independence meant, too, that the nationalist leaders inherited their former rulers' administrative systems. This colonial apparatus proved inadequate for the government of independent states.

At independence, African states shared several features. They all searched for new identities as nation-states. Besides the task of welding distinct nations into a state, most of these political entities were poor, predominantly rural, and overdependent on the vagaries of the world market.[38] But perhaps most influential was the authoritarian legacy of colonialism. Kasfir is correct that "the political culture bequeathed by colonialism contained the notions that authoritarianism was an appropriate mode of rule and that political activity was merely a disguised form of self-interest, subversive of the public welfare."[39] Following the colonial precedent, new administrations acted without widespread consultation, a shortcoming that still marks the contemporary African state. According to Falola,

> government and leadership have failed to acquire credibility, and in most cases the basis of power [legitimacy] lies in violence. Most of the governments began with huge support in the first few years of independence, but the promise of mass-based political parties quickly degenerated to one-party authoritarian states.[40]

The tragic dismantling of the checks and balances found in traditional political systems became obvious with the transfer of power to indigenous leadership. Whereas traditional leaders abided by the political norms and customs of their individual societies or ethnic groups, postcolonial leaders emulated colonialists' practices by imposing dictatorial power on their fellow citizens. If the primary goal of the colonial state was to maintain European domination, the goal of the new independent states became the establishment of indigenous domination. Although European powers made last-minute arrangements for multiparty systems, new leaders quickly centralized their power through single-party political systems.

At independence, African leaders found themselves with partially democratic colonial states.[41] Africa inherited British, French, or Belgian models of liberal democracy from the accelerated and panicky processes of rapid de-colonization. Only in the last decade of colonialism, when independence became a certainty, did the imperial powers incorporate democratic reforms into the colonial structures of exploitation, despotism, and degradation.[42] According to Udogu, "the colonial administrators socialized the African leaders in an authoritarian form of governance, but expected those to whom they handed the baton of leadership to become democrats in due course."[43] Democracy's elusiveness in Africa did not fulfill these expectations.

Paradoxically, the latter days of colonial autocracy encouraged democracy in order to perpetuate exploitative capitalism and continuing dominance by the former colonial powers. Ironically, withdrawal from the colonies enabled Europeans to regulate the colonial economies at a time when their focus had shifted from military to economic security. The undemocratic structures put into place by withdrawing colonial powers would later haunt the postcolonial national elite and be used to consolidate their authoritarian rule. In Sklar's words, "Africa's post-colonial states are successors to profoundly anti-democratic colonial forms of governing."[44]

African leaders never fully accepted the precepts of the European political model. Most tolerated it only as a means to their own selfish ends.[45] They argued that a competitive party system was inappropriate for African conditions, because political parties only represent and perpetuate social classes. Others rejected liberal democracy because of the Marxist argument that democracy only masks bourgeois domination. Given that mistrust of "bourgeois" democracy, one would expect African leaders to devote their energy to the betterment of the lives of their compatriots. Unfortunately, they simply replaced the colonizers and built support through local constituencies made up with kinship and ethnic groups. Ethnic constituencies thereby became crucial to the survival of new governments. In the meantime, they either ran the opposition underground or defused it by co-opting into government members willing to bestow their political support and personal loyalty in return for political compensation.[46]

Chazan and her colleagues believe that:

> because state institutions in Africa are fragile and command only limited public acceptance, informal networks of personal relationships emerge in society to link a relatively powerful and well-placed patron with a less powerful client or clients for the purpose of advancing their mutual interests.[47]

In the same vein, Lemarchand observes that "clientelism can lead to a pyramiding of client–patron ties, and, through the recruitment of new brokers, to an expansion of local or regional reciprocities on a more inclusive scale."[48]

Power evolved around individuals and constitutions were ignored, altered, or set aside. Many believed that Africa should develop its own forms of democracy, more suited to its history and culture.[49] That position was even praised by some scholars. Ruth Morgenthau[50] for example, hailed the one-party regime as a necessary and inevitable modernizing agency if different ethnic groups were to be mobilized and constituted into one nation. At the same time, Frantz Fanon already saw in such a system the root of all the problems the continent might face. In his condemnation of the corruption of Jean-Jacques Rousseau's "General Will" in the form of the one-party doctrine in Africa, Fanon said poignantly: "the single party is the modern form of the dictatorship of the bourgeoisie, unmasked, unpainted, unscrupulous, and cynical."[51] Through one-party political systems, new leaders crafted pervasive clientelistic networks that ensured the flow of power through their hands rather than through formal institutions that might impose unwanted constraints on them.

According to Schraeder, the first generation of African leaders faced the "great expectations-minimal capabilities" paradox. In the face of popular expectations that higher wages and better living conditions would quickly follow from independence, new leaders lacked both the will and the capabilities to satisfy these demands, chosing instead to promote the concentration of state power at the expense of civil society.[52] Describing postindependence power in Africa, Schraeder paints six distinct patterns. The "Africanization of state institutions" allowed the replacement of departing colonial administrators with African politicians and civil servants. Through bureaucratic expansion and the growth of parastatals African leaders sought to strengthen state power by expanding the number of civil servants, and by creating state-owned or state-controlled corporations. The dismantling of institutional checks and balances gave African leaders *carte blanche* for unaccountable behavior and unchallenged authority. Co-optation and silencing of civil society clearly contributed to the consolidation of unshared power. While the "expansion of the coercive apparatus" instilled more fear in the populations, the "creation of personal rule networks" transformed the nature of authority, in that power is ultimately vested in an individual leader as opposed to legally based institutions.[53]

The rise of centralized and authoritarian African states led to a series of economic, political, and social developments that would later be referred to as the crisis of the African state.[54] Severe economic crisis and the unexpected resurgence of civil society weakened African leaders' hold on power. After decades of corruption and economic mismanagement, the predatory states[55] lost their legitimacy and effectiveness, turning into lame Leviathans[56] and shadow states.[57] Attempting to understand the dismal performance of postindependence Africa is a Herculean task that volumes of books and articles have tried in vain to perform. However, the bulk of the literature on Africa's never-ending crisis does cite the state as the Gordian knot of Africa's economic and political nightmare.

The Contemporary African State: A *Res Privata*

Prior to the 1970s and 1980s, which were decades of disenchantment for the African state, the state was ascendant in the 1950s and 1960s. The unsuccessful attempts to strengthen state institutions gave way to pessimism about the profligacy, fragility, and incapacity of the African state and its leaders. Consequently, perspectives informed by increasing evidence of the state's incoherence, incapacitation, and weaknesses replaced more optimistic views about the state and its potential.[58] Subsequent efforts in the 1990s focused on completing the swing of the intellectual and policy pendulum away from the African state toward civil society, in the expectation that this will provide an alternate resource base for engineering and sustaining the development of the continent.[59]

African states have been recently depicted as "collapsed," "failed," or "quasi-states,"[60] epitomizing a corrupt institution incapable of fulfilling its basic duties. Despite its natural endowments, Africa continues to lag behind other continents because its leaders have failed to make efficient use of its resources. The autocratic trend of the early days of independence worsened with time, placing contemporary Africa at a critical juncture.[61] African leaders have expanded the scope of state power without increasing the state's capacity to use that power to create wealth for the populations.

In a deliberate way, the state, the regime, and the party, even individual personalities become blurred, making the "public" and the "private" very difficult to distinguish.[62] The African state has become an instrument of elite manipulation and of self-aggrandizement. Access to the state and its resources became key to the accumulation of wealth. Having robbed the state, wealthy politicians used their surplus to invest in social networks, build their own clientele and position themselves for access to wider patronage networks of the state.[63] By reproducing the structures of the colonial state and extending patronage through them, postcolonial states in Africa failed to resolve the inherited contradictions of the colonial system in that patronage networks have now been extended to triangular links of state officials, local middlemen, and international capital.[64]

The behavior of postindependence leaders created what Gunnar Myrdal called the "soft" state. African states are characterized by a general absence of discipline, particularly in the conduct of public business. Powerful officials often circumvent laws and regulations in their own behavior and apply them inconsistently to others. Corrupt practices are commonplace in order to secure objectives other than those officially stated. The "civic public realm" lacks the legitimacy enjoyed by the "primordial public realm" and thus, there is a tendency to enhance the latter by taking from the former. Although gift-giving and petty corruption existed in precolonial and colonial Africa, these phenomena could not compare to the kleptocracy that has now emerged, in which the elite systematically plunder the state's wealth.[65]

Instead of using the state to create conditions conducive to improving the well-being of their citizens, African leaders have generated on the continent what Bayart[66] dubbed *la politique du ventre*, or the politics of the belly. Contemporary leaders' behavior led to the belief throughout the continent that politics is all about "eating" or "devouring" the state's resources. Rich and poor, elites and masses, "big men" and "small boys," all share the same opportunistic and materialistic view of politics and the state. Instead of the political and economic forms of modernity, the pattern of state–society relations, the patronage systems, and ethnic communities and identities created an "uncivil nationalism" and a personal rule.[67]

Expediency and necessity determine political action in personal regimes. Actions are determined by the resources at one's disposal well as obligations and attachments to friends, kin, and factional allies. In Jackson and Rosberg's view,

> [p]ersonal rule is a form of monopolistic rather than pluralistic politics. Personal regimes consist primarily of the internecine struggles of powerful individuals, civilian or military, for power and place and secondarily of the actions of outsiders who desire to enter the monopoly, influence members within it, or displace it with their own personal regime. Politics tend to be closed to public participation and observation and even to be secretive.[68]

Through a web of strategies, African leaders have privatized their state. Rather than carrying out the regular functions assigned to the state, including oversight and supervision of the nation's resources, effective and rational revenue extraction, social services, and the maintenance of law and order, the "personally appropriative" African state serves only the private interests of its leaders. While external circumstances and pressures are relevant, it is rather patrimonialism that diverts the resources, energy, capacity, and political will of African states away from the tasks of development and democratization into the enrichment of a rapacious horde of venal officials. The crisis of the state in postcolonial Africa is a function of its nature as an authoritarian control structure preoccupied with the political survival and material interests of those who control it.

In a seminal article on state formation in Africa, Diamond argues that ruling classes and the class character of the rulers in Africa is based on political power. He unifies the Weberian and Marxist concepts of state and politics and adds a new look at the historic and current background of political elites in political power. Through an excellent description of the overdeveloped but inefficient postcolonial African state, Diamond explored the difficulties facing the African state.[69]

The liberal paradigm sees the state as a benevolent arbitrator of the various conflicting interests in society, whereas the Marxist perception of the state is a tool in the hands of the ruling class, which uses it to advance and perpetuate its interests. The African patrimonial state more closely reflects the latter view, in that different factions within society are locked in battle for the appropriation of state resources. According to Marenin, "the nature of the state [in Africa] . . . is found in the organizational processes by which contending coalitions of groups manage to institutionalize and reproduce their wishes and inter-ests."[70] The state disappears only to be replaced by personalistic poli-tics for which state structures are but an object of manipulation with no legitimate claims to a distinct existence or purpose. Some have argued that a confluence of pressures will reconfigure the structure of state–society relations in African states for some time to come.[71]

Most African ruling groups, civilian and military alike, have responded to nation-building by relying on a centralist and corpo-ratist tradition inherited from colonial powers along with a wide vari-ety of authoritarian techniques to create centralizing, patrimonial administrative states. Instead of crafting new states capable of improv-ing the living standard of their people, African leaders recreated states very similar to the colonial ones and patrimonialized them. The "modal" state squats on its people like a bloated toad, simultaneously "overdeveloped and underdeveloped,"[72] captured by and used for private interests, unwilling and unable to serve any conception of the public good. A review of the literature on the African state indicates that the African state is extensive, fragile, prebendal, and elitist.[73] A combination of any of these traits represents one of two situations: an image in which personal and social forces dominate the state, and another in which the state overpowers social forces. In either case, the ordinary citizen clearly loses.

Conclusion

The centrality of the state in Africa cannot be overstated. Efforts to promote democratization on the continent have thus far targeted the wrong institutional levels, missing those where bureaucratic authori-tarianism, patronage, and ethnic factionalism are entrenched. For ordinary people, the central problem lies in their daily contact with local authorities and agents of the state where instead of disinterested competence and fairness, they encounter incompetence, bias, venality, and corruption. So long as the state remains elusive and privatized, citizens cannot develop trust in their state, and will continue to rely on the personalized, protective ties of clientelism. To reduce the multiple manifestations of the African state to one overall conceptual entity might be a bit presumptuous since there are as many states as there are African countries. Although this may be true *stricto sensu*, it can also be argued convincingly that in virtually all African states, at least at this particular stage of their historical development, state–society relations are primarily defined by patrimonialism.[74]

The colonial experience in Africa was largely negative. European powers maintained their rule by the use of force. Colonial governments were authoritarian, disruptive to local economic systems, and essentially exploitive in character. They imposed arbitrary boundaries all over Africa and "colonized" the minds of Africans. Colonial powers imported state institutions while leaving behind doctrines such as constitutionalism, civil liberties, and liberalism. The idea of the nations as sacred corollaries of the state never materialized in colonial Africa, where colonial states represent the antithesis of national states.[75] Contemporary African states lost the positive attributes of the precolonial traditional system, and adopted the worst of the colonial system, creating a hybrid or a "vampire" state[76] that sucked dry every drop of state resources.

Chapter 4

Corruption in Africa

Institutionalization of corruption [in Africa]: no rational results can be expected from dealings involving the government, including its executive, judicial and administrative branches (from ministers, generals, judges, directors of departments, down to police officers, customs officials and post office clerks). Nothing will "get done" without the payment of a hierarchically determined bribe or kickback as a matter of routine.

Zaki Ergas, "Conclusion."

In his very first year in office, WB President, James Wolfensohn boldly identified corruption as a major global problem. In his view, extensive corruption in developing and transitional economies undermines public support for spending on overseas aid. The impression that aid money ends up in Swiss bank accounts gave rise to obvious signs of aid fatigue. Besides its effects on aid, corruption also deters investment, undermines good governance, distorts government policy, and leads to a misallocation of resources:

In a corrupt environment, resources may be directed towards non-productive areas—the police, the armed forces and other organs of social control—as the elite move to protect themselves, their positions and their material wealth. Resources otherwise available for socio-economic development will be diverted into security expenditure. This, in turn, can cause the weakening of market institutions as rent-seeking, rather than investment becomes the major objective of policy makers.[1]

In addition, corruption clearly bears down most heavily on the poorest sections of society who ultimately bear the cost of the distortions and deprivations it generates. Aware of the importance of combating corruption, UN Secretary-General Kofi Annan affirmed that development in Africa "implies good governance, competent elites, and above all, the disappearance of corruption."[2] In December 1996, the United

Nations adopted a declaration against international corruption and bribery enjoining member-states to strive to eliminate these and associated pathologies by criminalizing bribery of foreign officials as well as ending opportunities that promote briberies.[3] However, efforts at curtailing corruption in the world in general and in the Third World in particular have yet to eliminate this phenomenon.

Corruption, Development, and Poverty

Although petty corruption existed in the past, contemporary society faces a social scourge with consequences beyond imagination. The sudden upsurge in corruption, especially in poor countries, undermines any serious efforts to take these regions out of misery. The diverse manifestations of corrupt transactions have been identified as ranging from:

> Acceptance of money or other rewards for awarding contracts, violations of procedures to advance personal interests, including kickbacks from development programmes or multinational corporations; pay-offs for legislative support; and the diversion of public resources for private use, to overlooking illegal activities or intervening in the justice process. Forms of corruption also include nepotism, common theft, overpricing, establishing non-existent projects, payroll padding, tax collection and tax assessment frauds.[4]

In a seminal article, Krueger introduces the concept of rents that are present in government monopolies. Competitive rent seeking is a factor in societies where governments control sectors of the economy. He analyzes the opportunities created through state-owned enterprises, quantitative restrictions, and tariffs that lead to rent seeking.[5] Having defined rents as "the extra amount paid to somebody or for something useful whose supply is limited either by nature or through human ingenuity," Mauro argues that rent seeking is the essence of corruption, and that rent seeking is the government's capacity to interfere with the market, to create monopolies or otherwise restrict competition so that some industry or individual can realize a rent. It concludes that corruption negatively affects investment and growth.[6]

Grand corruption, in the form of *kleptocracy* and *lootocracy*, seriously impacts the economic development of countries already struggling to catch up to developed nations. Drawing on insights from the fields of political science, game theory, economics, sociology, and law, some have provided a framework for the analysis of political corruption, by examining how political corruption can be defined and how it operates in practice,[7] while others have elucidated the political economy of corruption, focusing on causes and consequences of corruption, and measures to curb corruption. For instance, Arvind Jain proposes a shift away from the study of bribery-type activities to grand corruption that distorts economic policies.[8]

In a major reference work on corruption, Rose-Ackerman views governmental corruption as an economic, cultural, and political problem that limits investment and growth and leads to ineffective government.[9] Assessing the economic impact of corruption, she posits that:

> All states, whether benevolent or repressive, control the distribution of valuable benefits and the imposition of onerous costs. The distribution of these benefits and costs is generally under the control of public officials who possess discretionary power. Private individuals and firms who want favorable treatment may be willing to pay to obtain it. Payments are corrupt if they are illegally made to public agents with the goal of obtaining a benefit or avoiding a cost. Corruption is a symptom that something has gone wrong in the management of the state. Institutions designed to govern the interrelationships between the citizen and the state are used instead for personal enrichment and the provision of benefits to the corrupt. The price mechanism, so often a source of economic efficiency and a contributor to growth, can, in the form of bribery, undermine the legitimacy and effectiveness of government.[10]

In her attempt to isolate the most important situations where widespread corruption can determine who obtains the benefits and bears the costs of government action, Rose-Ackerman proposes four overlapping consequences of corruption:

- *Bribes clear the market*: The government may be charged with allocating a scarce benefit to individuals and firms using legal criteria other than willingness to pay.
- *Bribes act as incentives*: Officials in the public sector may have little incentive to do their jobs well, given official pay scales and the level of internal monitoring. They may impose delays and other roadblocks.
- *Bribes lower costs*: Those engaged in legal pursuits seek to reduce the costs imposed on them by government in the form of taxes, customs duties, and regulations.
- *Bribes permit criminal activity*: Illegal businesses frequently purchase benefits from the state. In extreme cases illegal businesses and organized crime bosses dominate the police and other parts of the state through corruption and intimidation.

Several scholars have explored the complex contours of corruption. Cooksey expounds on two sets of arguments: first, corruption reduces the size of the economic cake in any given national context, condemning varying segments of the population to poverty. Second, the poor suffer directly from systematic corruption, for instance by being excluded from access to public services such as clean domestic water. In addition, corruption may breed patterns of public investments biased toward large, high-cost capital-intensive projects at the expense of broad-based, human capital enhancing investments.[11] Similarly, Carvajal argues that the factors sustaining large-scale corruption also inhibit development. By reviewing the history and evolution of a government agency for small farmers in a developing country, Carvajal shows that while extracting wealth, corrupt power networks generated waste, reduced production, and caused acrimony among their victims. Development requires the ability to detect and neutralize corrupt networks.[12]

In a preliminary step to analyzing the possible impact of the linkage between offshore interface (finance centers and tax heavens) and corruption on economic development, Hampton explores the relationships among corruption, offshore finance centers and economic development. He maintains that moral outrage at the "cancer of corruption" needs to be considered alongside the double standards of Western companies that routinely supply bribes to win contracts in poor countries, thus prolonging rent-seeking behavior. Hampton argues effectively that the growth of offshore interface may be outpacing any attempts at regulation by the business communities or governments.[13] Banerjee develops a theoretical model to explain why government bureaucracies are often associated with red tape, corruption, and lack of incentives. The model identifies two specific ingredients that together can provide an explanation: the fact that governments often act precisely in situations where markets fail, and the presence of agency problems within the government. Poverty and low levels of development only exacerbate these problems.[14]

Cartier-Bresson alleges that most studies of corruption concentrate on occasional and unorganized behavior and analyzes instead networks of corrupt actors who interact in regular, organized corruption. He concludes that the study of networks has more to offer for an understanding of corruption than the classic political economy approach.[15] Campos and Line, on their part, provide empirical evidence that it is not only the level of corruption that affects investment but also the nature of corruption. Different corruption regimes have different effects on investment, with unpredictable corruption regimes doing the most harm. The level of corruption also matters.[16]

Corruption spans a whole spectrum of unethical, immoral, illegitimate and illegal human activities. The WB defines corruption as the "abuse of power for personal gain,"[17] capturing the general essence of grand or institutional corruption. But corruption also includes the "use of privileges by office holders and those in statutory or functional equivalent positions for personal benefit."[18] The OECD Convention on Combating the Bribery of Foreign Public Officials and the European Council's Civil and Criminal Conventions on Combating Corruption, underscore that corruption includes active and passive bribery of public officials, breach of trust, and nepotism.[19] However, corruption can be defined more broadly as "the behaviour of persons entrusted with public or private responsibilities who neglect their duties to achieve unjustified benefits."[20] This means that the term covers not only the public sphere but also the private and semipublic sphere, ethical standards in civil society, and the practices of exploiting positions of trust held by private individuals in business in addition to political corruption.[21]

The OECD commission described three different levels of corruption based on the parties involved and the interest served:

- At government level ("grand corruption, lootocracy, kleptocracy"— "greed not need"): Here the state is considered as plunder for client structures of the ruling elite. This is done, for example, in the context of land reform by allocating land to high office holders and political cronies, in fraudulent privatization of state enterprises, granting import and export licenses, and manipulating public tenders for major contracts.
- At the level of the interface between citizen and state ("petty corruption"): This relates to officials demanding smaller sums from the citizens to "overlook" real or imagined irregularities, to "pay" for public goods and services, for example, access to schools, health care in hospitals, and so on. The term "petty corruption" relates solely to the sums involved; however, its significance for the poor population in particular is very great, and the devastating influence of this corruption on the relationship between citizen and state should not be underestimated.
- At the level of political life ("political corruption"): Attaining political influence through illegal means contributes greatly to corruption, as a way of rewarding political allies, client structures, and relatives.

Corruption, Development, and Politics in Africa

Africa, like the rest of the developing world, faces corruption as a preeminent problem. Corruption, whether rare, widespread, or systemic, has now reached cancerous proportions with a negative impact on the development of the continent. The economic consequences of pervasive corruption, in conjunction with recent trends toward democratization, have increased the pressure for accountability and transparency for those in public office. While political corruption is undoubtedly a global phenomenon, the nature of states of Africa, as discussed in chapter 3, renders the consequences especially dire, leading in extreme cases to state collapse. Statistical evidence suggests that countries with high levels of corruption experience poor economic performance. Corruption reduces domestic investment, discourages foreign direct investment, inflates government spending, and shifts government spending away from education, health, and infrastructure maintenance toward less efficient (more manipulable) public projects.[22]

In an important book that has shaped much of the thinking about corruption, Klitgaard provides a thorough analysis of the phenomenon and its consequences. Bribery, extortion, fraud, kickbacks, and collusion have resulted in developing economies, predator elites, and political instability.[23] Della Porta and Mény argue eloquently that corruption is central to the "vicious circles" that sustain clientelism, electoral fraud, administrative inefficiency, and criminal activities.[24] Exploring the role of institutions in helping achieve growth and development in Africa, Ateba shows why the *ad hoc* policies implemented by IMF and the WB in most sub-Saharan African countries have led to insignificant results. The failure to ensure the transition to a market economy seems to be due to the lack of recognition that African institutions are inefficient. The programs and policies that were implemented did not internalize the opportunistic and rent-seeking behavior of the economic agents who live in these regions.[25]

In an insightful book published just after many African states became independent, Andreski analyzes the obstacles facing the new states on the road to prosperity, internal peace and elementary freedoms. He focuses on the network of vicious circles and problems which, at the time the book was published, other authors and international agencies overlooked Andreski's chapter on "kleptocracy and corruption as a system of government" resembles, to an unpleasant degree, the present situation in many African countries.[26] According to Andreski, the use of public office for private enrichment became, with few exceptions, the normal and accepted practice in newly independent African states:

> After only a few years in office the top politicians have amassed fortunes worth a hundred times the sum of salaries received. Many of them have simply transferred bid sums from the treasury to their private accounts, but the practice of getting cuts on government contracts constitutes the chief fount of illegal gains.[27]

Based on evidence from Nigeria, which, continues to serve as the leading example of corruption in Africa, Andreski describes graft or corruption on the continent:

> Collection of taxes, excise and custom duties offer ample opportunities for graft. With the aid of bribes people can have liabilities drastically reduced or may even avoid taxation altogether, whereas those who refuse to play will receive most stringent assessments—which in cases where the amount of income cannot be exactly proven, could become exorbitant and crushing. Thus cupidity and the desire to evade the legal liability, and on the other hand the fear of victimization, enmesh everybody who runs business (regardless of the size) in a network of bribery.[28]

While those engaging in petty corruption take part in the "corruption business" based on the power they wield, powerful politicians and their civil servant counterparts rob the government and their citizens with ease. Their behavior clearly allows corruption to become an accepted practice. Andreski's narration uncovers the seeds of contemporary Africa's corruption problem:

> The forms of bribery and embezzlement are profusely variegate and many of them must appear incredible to people who have always lived in better ordered countries. I have known hospitals in West Africa where the patients had to pay nurses to bring them a chamber pot; where the doctors (who were receiving a salary from the state and were supposed to treat the sick free of charge) would look only at those patients who had given them money, and saw those first who paid most, regardless whose condition was most urgent. Those in charge of the dispensary stole the medicaments and then sold them either to the patients on the premises or to the traders. The doctors did the same, taking the medicaments for use in their private consulting rooms. Patients unable to pay got injections of coloured water. Many who did pay were cheated and got exactly the same.[29]

In his take on the issue, Médard demonstrates how international business uses corruption to obtain market share in Africa and other Third World regions. He brilliantly exposes the French–African neocolonial and clientelist relationship and its negative impacts on the continent.[30] Médard sees corruption, the misuse of public office for personal gain, as a defining characteristic of African governments. Médard's view of corruption shapes an analysis of bribery and embezzlement as contributing to a neo-patrimonial state, where corruption is systemic and the distinction between public and private is nonexistent.[31] De Sardan argues that corruption in Africa is socially embedded in the "logics" of negotiation, gift-giving, solidarity, predatory authority, and redistributive accumulation. He presents six general theses on corruption in Africa, which place it within a broader "corruption complex." De Sardan emphasizes the routine nature of corruption, its stigmatization despite the absence of effective sanctions, the apparent irreversibility of corruption, the absence of correlation with regime types, and corruption's legitimacy in the views of its perpetrators. He contends that any anticorruption policy must acknowledge this cultural argument.[32]

Chabal and Daloz argue that while corruption may appear to be peculiarly pathological African condition, it is in reality nothing more than a judicious behavior. In their view, corruption forms an integral part of the African neo-patrimonial and clientelist political systems, perceived of as the "informalisation of politics" and the "re-traditionalisation" of society. In economic terms, clientelism and corruption produce a system of patrimonial networks enriched at the expense of the continent's growth.[33] They believe that:

> Corruption in Africa concerns the whole of the population and operates essentially according to vertical relations of inequality. It is not confined to given sectors of economic activity, even if the "purchase" of favours within certain key administrative areas (most particularly connected with the control of trade licences) or in some highly sensitive geographical areas (such as borders) is obviously highly desirable. In truth, access to the right people in such circumstances can be richly rewarding. Outside one's own community (however loosely defined), where rules of civic behaviour apply, there is an assumption that graft presides over all forms of exchange.[34]

A comparative analysis of corruption shows that both the nature of the sedimentary state and the texture of a society's political culture are more telling indicators that the complexion of a regime or of its economic system. In other words, corruption permeates regimes of all ideologies. Kurer argues that the adoption and persistence of many failed development strategies can be attributed to political clientelism, factionalism, corruption, and the exchange of material benefits for political support in each country. In his contribution on predatory states, extraction, and clientelism, Kurer explores the political foundations of economic development policies.[35] Corruption varies across government agencies in the same state and sometimes within the same agency. Although most of the literature takes the perspective of winners in an emphasis on inducements and pressures for entry into corrupt exchanges, any serious assessment of corruption must take a country's politics into account. It is critical to understand who distributes the benefits of corruption. Combating corruption requires an analysis of the distribution of benefits in order to formulate a feasible, multidimensional effort. Maybe this lack of understanding explains why so few countries are successful in curtailing corruption in Africa.

Conditions on the continent seemingly suggest that Africa's political culture is especially propitious to corruption. However, there are African countries that do not make the list of most corrupt nations. Each country or region is unique in its own history and culture, its political systems, and its stage of economic and social development. In its 2004 report, *Global Witness* exposed corruption in Congo-Brazzaville, Angola, Equatorial Guinea among others. In these countries,

> governments do not provide even basic information about their revenues from natural resources. Nor do oil, mining and gas companies publish any information about payments made to governments. Huge amounts of money are therefore not subject to any oversight and crooked elites can extract all sorts of "facilitation payments" from firms that would probably prefer not to pay bribes.[36]

Congo-Brazzaville is one of the petro-states most closely associated with the legacy of influence peddling and dirty deals in Africa by the now-notorious French state oil company *Elf Aquitaine* (now *Total*). *Elf* treated Congo as its colony, buying off the ruling elite and helping it to mortgage the country's future oil income in exchange for expensive loans. The company even financed both sides of the civil war, as it also did in Angola. Although former senior *Elf* officials have been jailed in France for misuse of company assets, their legacy of opacity endures. Despite huge existing debts and a supposed program of cooperation with the international community to restructure Congo's finances, the government has entered into ever more arcane and tortuous deals to avoid financial scrutiny from the international community and its own citizens. Indeed, the national oil company *Société Nationale des Pétroles du Congo* makes a multimillion dollar profit but, according to the IMF, does not pay a single penny of this money into the government's coffers.[37]

In Angola, new evidence from IMF documents confirms Global Witness' previous allegations that over US $1 billion per year of the country's oil revenues, about a quarter of the state's yearly income, has gone unaccounted for since 1996. Meanwhile, one in four of Angola's children die before the age of five and one million internally displaced people remain dependent on international food aid. This report highlights the latest revelations from the "Angolagate" scandal, in which political and business elites in France, Angola, and elsewhere exploited the country's civil war to siphon off oil revenues. Most recently, a Swiss investigation uncovered evidence of millions of dollars being paid to President Dos Santos himself. The government continues to seek oil-backed loans at high rates of interest that are financed through opaque and unaccountable offshore structures. Concern exists that Angola's elite will now simply switch from wartime looting of state assets to profiteering from its reconstruction.[38]

In Equatorial Guinea, oil companies appear keen to do business with the brutal regime of President Obiang Nguema. The country's government has been tarnished by allegations of corruption, political violence, human rights abuses, and narcotics trafficking. Although the country's oil boom has resulted in a dramatic increase in GDP, its living standards remain among the worst in Africa. This may be because much of the country's oil money stays abroad. Journalists have recently uncovered evidence that major U.S. oil companies are paying revenues directly into an account under the president's control at Riggs Bank in downtown Washington DC.[39]

According to *Global Witness*, Riggs Bank has also managed the purchase of million-dollar mansions for Obiang and his family. The line between state revenues and the president's personal finances seems unclear. The government maintains that it is completely open and transparent about its oil revenues but, so far, the only way that any information has entered the public domain is on the initiative of the international media.[40]

Bostwana has been regarded as an island of stability in a sea of turbulence, a long-standing democracy that has never known military government. In addition, Bostwana's record on administrative probity is unequalled in tropical Africa until the late 1980s and early 1990s, when the country experienced a series of financial scandals that resulted in the creation of a Directorate on Corruption and Economic Crime. Some have characterized Botswana as marked by restrictive corruption. Charlton tries to explain this very deviant case by factors like democratic procedures, a non-corrupt elite culture, and the long presence of British expatriates.[41] In the same vein, Good explains the deviant Botswana case as resulting from rapid economic growth, multiparty democracy, and the relatively efficient central state. However, such political–economic scandals as illegal land transactions, mismanagement of parastatals, and dubious central bank loans indicate increasing corruption. Good argues that with the coalescence of economic and political power and the predominance of the ruling elite, corruption and mismanagement are unlikely to be eliminated,[42] making Botswana another corrupt nation in Africa.

Kenya's corruption stems from earlier governments' lack of legitimacy. Ethnic competition and patron–client relationships have undermined both political stability and policy-making. The government uses its resources to purchase support while increasingly repressing its opponents. As a consequence, the public sector is overstaffed and corruption defeats its capacity to deliver services. Kenya has accordingly suffered an economic decline.[43] Hope remains that only democratization can work against corruption in Kenya and President Mwaibaki, a crusader against corruption might be the best chance for Kenya.[44]

Even tiny Malawi is not spared the scourge of corruption, as described in Kaunda's laudable study. He identifies a structural continuity in the organization of Malawi's political economy in the three phases of the country's evolution from colonial rule, through the one-party era, to the current multiparty system. Kaunda emphasizes the political centralization of the one-party era, its promotion of economic concentration and how that benefited a minority, principally the national political leadership. He also maintains that the reintroduction of political pluralism has not been accompanied by a rearrangement of the economic forces. Further, the lack of a vision for future national development, combined with economic mismanagement and corruption, do not promise to bring about widespread national development. Growing social and economic inequalities and grand corruption jeopardize the maintenance of democracy.[45]

In Uganda, firms perceive corruption to be one of the most serious impediments to conducting business. Based on a survey of private enterprises in Uganda, Svensson shows that firms typically have to pay bribes when dealing with public officials, with the amount of the bribe depending partly on company-specific characteristics. His study finds that corruption constitutes a heavy burden on firms relative to other costs of operation. The adverse effect of bribery on firm growth is found to be more than three times greater than that of taxation.[46] In another study, Ouma characterizes Uganda's policies since 1979 as unstable, unpredictable, and conflicting. He argues that corruption in Uganda is a product of self-aggrandizement, unrealistically low remuneration of public servants, and bitter political and armed struggles aimed at gaining access to and retaining state power. He demonstrates how corruption leads to loss of much needed revenue and human talent for development, distorts priorities for public policy, and shifts scarce resources away from the public interest. The natural distrust that results is incompatible with the requirements for successful public policy. In his view, political instability, corruption, and underdevelopment are mutually reinforcing.[47]

Despite former president Chiluba's rhetoric of righting decades of wrongs and fighting corruption in Zambia, one country study concludes that corruption is even more widespread in Zambia under the

Chiluba regime than what it was under Kaunda, due to the utter contempt for probity and constitutional procedures with regard to public financial management and the regime's voracious appetite for wealth. The Zambian government has been forced to act on corruption. However, the prospects are meager because the pressure is coming more from external actors, such as the World Bank, the IMF, and aid donors, rather than from the disorganized internal opposition and the weak civil society.[48]

Obviously, the countries listed above are not the only corrupt nations in Africa. The challenge might be to find noncorrupt candidates on the continent. However, some have moved beyond corruption to sheer stealing by joining an organized lawless banditry in the form of kleptocracy and lootocracy. These are nations in which leaders spare no effort to "privatize" public funds through robbery.

Kleptocracy and Lootocracy as Systems of Government in Africa

Kleptocracy and lootocracy involve grand corruption, as opposed to routine or petty corruption, and could be defined as the misuse of public power by heads of state, ministers and senior officials for private pecuniary gain. Highly placed individuals exploit their positions to extract large bribes from representatives of transnational corporations, arms dealers, drug barons, and appropriate significant pay offs from contract scams, or who transfer huge sums of money from public coffers into private bank accounts. Kleptocracy and its highest form, lootocracy, represent an unashamed pillaging of the public treasury and the self-enrichment through all kinds of frauds. According to Andreski,

> the essence of kleptocracy is that the functioning of the organs of authority is determined by the mechanisms of supply and demand rather than the laws and regulations; and a kleptocratic state constitutes a curiously generalized model of laissez-faire economics.[49]

In Rose-Ackerman's view:

> Kleptocrats view the regulatory system as a source of personal profits. Thus regulations and licensing requirements may be imposed that have no justification other than to create a bottleneck that firms will pay to avoid. Efficient regulatory reforms will be opposed by the kleptocrat if the reforms would convert illegal into legal pricing systems. The kleptocrat will focus subsidies on individuals and business firms willing to pay for them. Of course, even corrupt autocrats may need to satisfy the

mass of the population in order to maintain power, but they will also promulgate programs that induce the wealthy to pay for benefits. The ruler . . . might institute a system of investment subsidies with discretion to distribute these benefits. No one can obtain these benefits as a matter of right. Everyone must bid to obtain them from the ruler. The allocation of scarce foreign exchange and access to credit are additional sources of rents for rulers.[50]

Powerful kleptocrats facing weak private actors and passive or cooperating civil society not only extract rents but also organize the state to create rents regardless of their impact on the economy and society. Rent seeking is harmful to growth for two reasons. First, rent seeking tends naturally to have increasing returns. The effect is that high levels of rent seeking are particularly harmful to innovation, a key element in economic growth and rent seeking is therefore costly to growth. Second, political power in Africa has come to be associated with spectacular economic mismanagement, grand corruption, and a style of political competition approximating open warfare. The rulers of the customs post states draw the bulk of their economic resources from the control of foreign trade, the diversion of food aid, the preferential allocation of import licenses, and smuggling. In what Bayart calls the "politics of the belly,"[51] survival by all means becomes the key issue. Politics becomes a life-and-death struggle for power and a share of the national cake. Corruption and predation extend beyond the powerful, blurring the boundaries between crime and legality.

In a survey paper, Tanzi analyzes the consequences of the costs of corruption in terms of economic growth. He also emphasizes that the fight against corruption cannot be independent from the reform of the state. Unless certain reforms are made now, corruption is likely to continue to be a problem in the developing world in general, and in Africa in particular, regardless of future actions aimed at directly curtailing it.[52] Both political and bureaucratic corruption negatively impact government revenue and spending. Corruption reduces government revenue while pushing for higher government spending, thus contributing to larger fiscal deficits. It also distorts the tax system and renders public spending less productive. Kpundeh rightly argues that political actors or leaders can rely on an arsenal of resources to develop and implement sustainable economic reform and anticorruption strategies. However, political leaders still lack the necessary political will since it depends on the types and levels of corruption, leaders' security, democratic checks and balances, public constituencies and participation, an independent press, and transparent accountable government.[53] As long as African leaders continue to empty the coffers of their countries with impunity, they lack an incentive to curtail corruption.

Kofele-Kale argues that indigenous plunder of national resources can, and should be made a crime according to international law. He provides excellent examples of grand corruption in Africa. The extent of the phenomenon and its damage to the continent compel the author to suggest that massive corruption and presidential graft be named "patrimonicide," the deliberate killing of one's nation. "Patrimonicide," or indigenous spoliation, should be taken as seriously as genocide, according to Kofele-Kale, by the international community. He calls for international legislation to overcome this important problem, because, ultimately, continued examples of presidential graft, leaders' economic predation, corruption, and primitive extraction from Africa do not bode well for the continent.[54]

In an edited volume, Hope and Chikulu analyze corruption in Africa, exposing its causes, its impacts, and suggesting possible solutions. From a theoretical point of view, the first part analyzes the political, economic, and cultural bases of corruption in Africa, the kleptocratic system, aid abuse, Western policies, and African control efforts. The second part, however, tackles the study of the phenomenon in such countries as Zambia, Ghana, Sierra Leone, South Africa, Cameroon, Ethiopia, Nigeria, and Botswana. To various degrees, the countries involved in the study displayed ingenious ways to plunder national resources.[55] While most traditional African leaders and societies had little or no corruption, there is no evidence of any precolonial African community brought to ruin because of corrupt leaders or where bribery was institutionalized. The same can hardly be said of contemporary African leaders.

Harsch argues that corruption is a form of neo-patrimonialism, primitive extraction that has fundamentally hurt, and will continue to retard Africa's development endeavor. As the primary mechanism of dominant-class formation, corruption seems to be the best tool to accumulate wealth in a steady and fast manner. Although popular pressures are welcome on the struggle against autocratic regimes, their effectiveness in fighting corruption is in doubt. In Harsch's view, only an all-out war and genuine effort to defeat the villains and overthrow corrupt regimes.[56] Corruption encourages criminality because those with no access to public funds search for other means to reach their malevolent goals:

> Criminality thrives in disordered societies such as Africa's simply because it can operate easily in the interstices of the existing networks which delineate the competitive boundaries between "official" activities and those of the parallel sector. The overlap between formal and informal as well as the intense rivalry between patrons create an ideal framework for the spread of criminal activities. This criminal world is

diverse—from small-scale racketeering to wholesale pillage—but what makes it particularly effective in Africa is the frightening ease with which it can use violence. Devoid of police protection, people will thus either turn to patrons for succour or, inevitably and reluctantly, they will seek help from the bosses of other local criminal gangs.[57]

Patrons are the key players in illicit activities in Africa since success depends on the ease with which economic transactions can evade official control. Economic delinquency is overwhelmingly due to the ruling classes' activities. Although it is true that Africa remains economically unproductive, and that the pursuit of rents or unearned fees has become more prevalent, there is a development of illicit activities and financial flows considered improper or even criminal by nature. According to Bayart and Daloz,

> The extension of forms of behaviour which are at or beyond the bounds of legality cannot simply be interpreted as a reflection of a fall in general moral standards. Ethical values and moral judgements are astonishingly ambivalent. All over Africa, the so-called "dinosaurs" who hold power are also models of successful personal enterprise and the very epitome of witches. The legitimation of illicit activity by people at all social levels, by recourse to arguments such as that it creates jobs and wealth, and that it is often the only way of getting ahead, goes hand in hand with the widespread popular condemnation of existing governments. It could be said that the wealth of those in power is no more legitimate that that generated by the cocaine trade or any other activity which is regarded by the international community as criminal in nature.[58]

Coolidge and Rose-Ackerman note the negative impact that government officials' rent seeking has on African economic growth. They distinguish between benevolent autocrats involved in economic mismanagement and kleptocrats, arguing that kleptocrats have a greater incentive to be corrupt because of the shorter window of opportunity. In conclusion, they urge the WB and the IMF to use caution in lending to governments with kleptocratic leaders.[59] Bayart, Ellis, and Hibou wrote another excellent book on the criminalization and "privatization" of politics and public funds in contemporary Africa, with a theoretical approach to the term "kleptocracy" and numerous examples of political corruption, fraud, primitive extraction, extortion, and other forms of power-abuse by African leaders. They provide a thorough explanation of corruption in Africa and discuss its international ramifications.[60]

In many African countries, crime reigns supreme and looting of government coffers seems acceptable. Powerful groups reserve to themselves, with complete impunity, "the possibility of disobeying their own rules and their own laws," which has the effect of creating "a vast economic sector" that lies outside the law.[61] Kleptocrats control the state but not the entire economy. They may have a weak and disloyal civil service, a poor resource base, and a vague and confusing legal framework. The kleptocrat has to support interventions that do not increase overall national income because they provide personal benefits to the head of state.[62] To overcome the hurdles of kleptocracy, the rulers turn to lootocracy, a highly corrupt system in which they are in full control of economic and political apparatus. Besides setting monopoly prices and restricting supply to maximize rents, lootocratic rulers strive for productive efficiency, but restrict the output of the entire economy to maximize their own profits. Raw materials and other national resources are viewed as personal goods to be sold on international market, with the implicit or tacit complicity of the international community. In plain terms, Hauss defines lootocrats as "political and bureaucratic officials who have used their position for tremendous personal and who, like the European bourgeoisie Marx wrote about have been able to protect their wealth and power."[63]

Edvabaro's dissertation uncovers the extent of corruption in Nigeria. Having emphasized the neo-patrimonial nature of Nigerian politics, he elucidates on how lootocracy helps the ruling elite, both civilian and military, acquire wealth at the expense of the majority. If his study of the political history of Nigeria is any guide, reforming the corrupt system of Nigeria will remain a perennial and Herculean task.[64] Nigeria is truly a paradise on earth, a country blessed with good soil, warm climate, enormous natural resources, and people, with over four hundred nationalities totaling over hundred and twenty million souls. Its culture is rich and varied; the people are dynamic and enterprising. Although well endowed with natural and human resources, Nigeria remains a paradise of paupers. The sixth largest oil-producing country in the world is ironically the sixteenth poorest nation on earth. Incredible poverty is the lot of the toiling masses who are therefore easy prey for the vultures of disease and ignorance. Yet, this is also a nation of palatial mansions built by those who had neither farms nor factories, who have imposed themselves on the nation to loot the treasury in collaboration with Western international gangsters. And, as the ranks of the looters swelled through the bandwagon effect, the ranks of the diligent middle class thinned.[65]

On the social scene, education has been devastated by the ripples of the debt burden. Corruption crept into the system and turned "Free Education" into "Fraud Education," with criminally low funding, most of which disappeared either into private pockets of corrupt officials or nonperforming contractors. Increasingly, survival skills needed for life are being neglected while everything is being done to obtain a certificate. Worse still, because the many who have left school have no job, some youths now consider education a waste of time. Rather than attending schools without job prospects, some young girls have taken to prostitution in unprecedented numbers at home and abroad. This has led to the harmattan-fire spread of AIDS as the rich prostitutes return home laden with dollars and the AIDS virus.[66] Long queues at gas stations only add to the list of unconceivable ironies on the continent.

The Democratic Republic of the Congo, formerly Zaire, remains another model of lootocracy. Under the corrupt, mediocre, and inept leadership of the late Mobutu, Zaire was turned into the private coffer of the "Leopard of Gbadolite." In his bloated and inefficient state, Mobutu and his cliques controlled everything that moved. In a comprehensive work on corruption, nepotism, and presidential graft in Mobutu's Zaire, Willame provides detailed documentation outlining the mechanisms of corruption and power-abuse in one of the worst examples of kleptocratic rule that the modern world has known.[67] Zaire exemplifies the political and economic trajectory of African states and the activities of their rulers, who create "shadow states" to plunder their countries. When autocrats and narrow interest groups win control of the state in Africa, many have expanded the role of government in an effort to enrich themselves.[68]

Rose-Ackerman gives another unwavering assessment of Mobutu's Zaire:

> In Zaire, President Mobutu and his associates can be described as "looting" the state. Mobutu placed a third of the state budget under his control and reportedly siphoned off a quarter of gross receipt from copper exports. But Mobutu too had to share his corrupt gains with both high-level cronies and low-level customs inspectors and other officials. Corruption and predation undermined the formal private sector, and grandiose infrastructure projects were used as sources of payoffs for the President and his associates.[69]

In a comparative study of lootocracies, Wedeman tries to explain different patterns of corruption, focusing on looting, scraping, and rent-collection, and development in Zaire among other countries.[70] Mobutu reportedly had more than US$5 billion in overseas bank accounts, in addition to his gorgeous palaces all over Europe.[71] In a good example of how wealth could be a curse, the Democratic Republic of the Congo continues to suffer despite its tremendous riches because of rebels and government officials trying to exploit to their own benefit national resources.

The late Houphouët-Boigny of Côte d'Ivoire was also considered a lootocrat. He boasted of having billions abroad,[72] and used his "personal wealth" to build the replica of the Basilica Cathedral in Yamoussokro, his birthplace. Bongo of Gabon is also believed to have taken billions out of the treasury of his country. In recent politico-financial trials about the French oil conglomerate *Elf*, Bongo's name has been mentioned several times. Kodjo Agbéyomè, a former prime minister of Togo, has accused late President Éyadéma of ordering a series of scandalous embezzlements, through constant, periodic, and unscrupulous withdrawal from the coffers of several national corporations and firms.[73] Biya of Cameroon, whose regime tops a list of corrupt nations, cannot pass an oath of honesty. Former Presidents Abacha and Babangida of Nigeria, Taylor of Liberia, Ould Taya of Mauritania, and Yayah Jammeh of the Gambia, to name but a few, are all believed to have involved in the looting of the national resources of their countries.

Corruption at the top creates expectations among bureaucrats that they should share in the wealth and reduces the moral and psychological constraints on lower-level officials. Low-level malfeasance that could be kept under control by an honest ruler becomes endemic with a dishonest leader. Consequently, bureaucrats design all kinds of schemes or strategies to collect bribes. One such scheme is the use of forged document to reach illicit gains. Some believe that

> False documents are a Nigerian specialty, although forgeries are to be found throughout Africa, in such quantity that banks will no longer accept property title deeds as loan guarantees, while European immigration services routinely suspect African passports of being forged, including (or perhaps especially) diplomatic passports . . . In Mozambique, Côte d'Ivoire, Senegal and Benin, among many other countries, any document imaginable can be bought, including false immigration documents, false health or sickness certificates, false official texts or laws, [and] false driving licences.[74]

The straddling of positions of power and accumulation by individuals has a marked effect on the actual results of public policy interventions, and serious endeavors should be undertaken to fight corruption in Africa if the new political renaissance is to have any sense.

Fighting Corruption Is a Requisite for Development

In their attempt to justify corruption, many argue, that the "informal sector" is a good thing for employment and housing. However, there is more disagreement about corruption and the black market economy.

Ultimately, corruption hurts more than it helps the ordinary citizen.[75] No serious effort to rid Africa of underdevelopment should ignore the scourge of corruption. Those living on the wealthiest continent continue to be the poorest individuals among in part because of corruption, kleptocracy, and lootocracy. Given the extent of the gangrene, words alone would not counteract the problem. Genuine and important moves are required to halt Africa's free fall.

In his classic article, Becker analyzes the effect of punishment on an individual's willingness to engage in an illegal act. In his view, the optimal level of punishment is largely a function of the cost of enforcement, investigation, and punishment. In the end, the optimal levels of sanction depend upon the overall cost of enforcement.[76] In his exploration of possible means to curb corruption, Ateba is very critical of the IMF and WB because their policies failed to address the issue of corruption on the continent. In his views, these IFIs have yet to acknowledge that corruption has rendered African institutions too weak to engage in a smooth transition to market economy. In fact, opportunistic and rent-seeking behavior accounts for much of the bad performance of African economies.[77] A 1997 UNDP study, beginning from the assumption that corruption is a symptom of something wrong in the management of the state, explores the extent of corruption in Africa. It presents options to combat corruption. Efforts to curtail endemic corruption require not piecemeal reform but instead a multifaceted approach, including the cooperation of the donor community.[78]

Cooksey argues that aid, instead of achieving stated objectives, has fuelled corruption in recipient countries, and allowed incumbent ruling elites to buttress themselves against the logic of market reform political pluralism.[79] Until recently, aid agencies have tolerated high levels of corruption among recipient governments. Legacies of this laxness include failed structural adjustment programs, lack of investment and job creation, and widespread market failure. At its worst, aid can fuel corruption among recipients and undermine aid effectiveness. Thus, corruption in aid can only be tackled by increasing transparency and accountability on both givers' and recipients' side. Unless and until donors begin to accept that they are as much a part of the corruption problem as aid recipients, it will be difficult to address the underlying causes of corruption in aid.[80]

Klitgaard wonders why some countries do not take more serious steps to reduce corruption. He believes that if countries have trouble fighting corruption, it may be because they lack sufficient will or sufficient local capacities, such as proper strategies and structures, including incentives, to prevent corruption. In some instances, costs constrain local capacities; in other cases a lack of know-how or effort limits capabilities. Klitgaard argues that international cooperation can help individual countries to develop the necessary will and capacities. He proposes several new initiatives in which international cooperation could play crucial roles in combating corruption. One is the sponsorship of regional diagnostic studies. His study helps identify systematic improvements that might be made and suggests how to ensure the permanence of improvements through monitoring.[81]

In an edited volume with an interdisciplinary approach to analyzing corruption, Robinson tackles the complexity of fighting corruption in the Third World. Corruption is a complex, multifaceted phenomenon that pervades all societies to varying degrees, which is not amenable to quick-fix solutions.[82] The sketchy results of Uganda's current strategy to fight corruption buttress Robinson's point. Like many countries on the African continent, Uganda deemed it necessary to reduce and control corruption within the public sector. As awareness of the deleterious and debilitating effects of corruption has grown, so too have both internal political factors and external pressures from aid donors to push for fundamental change in this respect. In terms of the donors, many have stipulated specific conditions relating to a good governance agenda based upon adherence to public integrity and minimum standards of public conduct. Sensitivity to pressure also stems in part, from a wish by government to be seen to be actively responding to donor concerns. Internal pressures stem from a growing desire by the public to demand accountability from those in government.

In his work, Theobald maintains that the phenomenon of political corruption can be understood only against a background of social and economic change. Both the negative and positive sides of corruption are listed and reviewed. He also identifies a number of remedial measures to control corruption although arguing that its elimination cannot be realistically anticipated until certain fundamental changes have taken place. The most important of these are the rise of predominance of universalistic norms, the emergence of new centers of power outside the bureaucracy and the development of competitive party politics. Such changes, however, much to Africans' chagrin, can come about only after a long period of social and economic development.[83]

Several papers presented at the 1997 Vienna conference entitled "*Institutionalising horizontal accountability: How democracies can fight corruption and the abuse of power*," provided their input on the debate on fighting corruption. Liberal democracies require governments that are not only accountable to their citizens but also subject to restraint and oversight by other public agencies. These are referred to as institutions of "horizontal" accountability, and allude to the capacity of state institutions to check abuses by other public agencies and branches of government. Instead of analyzing the role of parliaments in overseeing the executive, the papers focus on independent, nonelective, specialized bodies of oversight, including electoral administrations, judicial systems, anticorruption bodies, and central banks. These autonomous institutions of accountability are typically insulated from state officials and from the people as well. As long as they are unaccountable themselves, agencies of accountability are therefore vulnerable to charges that they are undemocratic. To the key question of "who shall guard the guardians?"[84] participants believe that civil society should play its role as effective watchdog of government activities.

In a sourcebook on integrity emphasizing accountability measures and attitude changes over the reform of substantive programs to reduce corrupt incentives, Pope identifies five main areas of reform as crucial to the implementation of an anticorruption system: public programs, government reorganization, law enforcement, public awareness, and the creation of institutions to prevent corruption. Pope points out that anticorruption efforts are a long-term process that requires open support from the top and reinforcement of attitudes and conduct at all levels.[85] A great deal of hope is put in democratic transition. However, Szeftel argues that democratization and "good governance" strategies in Africa have failed in curtailing corruption because the strategies imposed on African governments have been inadequate. In particular, downscaling of the state, deregulation and privatization have reduced the state's capacity to implement policy and created new conditions in which corruption can flourish.[86]

Conclusion

African leaders must be determined to fight corruption so as to free resources for growth and development. Corruption generates distortions by allowing prices to deviate from marginal cost pricing. Corruption impacts negatively on growth and development in several ways:

- It reduces public revenue and increases government spending hence contributing to large fiscal deficits and making it more difficult for a government to run a sound fiscal policy;
- It reduces investment and the productivity of public investment and infrastructure;

- It tends to increase income inequality by allowing those in influential positions to take advantage of government activities at the expense of the rest of the population;
- By distorting markets and the allocation of resources, corruption interferes with the government's ability to impose necessary regulatory controls and inspections to correct market failures and reduces the fundamental role of government, for example, in the enforcement of contracts and property rights; and
- By reducing foreign direct investment because corruption has the effect of a tax.

Obadan notes that corruption survives under conditions of bad leadership, scarce resources, and government domination of resource allocation, when public sector wages are low and rules are unreasonable and unclear, when controls are pervasive and excessive regulations, when transparency and accountability are not taken seriously, and when punishment is not likely.[87]

Democratic transitions will not *ipso facto* reduce corruption mainly because they do not address the structural, social, and cultural roots of corruption. According to Chabal and Daloz,

> democratic reform on the Western model—that is the political institutionalization of the bureaucratic and legal order—would undoubtedly have brought about greater accountability, more transparency and a more effective system of checks and balances. Despite changes to the façade of governance, the introduction of multiparty elections into Africa has not yet had the desired effects. In reality, not much has changed.[88]

The continent has a long way to go in fighting corruption and the current bickering in several African countries over appropriate strategies illustrates the difficulties ahead.

Chapter 5

Africa at its Nadir

Economics, politics and globalisation may have conspired to create the deadly triangle of diamond and other resource wars in Africa ... there is a thread that runs through all [the] threats to security and state survival: spoils politics where violence and reward become mutually reinforcing. Democracy cannot work where warlords are rampant.

WJ. Breytenbach, "Rulers, Rebels and Mercantilists."

Many in the media describe contemporary Africa as a "continent in crisis," a "region in turmoil," "on a precipice," and "suffering."[1] These images recall sensationalist accounts by nineteenth-century missionaries eager to convince others of the continent's need for "civilization" and "salvation," but they also reflect today's realities in Africa. Abusive and autocratic governance underlies economic decay, state collapse, ethnic violence, civil war, and humanitarian disaster in Africa. The very nature of the state in Africa and the lawlessness predispose the continent to massive corruption, nepotism, and the personal whims of a handful of dictators. The image of Africa as a sick continent remains firmly entrenched in many minds because African leaders have yet to show their determination, through concrete actions, to alter such an image. An overview of the horrors of civil wars, the tragedy in Rwanda, and the ravage of HIV/AIDS all show Africa at its worst.

Conflicts, Violence, and Distribution of Wealth

The end of the cold war has failed to make the world any safer for Africans. Wars have not only persisted, but also worsened, continuing to hamper economic and social development on the continent. Like other societies, traditional Africa experienced conflicts and wars that often arose out of rivalries among empires and kingdoms bent on expanding their territories. However, conflicts in contemporary Africa are of a totally different nature. Violent social and ethnic conflict has emerged as a dominant feature of political life in much of Africa today. At the core of these contemporary conflicts lies a failure of nation-building in Africa. Even border wars and ethnic conflicts, though they pose genuine issues, could have been resolved from a more conciliatory perspective. Sometimes deeply rooted, often irrational, always bloody and merciless, these wars oppose former neighbors, friends, and associates to each other. Whatever their origin, these new conflicts stem essentially from bad governance. Differences in ethnic and regional origins or religious beliefs, and the existence of mineral resources, such as diamonds, are not specific to countries affected by civil war. The reality is that these differences do not lead inevitably to war. They become hot issues only when they are continuously manipulated by the irresponsible governing elites for their own or others' benefit.

In the last four decades, Africa has witnessed several civil wars, many colored by ethnic conflict. Wars of the last decade claimed over two million victims, making ethnic conflict one of the leading causes of displacement and death in Africa. Often, the Western media seems to dismiss such conflict as African "tribalism."[2] In other words, ethnic conflict is seen as an inherent characteristic of African society. Some authors draw attention to the role of colonialism in the development and promotion of ethnic identification. Leroy Vail, for example, explores how ethnicity in Africa has been crafted, deliberately or not, by European missionaries and intellectuals, colonial administrative officers, and even ordinary Europeans living in the colonies. Missionaries and anthropologists lumped fairly disparate groups together and often assisted in the creation of common language for groups of people of similar, but distinct, kinship and language.[3] The use of indirect rule also promoted and rewarded ethnic identification because it involved using chiefs and headmen to govern in exchange for income and patronage. Ultimately, Africans embraced the ethnic identities manipulated or created by colonialists through their adaptation to the new realities of tribalism. In the end, colonialism left African states with several manipulated ethnic groups that lacked an idea of nationhood.[4]

At independence, African governments adopted new constitutions that greatly centralized the political framework, discouraged or destroyed multiparty systems, weakened legislative authority, and conferred sweeping powers on the president. Decision-making became more concentrated, central bureaucracies gained power at the expense of local government, and popularly elected institutions declined. But, much to the dismay of new leaders, Africans refused to give up their rights as citizens and embarked on challenging their autocratic states. The rapid construction of African political and economic systems, though quite noble as a goal, generated resentment among Africans because of the means utilized to achieve it. That early dispute over the proper and faster road to development opened up the first salvo of conflict on the continent. Convinced that they got it right, new African leaders tolerated no dissent and characterized any opposite view as a neocolonialist betrayal.

The growth of single-party political systems dominated by a charismatic leader became the hallmark of postindependence political development in Africa. In most cases, these same parties had previously organized nationalist resistance to colonial rule and established efficient networks of local branches at the village level. The success of the leadership in rallying popular support for independence brought the party to power with widespread electoral strength. To oppose the nationalist party often meant being branded as a traitor or a supporter of colonialism. In consequence, even after independence the party in power often regarded the opposition as an unnecessary interference in the pressing tasks of development and modernization.

As independence receded into the past, popular enthusiasm abated. The new governments faced increasingly complex problems of economic transformation and social change. These problems required leadership to make unpopular decisions, particularly in taxation and control of imported goods. These decisions alienated former followers. The desire to remain in power, coupled with the mounting frustrations in projected economic development, created tensions within the ruling group, and that frequently led to harsh measures of repression against those who opposed the government's aims. The growing discontent with the failure of the political leaders to produce the expected results, combined with the hardships of economic stagnation and dictatorial rule, generated conflicts of all kinds, including boundary claims.

International boundaries are the most fundamental part of Africa's colonial inheritance. Modern African states mirror almost exactly the contours of the European colonies that they replaced. Despite the obvious drawbacks of an anachronistic political framework, and problems with the boundary lines themselves, African countries agreed to keep their colonial boundaries when they accepted an OAU policy requiring that "all member states pledge themselves to respect the borders existing on their achievement of national independence."[5] However, the survival of these artificial entities depended on the existence of a proper state. As a tool of enrichment for the few, the African state became subject of contestation and dispute. Those who believed themselves to be discriminated against demanded a more balanced treatment through a redrawing of the boundaries.

Given that cultural groups on the continent vastly outnumbered the states created out of former colonies, boundaries necessarily cut across culture group areas. In addition, many ethnic groups overlap with each other. According to Reed,

> arbitrary and ill-defined borders not only blur the effective territorial jurisdiction of African states, they make the identification of populations over which African states "rule" difficult at best and impossible at worst. Arbitrary borders mean that population groups have more often than not been divided between various states, rather than united in one.[6]

For example, in West Africa, such nomadic people as the Fula or Fulani intermingle with sedentary people such as the Madinka and Wolof in the west and the Hausa in the east, and the Ewe straddle Ghana and Togo; in Central Africa, the Azande are found from Sudan to the Central African Republic. Villages frequently contain two or more different ethno-linguistic groups. Boundaries that ignore cultural and ethnic realities have deleterious effects where central governments fail to meet the basic needs of their constituent groups. While there have been petty border disputes in West Africa, between Mali and Burkina Faso, and Benin and Niger, more serious attempts to alter boundaries occurred between Somalia and Ethiopia, Eritrea and Ethiopia, and Libya and Chad.

The lack of fit between the states and ethnicities means that almost every independent African country has been threatened by irredentism or territorial claims by other states. The uneven way in which European powers carved up the continent underlies these secessionist movements. As a result of European competition, some states are land-locked, others are odd-shaped, and many have ambiguous boundaries. Some are too small to be economically or politically viable, while others are so large that they encompass many disparate groups of people. African states lack cohesion and unity in contradistinction to the nation-state concept imposed on the African polity from the outside.[7] In extreme cases, some states have faced serious secessionist threats from groups claiming an entitlement to a state of their own. Civil wars ensued at enormous human and economic cost. Besides the notable case of the Biafra secession in Nigeria, Casamance remains an intractable situation in Senegal.

Civil conflicts lead to extraordinary hardship, mass killings, flows of refugees and internally displaced persons, and large numbers of disabled people, orphans, widows, and widowers. They also destroy infrastructures and productive economies. Public opinion finds these losses unacceptable. In addition, the longer they last, the more these conflicts generate a new culture and indeed a whole new society. With daily killing and pervasive impunity, a culture of violence takes root. The population soon becomes a militarized society as groups, families, and individuals get armed in self-defense or to prey on others. Furthermore, a lasting domestic conflict leads to the criminalization of the state and the economy[8] as trafficking in drugs, minerals, and arms flourishes.[9]

Poverty and uneven access to resources contribute heavily to most African conflicts. Several years of conflict in Angola found their rationale in such resources as oil and diamonds. Cold war ideological stances aside, Savimbi was also concerned about the distribution of the wealth of Angola. Until his death in 2002, he dedicated his whole life to controlling vast diamond areas. In the Democratic Republic of the Congo, diamonds, gold, and other such minerals as columbite-tantalite and coltane, as well as the land rights of the Banyamulenge in Kivu explain ongoing wars. In Liberia and Sierra Leone, civil wars revolved around control of the economy since political control determines economic power. Even in Sudan, age-old religious differences between an Islamic north and a non-Islamic south became a resource war after the discovery of oil. Widespread poverty and uneven access to wealth-creating resources also lie at the center of conflicts in Congo Brazzaville, Senegal, Guinea-Bissau, and Somalia.[10]

Of course, the risks associated with these conflicts including massive violation of human rights, migration, health issues including the spread of HIV/AIDS, environmental degradation, and threats of spillover, also play a crucial role in the search for peace. Nevertheless, armed conflicts spread beyond areas where war has been endemic for decades to parts of the continent that had previously been spared. The true test of the new *African Union* will be its ability to handle dissent and conflict among and within its member states in order to avoid another Rwanda.

Rwandan Genocide as Humans' Nadir: The Choice to Remain Indifferent

Precolonial Rwanda was based on the kinship of one ruling clan. A society possessed chiefs, such as land chief, a cattle chief, or a war chief to carry out its various functions. All the eight million inhabitants of Rwanda, though divided into three ethnic groups, share the same language, Kinyarwanda, and the same territory. They share common physical features, a common culture, and a common past.

The Rwandan population consists of 89 percent Hutu, 10 percent Tutsi, and 1 percent Twa. A prelude to the genocide was Belgium's establishment of a social hierarchy after acquiring Rwanda from Germany following World War I. Belgium categorized the Africans according to the number of cattle that an individual owned. Therefore a "Tutsi" was someone who owned more than ten cows, while a "Hutu" was someone who owned fewer than ten cows. Subsequently, the Tutsi became the aristocrats and were favored by the Belgians, while the Hutu remained as peasants. This instigated an intense competition for power between the Hutu and the Tutsi. This social hierarchy differed significantly from precolonial practice.[11]

When Rwanda emerged as a major kingdom in the eighteenth century, its rulers measured their power in the number of their subjects and counted their wealth in the number of their cattle. Giving or lending cattle was a way of winning supporters, and a large number of supporters helped to win cattle, both in conflicts with other members of the elite and in adventures abroad. However not all cattle-owners held official positions. Although they constituted a minority, the Tutsi imposed on Hutu a system of feudal overlordship that bordered on a caste system, monopolized military and political power, and controlled land and labor. The Tutsi aristocracy was itself firmly subordinated to the *mwami* or king, who ruled absolutely as supreme leader, legislator, and judge. The Germans, who established a colonial administration at the turn of the century, and the Belgians who replaced them after the World War I, ended the occasional open warfare that had taken place within Rwanda and between Rwanda and its neighbors. Both Germans and Belgians sought to rule Rwanda at the lowest cost and the greatest profit. To do so they made use of the impressive indigenous state, but the colonialists found its complexities troublesome. Multiple hierarchies, which had allowed the ruler to maximize his control by playing off rival officials, now permitted both ruler and his subordinates to evade control by the colonialists.[12]

The dense precolonial administration within central Rwanda, in which the least important representatives of the ruler sometimes governing only a few hundred people, required a relatively high proportion of local goods and labor for its support. The colonialists preferred to have these resources at their own disposal, in order to cover their expenses and to pay the costs of building an infrastructure that would link Rwanda to the world economy. At the same time, the Belgians saw the autonomous enclaves, where central control was light, as potentially disruptive anomalies. In the 1920s, the Belgians began to alter the Rwandan state in the name of administrative efficiency. While professing to keep the essential elements of the system intact, they eliminated the competing hierarchies and regrouped the units of administration into "chiefdoms" and "sub-chiefdoms" of uniform size. They used force to install state officials in the autonomous enclaves, destroying the power of the heads of lineages and of local small states. They made uniform the goods and services that local officials could demand, thus reducing, they thought, the burden on the population.

By assuring a Tutsi monopoly of power, the Belgians unintentionally set the stage for future conflict in Rwanda by implementing the racist convictions common to most early-twentieth-century Europeans. They believed that Tutsi, Hutu, and Twa were three distinct, long-existent, and internally coherent blocks of people, who were local representatives of three major population groups, the Ethiopid, Bantu, and Pygmoid. Unclear whether these populations were races, tribes, or language groups, the Europeans nonetheless believed the Tutsi to be superior to the Hutu and the Hutu superior to the Twa, just as they knew themselves to be superior to all three. Because Europeans thought that the Tutsi looked more like themselves than did other Rwandans, they found it reasonable to suppose them closer to Europeans in the evolutionary hierarchy and hence closer to them in ability. Believing the Tutsi to be more capable, the Europeans found the Tutsi rule of the Hutu and Twa as reasonable as their own rule of Africa. Unaware of the Hutu contribution to building Rwanda, the Europeans saw only that the ruler of this impressive state and many of his immediate entourage were Tutsi, which led them to assume that the complex institutions had been created exclusively by Tutsi.[13]

Not surprisingly, Tutsi welcomed these ideas about their superiority, which coincided with their own beliefs. In the early years of colonial rule, Rwandan poets and historians, particularly those from the milieu of the court, resisted providing Europeans with information about the Rwandan past. But as they became aware of European favoritism for the Tutsi in the late 1920s and early 1930s, these poets and historians provided information selectively to reinforce this predisposition. They supplied data to the European clergy and academics who produced the first written histories of Rwanda. The collaboration resulted in a sophisticated and convincing, but inaccurate, history that simultaneously served Tutsi interests and validated European assumptions. According to these accounts, the Twa hunters and gatherers were the first and indigenous residents of the area. The somewhat more advanced Hutu cultivators arrived later to clear the forest and displace the Twa. Next, the capable, if ruthless, Tutsi descended from the north and used their superior political and military abilities to conquer the far more numerous but less intelligent Hutu. This mythical history drew on and made concrete the "Hamitic hypothesis," the then-fashionable theory that a superior Caucasoid race from north-eastern Africa was responsible for all signs of true civilization in Africa. This distorted version of the past revealed more about the intellectual atmosphere of Europe in the 1920s than the early history of Rwanda. Packaged in Europe, this history was returned to Rwanda where it was disseminated through the schools and seminaries. Rwandan held European education in such high esteem that this faulty history was accepted by the Hutu, who stood to suffer from it, as well as by the Tutsi who helped to create it for their own profit. People of both groups learned to think of the Tutsi as the winners and the Hutu as the losers in every great contest in Rwandan history.[14]

It is in this context that disenfranchised Hutu began calling for radical reforms and an end to Tutsi domination. However, upon the death of *Mwami* Matari III in 1959, radical Tutsi seized power and the opportunity to eliminate Hutu leaders. In a counterattack, Hutu activists staged a widespread uprising in which countless Tutsi perished. Thousands of Tutsi followed their king into exile in neighboring countries. By the time Belgium initiated the transition to independence the Hutu had become the new dominant force in Rwandan politics. After communal elections in October 1960, and a UN-supervised referendum in 1961 that approved a republican constitution, Rwanda was on its way to statehood. When parliamentary elections brought PARMEHUTU (Party of the Movement for the Emancipation of Hutu/Bahutu), and President Grégoire Kayibanda to power in 1962, it became obvious that the Hutu were ready to exercise their newly acquired control at the expense of their rival Tutsi. The Hutu Revolution had begun.[15]

By 1963, hardly a year after independence, violence erupted once again when Tutsi guerrillas, unhappy about their reversed fortune, conducted vicious raids that provoked Hutu. This conflict cost lives on both sides, and drove thousands of Tutsi into exile. By the end of the 1960s, several hundred Tutsi had fled Rwanda, and those who remained faced persecution. Tutsi atrocities against Hutu in neighboring Burundi fueled Hutu anger in Rwanda. But even within Rwanda, rivalries between Hutu from the north and the south complicated the equation. The military felt obligated to intervene and General Juvénal Habyarimana, a moderate Hutu, staged a coup against Kayibanda in 1973. After replacing PARMEHUTU with a single-party, the Revolutionary National Movement for Development, Habyarimana managed to control the situation until the 1990s when Rwandan Tutsi refugees in such neighboring countries as Uganda and Tanzania rediscovered their old-age dream to return, and started launching attacks from their sanctuary.

Under pressure from the main Tutsi guerrilla group, the Rwandan Patriotic Front (RPF), called for political reforms and the repatriation of Tutsi refugees, Habyarimana opened up the political system by instituting multiparty politics, setting a term limit on the presidency, and prohibiting political activity by both the army and the judiciary. To show his goodwill, he nominated a Tutsi, Dismas Nsengiyaremye of PARMEHUTU, now rechristened the Democratic Republican Movement, to the new post of Prime Minister. Whether his actions were skillful political maneuvers or something more sincere, Habyarimana made a genuine effort to reduce ethnic tensions in Rwanda. The transitional government extended a formal invitation to the RPF, which the RPF declined, forcing a series of negotiations. In August 1993, the RPF leader, Colonel Alex Kanyarengwe and the government, agreed to form a united government. However, on April 6, 1994, Habyarimana died in a mysterious plane crash with the president of Burundi, ironically, on their way back from a conference to end the ethnic strife in their countries.[16]

Rwanda's history took a more tragic turn with that accident, which was used by supporters of the regime to launch a well-planned program to eliminate all opposition. A few hours after the plane crash, members of the Presidential Guard and other soldiers engaged in sharp rhetoric against the minority Tutsi, sweeping through Kigali, the capital city, with lists of prominent opposition leaders and critics of the Habyarimana regime to assassinate. The murder of the prime minister, Agathe Uwilingiyimana, and other moderate leaders created a political vacuum. In the following days, the unthinkable happened. According to Longman:

> a plan that had been in preparation for months was set in motion, carrying violence in every corner of the country. In each community, trained civilian militia, directed by local officials and supported by soldiers, attacked and looted the homes of moderate Hutu and members of the Tutsi minority; then they systematically slaughtered those who sought refuge in churches and other public buildings. By July, as many as one million people were dead, more than two million had fled into exile, and the remnants of the government had escaped into [then] Zaire in advance of a military victory by the largely Tutsi Rwandan Patriotic Front (RPF).[17]

That carnage clearly shocked the world with painful images of dismemberment, displacement, starvation, and bloated corpses floating down the Kagera River into Uganda and Lake Victoria. The Rwandan Armed Forces (FAR) and Hutu militia (the Interahamwe) set up roadblocks and went from house to house, killing Tutsis and moderate Hutu politicians. Thousands died on the first day. Some UN camps sheltered civilians, but most of the peacekeeping forces, part of the United Nations Assistance Mission in Rwanda (UNAMIR), stood by while the slaughter continued. To intervene would have exceeded their monitoring mandate. With still no sign of additional UN deployments, the Security Council authorized the deployment of French forces in south-west Rwanda that would be known as *Opération Turquoise*. On June 22, 1994, the French created a "safe area" in territory controlled by the government. However, killings of Tutsis continued even in the safe areas. The Tutsi RPF forces captured Kigali. The Hutu government fled to Zaire, followed by a tide of refugees. The French ended their mission and were replaced by Ethiopian UN troops. The RPF set up an interim government of national unity in Kigali. Although disease and more killings claimed additional lives in the refugee camps, the genocide was over. An estimated 800,000 Rwandans had been killed in 100 days.[18]

In reality, signs of impending crisis were plainly visible in Rwanda in late 1993. Social conflicts escalated almost daily, reflecting an angry polarization between the state and the public. Yet it was still with "stupefaction" that, on December 17, 1993, the editors of the opposition journal, *Le Flambeau*, reported that the government was apparently planning a campaign of mass murder, "which the plotters will pass off as a civil war," to purge Rwanda of dissent. "Rwandan fascists and their chief have decided to apply 'the final solution' to their fellow citizens," *Le Flambeau* warned, calling for local self-defense and international pressure to bind the hands of "the mafia that finds itself at the head of Rwanda, which today, dissatisfied with its people, has decided to dissolve them."[19] The reaction of the international community was typified by the evacuation of foreign nationals at the beginning of the genocide, the removal of Belgian UN peacekeepers, and the reluctance of national governments and international bodies to commit resources to relieve the suffering of the victims. France and Belgium sent troops to rescue their citizens. American civilians were also airlifted out. Nobody intervened to rescue even those Rwandans employed by Western governments in their embassies and consulates.

In Kigali, the capital city of Rwanda, President Clinton apologized to the victims of genocide on March 25, 1998:

> The international community, together with nations in Africa, must bear its share of responsibility for this tragedy, as well. We did not act quickly enough after the killing began. We should not have allowed the refugee camps to become safe havens for the killers. We did not immediately call these crimes by their rightful name: genocide. We cannot

change the past. But we can and must do everything in our power to help you build a future without fear, and full of hope.[20]

Through the prism of Somalia, American officials saw Rwanda as another "failed state," just one more of a series of political disasters on the continent. In such a case, they reasoned, any intervention would have to be large-scale and costly and would probably produce no measurable improvement.

In Kigali, UN Secretary-General, Kofi Annan also apologized to the Parliament of Rwanda:

> The world must deeply repent this failure. Rwanda's tragedy was the world's tragedy. All of us who cared about Rwanda, all of us who witnessed its suffering, fervently wish that we could have prevented the genocide. Looking back now, we see the signs which then were not recognized. Now we know that what we did was not nearly enough— not enough to save Rwanda from itself, not enough to honor the ideals for which the United Nations exists. We will not deny that, in their greatest hour of need, the world failed the people of Rwanda.[21]

Bolder actions on the part of the United States and the United Nations could have spared the world of such a strategy, based on events leading to the genocide. Major General Roméo Dallaire, UN Force Commander in Rwanda, sent a fax to the UN's New York Headquarters on January 11, 1994, in which he urgently requested protection for an informant who outlined to him Hutu plans being made to exterminate Tutsis and to provoke and kill Belgian troops so as to guarantee Belgium's withdraw from Rwanda. This informant provided further details about the location of Interahamwe arm caches. Everything Dallaire's informant told him came true three months later.[22]

General Dallaire received, the same day, a reply that came from the desk of future Secretary-General Kofi Annan, then head of UN peace-keeping operations. Annan told Dallaire that the UN did not agree with his plan to raid the arm caches and furthermore, he must inform the president of Rwanda of what he had learned from the informant, even though it was the president's own inner circle that was planning the slaughter of Tutsis. Philip Gourevitch's book, *We Wish to Inform You That Tomorrow We Will Be Killed with Our Families*,[23] details how the UN ignored the famous January 11th cable while individual Rwandans sensed the imminent calamity. *The Triumph of Evil* also reveals report on how the 1994 Rwanda genocide could have been prevented.[24] Drawing on dramatic footage, previously con-fidential cables, and interviews with UN and U.S. officials, *Frontline* investigated early warnings of the coming slaughter.[25] Despite the warning, the West did not try to prevent it. And once the genocide started, the United States and the UN did not try to halt it. In just hundred days, the Hutu majority of Rwanda murdered an estimated 800,000 of their Tutsi compatriots. The pace of the Rwandan killing outstripped even the Nazis.[26]

In its indictment of the West's failure to act, *The Triumph of Evil* [27] chronicles significant points in the unfolding genocide. It shows how a UN peacekeeping force of over 2,500 was unable to protect Tutsis seeking sanctuary. How, as the massacres spread, the UN withdrew its force, abandoning Tutsi refugees. And, at a point when Rwanda was literally overflowing with corpses, the program shows how U.S. and UN officials still refrained from characterizing the slaughter as genocide so they would not have to get involved. In candid, on-the-record interviews, U.S. officials detail the many inter-agency meetings on the subject of the Rwandan genocide.[28] In the end, the Clinton administration hesitated to act because of the so-called Somalia syndrome, which originated only a few months earlier when a UN/U.S. peacekeeping mission in Somalia ended with the deaths of eighteen U.S. Rangers. The Clinton administration did not want to be dragged into another African quagmire. As Gourevitch bitterly notes at the conclusion of his report, the Clinton administration's failure to intervene in Rwanda "wasn't a failure to act. The decision was not to act. And at that, we succeeded greatly."[29]

By the evening of April 7, UN staff as well as the members of the Security Council knew that the Presidential Guard had killed Belgian peacekeepers, assassinated political leaders, and massacred civilians. In its first statement on the crisis, the Council deplored the slaughter of government leaders and many civilians, strongly condemning "these horrific attacks and their perpetrators." The council then demanded that the "Rwandese security forces and military units and paramilitary units" halt the killings.[30] At this point, the council could have declared a threat to international or regional peace and security and invoked its Chapter VII mandate, but instead it delayed a decision until the Secretary-General presented a written recommendation nearly two weeks later. From the declaration, Council members clearly knew that Rwandan government forces and militia were responsible for the slaughter, but it is not clear how many of them knew that many of the civilians were Tutsis targeted because of their ethnicity. Notes of the briefing that preceded the vote on the resolution make no mention of this information.[31]

Certainly the United States, French, and Belgian delegates knew that ethnic slaughter had begun and anticipated extensive disorder, as evidenced by their plans to evacuate their own citizens. Both the Belgians and the United States began planning to evacuate their citizens by the evening of April 7 and the French were considering the move the next day. General Christian Quesnot, then head of military affairs for the French presidency, recalled that "political as well as military leaders understood immediately that we were headed towards massacres on a scale far beyond any that had taken place before."[32] At a meeting on April 8, senior French military officers reportedly predicted that 100,000 Tutsi would die.

Yet the United States decided on the evening of April 7 that UNAMIR's mandate would not be broadened from Chapter VI to Chapter VII and it began to suggest even that UNAMIR be withdrawn. Several permanent members of the Security Council shared these views, probably meaning that at least the U.K. supported the U.S. position.[33] These UN diplomats—and presumably the UN staff who assisted them—insisted that UNAMIR remain neutral. To permit any apparent deviation from this position could result in military action against UNAMIR, a weak and lightly armed force unable to defend itself. Were UNAMIR attacked, member states might have to provide additional troops or funds to rescue it. They feared also creating a precedent that would have repercussions on other peacekeeping operations. They recalled the unfortunate consequences of an overly assertive policy in Somalia, where the lack of neutrality contributed to the mission's failure. Rather than intervene more actively to protect the population, all that the UN troops could do in Rwanda was to patrol and be visible in the city. Both the United States and the United Kingdom had considered total withdrawal in February,[34] and they continued to hold this position even after massive ethnic slaughter had begun.

Although UNAMIR could not actively protect Rwandans, Assistant Secretary-General Riza suggested that it might be able to assist foreigners if its mandate were changed.[35] From this comment, it appears strong signals from certain permanent Western members of the Security Council had caused the secretariat staff to consider applying different rules for foreigners and for Rwandans. By April 8, as massacres of Tutsi increased, Belgium moved from seeking to use UNAMIR to protect both Rwandans and foreigners to proposing that the force help just foreigners. A Belgian official, Claes, once more used public opinion as a pretext for policy. Public opinion, which in February would not accept passivity in the face of genocide, and which the day before would not accept UNAMIR hiding behind the limitations of its mandate in the face of many deaths, now was said to find the UNAMIR soldiers' obligation to "stay passive"[36] unacceptable if there were more Belgian victims.

The Secretary-General also foresaw the use of UNAMIR to assist foreigners, but he proposed helping UN personnel exclusively. He wrote from Europe to ask the Council to change the mandate and rules of engagement and to plan for recruiting an additional two or three battalions in order to make this assistance possible. However, that afternoon, Under-Secretary General for Peacekeeping, Kofi Annan, in effect rescinded the request made by Boutros-Ghali and told Belgian, U.S., and French diplomats that sending two or three battalions under UN command would be too costly in terms of time and money.[37] It would be preferable for national governments to send troops for a "humanitarian" intervention, in order to evacuate foreigners. With the problems of troops to be resolved in this way, the question of mandate no longer posed a problem. The United States in any case stated that there was "no need to change" the mandate "which was already quite broad enough (if interpreted flexibly)."[38] The French had also indicated that the question of restrictions in the mandate could be resolved without difficulty.[39] They all preferred not to discuss a broader mandate, probably because they realized, as had Annan, that any greater authority for UNAMIR would raise the issue of using that authority to protect Rwandans.

As the slaughter of the Tutsis continues, the United Nations finally agrees to send 5,500 troops to Rwanda. The Security Council resolution stated that, "acts of genocide may have been committed." However, arguments over financing and equipping of the mission delayed the deployment of the mainly African UN forces. The United Nations requested that the United States provide fifty armored personnel carriers. However, arguments between the United States and the United Nations over the costs ensued. A French parliamentary commission completed a nine-month inquiry into France's military involvement in Rwanda before and during the genocide. The commission concluded that most of the blame for the lack of action lies with the international community, particularly the United Nations and the United States. Although France made "errors of judgment," the government was absolved of responsibility for the killings. A week before the fifth anniversary of the Rwanda genocide, the Paris-based International Federation of Human Rights Leagues and the U.S.-based Human Rights Watch released a report titled "Leave None to Tell the Story." The 900-page report documents events before and during genocide. It also criticized the United Nations, the United States, France, and Belgium for knowing about preparations for the impending slaughter and not taking action to prevent the killings.

What is difficult to understand in retrospect, and quite discouraging for future efforts to prevent genocide, is how a mountain of seemingly incontrovertible evidence failed to warn the United States, the United

Nations, and other Western nations. Apparently, many observers dis-counted warnings of impeding genocide because such an outcome seemed too horrible to imagine. As Barnett writes, "few dared to imag-ine the apocalyptic possibility of genocide. Genocide is not simply a low probability form of violence that ranks at the bottom of any list of violent alternatives. It resides outside the realm of human imagination."[40]

Rwanda had been plagued with violence even before it achieved independence, and Africa's history is replete with ethnic animosities and hatred. However, nothing in known African history paralleled the Rwandan bloodbath. Sadly for those murdered, Rwandan and African politicians and institutions, the Catholic Church as an institution, the international community, and national, regional, and international media, all failed Rwanda and Africa. Incidentally, the tragedy occurred while Boutros Boutros-Ghali and Kofi Annan, both Africans, were holding the positions of UN Secretary-General, and Under-Secretary General for Peacekeeping, respectively. Although efforts at administer-ing justice are under-way through the UN International Criminal Tribunal for Rwanda in Arusha, Tanzania, the genocide will stain Africans and their history for centuries to come. While events in Rwanda clearly show humanity at its worst, the reactions, or lack thereof, of African leaders and institutions demonstrate a sad incapa-bility to deal with African problems that no amount of blaming the West will absolve. Not even the churches could help Rwandans.[41] While the continent hit its nadir with the genocide in Rwanda, the lack of a strong leadership to tackle the ongoing ravages of HIV/AIDS seems to reflect Africa's deliberate and continuing descent into hell.

HIV/AIDS and the Slow Death of a Continent

The bubonic plague is reckoned to have killed about thirty million people in medieval Europe.[42] The U.S. Census Bureau projects that AIDS deaths and the loss of future population from the deaths of women of child-bearing age means that by 2010, sub-Saharan Africa will have seventy-one million fewer people than it would otherwise. The numbers are staggering, but they do not begin to encompass the suffering and the dramas that put faces on the epidemic.[43]

Nowhere has the impact of HIV/AIDS been more severe than sub-Saharan Africa. Though unknown twenty years ago, AIDS now kills more people in sub-Saharan Africa, than any other disease. HIV/AIDS marks a severe development crisis in sub-Saharan Africa, the worst-affected region in the world. Even if exceptionally effective prevention, treatment, and care programs take hold immediately, the scale of the epidemic means that the human and socioeconomic toll will remain massive for many generations. The epidemic's toll continues to mount, even in countries already experiencing very high rates of HIV infection. The number of AIDS-related deaths among young adults in South Africa, for example, is expected to peak in 2010–2015, when it is estimated that there will be more than seventeen times as many deaths among persons aged 15–34 as there would have been without AIDS. At least 10 percent of those aged 15–49 are infected in twelve African countries.[44]

According to the international AIDS charity AVERT:

> Sub-Saharan Africa is the region of the world that is most affected by HIV and AIDS. An estimated 25.4 million people are living with HIV and approximately 3.1 million new infections occurred in 2004. In just the past year the epidemic has claimed the lives of an estimated 2.3 million people in this region. Around 2 million children under 15 are living with HIV and more than twelve million children have been orphaned by AIDS. The extent of the epidemic is only now becoming clear in many African countries, as increasing numbers of people with HIV are now becoming ill. In the absence of massively expanded prevention, treatment and care efforts, the AIDS death toll on the continent is expected to continue rising before peaking around the end of the decade. This means that the worst of the epidemic's impact on these societies will be felt in the course of the next ten years and beyond. Its social and economic consequences are already being felt widely not only in health but in education, industry, agriculture, transport, human resources and the economy in general.[45]

There is no doubt that most countries in sub-Saharan Africa have failed to bring the epidemic under control. Nearly two-thirds of the world's HIV-positive people live in sub-Saharan Africa, although this region contains little more than 10 percent of the world's population. There is a significant risk that some countries will be locked in a vicious cycle, as the number of people falling ill and subsequently dying from AIDS has a tremendous impact on many parts of African society, including demographic, household, health sector, educational, workplaces, and economic aspects.[46]

Obviously, large variations exist between individual countries. In some African countries, the epidemic is still growing despite its severity. Others face a growing danger of explosive growth. Cameroon saw a sharp rise in HIV prevalence among pregnant women, more than doubling to over 11 percent among those aged 20–24 between 1998 and 2000, and demonstrating how suddenly the epidemic can surge. In Somalia and the Gambia, the prevalence is under 2 percent of the adult population, whereas in South Africa and Zambia around 20 percent of the adult population is infected.[47]

In four southern African countries, the national adult HIV prevalence rate has risen higher than was thought possible and now exceeds 24 percent. These countries are Botswana (37.3 percent), Lesotho (28.9 percent), Swaziland (38.8 percent), and Zimbabwe (24.6 percent).[48] West Africa is relatively less affected by HIV infection, but the prevalence rates in some countries are creeping up. In west and central Africa HIV prevalence is estimated to exceed 5 percent in several countries including Cameroon (6.9 percent), Central African Republic (13.5 percent), Côte d'Ivoire (7 percent), and Nigeria (5.4 percent).[49] Until recently the national prevalence rate has remained relatively low in Nigeria, the most populous country in sub-Saharan Africa. The rate has grown slowly from 1.9 percent in 1993 to 5.4 percent in 2003. But some states in the Federal Republic of Nigeria are already experiencing HIV prevalence rates as high as those now found in Cameroon. Already around 3.6 million Nigerians are estimated to be living with HIV.[50]

HIV infection in eastern Africa varies between adult prevalence rates of 2.7 percent in Eritrea to 8.8 percent in Tanzania. In Uganda where a great deal of progress has been made the countrywide prevalence among the adult population is 4.1 percent.[51]

In its evaluation of HIV/AIDS' consequences on Africa, AVERT has come to the following conclusions:

- In many countries of sub-Saharan Africa, AIDS is erasing decades of progress made in extending life expectancy. Millions of adults are dying young or in early middle age. Average life expectancy in sub-Saharan Africa is now forty-seven years, when it could have been sixty-two without AIDS.
- The toll of HIV/AIDS on households can be very severe. Many families are losing their income earners and the families of those that die have to find money to pay for their funerals. Many of those dying have surviving partners who are themselves infected and in need of care. They leave behind children grieving and struggling to survive without a parent's care. HIV/AIDS strips the family assets further impoverishing the poor. In many cases, the presence of AIDS means that the household eventually dissolves, as the parents die and children are sent to relatives for care and upbringing.
- In all affected countries, the HIV/AIDS epidemic is bringing additional pressure to bear on the health sector. As the epidemic matures, the demand for care for those living with HIV rises, as does the toll amongst health workers. Health-care services face different levels of strain, depending on the number of people who seek services, the nature of their need, and the capacity to deliver that care.

- How schools and other educational institutions are able to cope is a major factor in how well societies will eventually recover from the HIV/AIDS epidemic. A decline in school enrolment is one of the most visible effects of the HIV/AIDS epidemic on education in Africa.
- HIV/AIDS dramatically affects labor, setting back economic activity and social progress. The vast majority of people living with HIV/AIDS in Africa are between the ages of fifteen and forty-nine—in the prime of their working lives. Employers, schools, factories, and hospitals have to train other staff to replace those at the workplace who become too ill to work.
- Through its impacts on the labor force, households, and enterprises, HIV/AIDS can act as a significant brake on economic growth and development. HIV/AIDS is already having a major affect on Africa's economic development, and in turn, this affects Africa's ability to cope with the epidemic.[52]

The statistics for adults and children living with HIV/AIDS, the statistics of the estimated number of deaths from AIDS, and the number of orphans in individual countries in sub-Saharan Africa at the end of 2003 are shown in table 5.1.

According to the Joint United Nations Programme on HIV/AIDS (UNAIDS), by 2025, Africa and the world could face three very different scenarios for AIDS. And depending on the actions taken today, up to forty-three million HIV infections could be averted over the next twenty years. These findings are from *AIDS in Africa: Three scenarios to 2025.* The report presents three possible projections for how the AIDS epidemic in Africa could evolve over the next twenty years based on policy decisions taken today by African leaders and the rest of the world.[53]

The scenarios set out to answer one central question: Over the next twenty years, what factors will drive Africa's and the world's responses to the AIDS epidemic, and what kind of future will there be for the next generation? The scenarios project was based on two key assumptions:

1) AIDS is not a short-term problem; AIDS will affect Africa twenty years from now. What is uncertain is in what ways and to what extent AIDS will shape Africa's future.
2) Decisions taken now will shape the future of the continent.

The scenarios also address the factors fuelling Africa's AIDS epidemics, including poverty, gender inequality, and underdevelopment. According to Dr. Peter Piot, UNAIDS Executive Director, "The

Table 5.1 The statistics for adults and children living with HIV/AIDS in sub-Saharan Africa 2003

Country	Adults	Adult rate %	Women	Children	AIDS deaths among adults and children	Orphans due to AIDS
Angola	220,000	3.9	130,000	23,000	21,000	110,000
Benin	62,000	1.9	35,000	5,700	5,800	34,000
Botswana	330,000	37.3	190,000	25,000	33,000	120,000
Burkina Faso	270,000	4.2	150,000	31,000	29,000	260,000
Burundi	220,000	6.0	130,000	27,000	25,000	200,000
Cameroon	520,000	6.9	290,000	43,000	49,000	240,000
Central African Republic	240,000	13.5	130,000	21,000	23,000	110,000
Chad	180,000	4.8	100,000	18,000	18,000	96,000
Congo	80,000	4.9	45,000	10,000	9,700	97,000
Côte d'Ivoire	530,000	7.0	300,000	40,000	47,000	310,000
Dem. Republic of Congo	1,000,000	4.2	570,000	110,000	100,000	770,000
Djibouti	8,400	2.9	4,700	680	690	5,000
Eritrea	55,000	2.7	31,000	5,600	6,300	39,000
Ethiopia	1,400,000	4.4	770,000	120,000	120,000	720,000
Gabon	45,000	8.1	26,000	2,500	3,000	14,000
Gambia	6,300	1.2	3,600	500	600	2,000
Ghana	320,000	3.1	180,000	24,000	30,000	170,000
Guinea	130,000	3.2	72,000	9,200	9,000	35,000
Kenya	1,100,000	6.7	720,000	100,000	150,000	650,000
Lesotho	300,000	28.9	170,000	22,000	29,000	100,000
Liberia	96,000	5.9	54,000	8,000	7,200	36,000
Madagascar	130,000	1.7	76,000	8,600	7,500	30,000
Malawi	810,000	14.2	460,000	83,000	84,000	500,000
Mali	120,000	1.9	71,000	13,000	12,000	75,000
Mauritania	8,900	0.6	5,100		<500	2,000
Mozambique	1,200,000	12.2	670,000	99,000	110,000	470,000
Namibia	200,000	21.3	110,000	15,000	16,000	57,000
Niger	64,000	1.2	36,000	5,900	4,800	24,000
Nigeria	3,300,000	5.4	1,900,000	290,000	310,000	1,800,000
Rwanda	230,000	5.1	130,000	22,000	22,000	160,000
Senegal	4,000	0.8	23,000	3,100	3,500	17,000
South Africa	5,100,000	21.5	2,900,000	230,000	370,000	1,100,000
Swaziland	200,000	38.8	110,000	16,000	17,000	65,000
Togo	96,000	4.1	54,000	9,300	10,000	54,000
Uganda	450,000	4.1	270,000	84,000	78,000	940,000
United Rep. of Tanzania	1,500,000	8.8	840,000	140,000	160,000	980,000
Zambia	830,000	16.5	470,000	85,000	89,000	630,000
Zimbabwe	1,600,000	24.6	930,000	120,000	170,000	980,000
Total sub-Saharan Africa	23,100,000	7.5	13,100,000	1,900,000	2.2 million	12,100,000

Source: UNAIDS Report on the Global HIV/AIDS Epidemic, July 2004.

scenarios are not predictions. They are plausible stories about the future. The scenarios highlight the various choices that are likely to confront African countries in the coming decades. Millions of new infections can be prevented if Africa and the rest of the world decide to tackle AIDS as an exceptional crisis that has the potential to devastate entire societies and economies."[54]

The three scenarios featured in the report are: "Tough choices: Africa takes a stand," "Traps and legacies: The whirlpool," and "Times of transition: Africa overcomes." *Tough choices* tells a story in which African leaders choose to take tough measures that reduce the spread of HIV in the long term. This scenario shows how, with scarce resources, governments and civil society are forced to confront tough choices in improving Africa's future and tackling underdevelopment. In "Tough choices," antiretroviral therapy is scaled up, from less than 5 percent treated at the start of the scenario to just over one-third by 2025. The roll-out of antiretroviral therapy increases steadily, reflecting the continued investment in health systems and training, as well as drugs manufacturing capacity within Africa. Compared to "Traps and legacies," an estimated twenty-four million HIV infections are averted over the next twenty years. Initiatives to support children orphaned by AIDS also increase, but the number of children orphaned by AIDS almost doubles by 2025.[55]

Traps and legacies is a scenario where AIDS depletes resources and weakens infrastructure. As a result, AIDS deepens the traps of poverty, underdevelopment, and inequality. In this scenario, the HIV prevalence across the continent by 2025 remains at around 5 percent of the adult population, with some countries above or below this level. Life expectancy drops across many countries, and the number of people living with HIV in Africa increases considerably. HIV prevention efforts are not effectively scaled up. Efforts to roll out antiretroviral therapy continue (over 20 percent of people who need Antiretroviral Drug (ARV) therapy have access to it), but huge obstacles remain, including a combination of underdeveloped and overwhelmed systems, and escalating costs.[56]

In *Times of transition*, AIDS is seen as an exceptional crisis requiring an exceptional response. AIDS is viewed in its broader development context. A series of transitions occur in the ways Africa and the rest of the world approach health, development, trade, and security. External aid increases considerably and there is sustained social and infrastructural investment. In this scenario, Africa's adult HIV prevalence rate drops considerably, external aid to Africa doubles, and ARV coverage is approximately 70 percent by 2025. Compared to "Traps and legacies," an estimated forty-three million HIV infections are averted by 2025.[57]

The scenarios suggest that, while the worst of the epidemic's impact is still to come, a great deal can be done to change the longer-term trajectory of the epidemic and to minimize its impact.[58]

In many countries of sub-Saharan Africa, AIDS is erasing decades of progress in extending life expectancy. Life expectancy reflects the conditions in a community, but also life expectancy affects conditions in the community. Average life expectancy in sub-Saharan Africa is now forty-seven years, when it would have been sixty-two years without AIDS. Life expectancy at birth in Botswana has dropped to a level not seen in Botswana since before 1950. In less than ten years time, many countries in southern Africa will see life expectancies fall to near thirty, levels not seen since the end of the nineteenth century.[59]

Tragically, mass killers are nothing new in Africa. Malaria still claims about as many African lives as AIDS, and preventable childhood diseases kill millions of others. What sets AIDS apart, however, is its unprecedented impact on regional development. Because it kills so many adults in the prime of their working and parenting lives, AIDS decimates the workforce, fractures and impoverishes families, orphans millions, and shreds the fabric of communities.

The costs it imposes force countries to make heartbreaking choices between present and future lives, and between health and dozens of other vital investments for development. Given these realities, African governments and their partners must act now to prevent further HIV infections and to care for the millions of Africans already infected or affected. The huge gap between Africa and the rest of the world in HIV infection rates and AIDS deaths, will likely grow even larger in the next century. Massive national and international actions are needed to end the stifling silence that continues to surround HIV in many countries, to explode myths and misconceptions that translate into dangerous sexual practices, to expand prevention initiatives such as condom promotion that can reduce sexual transmission, to create conditions in which young children have the knowledge and the emotional and financial support to grow up free of HIV, and to devote real money to providing care for those infected with HIV and support to their families. A trail of successful responses has already been developed by a small number of dedicated communities and governments. The challenge for the leaders of Africa and their partners in development is to adapt and massively expand successful approaches that between Africa and the rest of the world prevent the spread of the virus and assist those affected in living full and rewarding lives.

Across the southern quadrant of Africa, this nightmare is real. The word not spoken is AIDS, and here at ground zero of humanity's deadliest cataclysm, the ultimate tragedy is that so many people do not know, or do not want to know, what is happening. As the HIV virus sweeps mercilessly through these lands, a few try to address the terrible depredation. The rest of society looks away. Flesh and muscle melt from the bones of the sick in packed hospital wards and lonely huts. Corpses stack up in morgues until those on top crush the identity from the faces underneath. Raw earth mounds scar the landscape, grave after grave without name or number. Bereft children grieve for parents lost in their prime and for siblings scattered to the winds. The victims do not cry out. Doctors and obituaries do not give the killer its name. Families recoil in shame. Leaders shirk responsibility. The stubborn silence heralds victory for the disease because denial simply cannot keep the virus at bay.

The developed world is largely silent too. AIDS in Africa has never commanded the response that the West has brought to other, sometimes lesser, travails. It pays sporadic attention, turning on the spotlight when an international conference occurs, then turning it off. Although good-hearted donors donate, governments acknowledge that more needs to be done. In June 2003, U.S. President Bush earmarked $15 billions for the fight against AIDS in Africa and the Caribbean. Besides the fight against terrorism, AIDS was the other theme of President Bush's visit to Africa in July 2003. In his praise for Uganda's efforts to combat the dreadful disease, he did remind Africans of what it is going to take to bring AIDS under control on the continent.

Botswana, South Africa, Zimbabwe abut one another at the bottom of Africa, forming the heart of the epidemic. For nearly a decade, these nations suffered a hidden invasion of infection that concealed the dimension of the coming calamity. Now the omnipresent death reveals the shocking scale of the devastation. AIDS in Africa bears little resemblance to the American epidemic, limited to specific high-risk groups and brought under control through intensive education, vigorous political action and expensive drug therapy. In Africa the disease has bred a Darwinian perversion. Society's fittest, not its frailest, are the ones who die, leaving the old and the children behind. Everyone who is sexually active is at risk. Babies are infected by their mothers. Barely a single family remains untouched. Most do not know how or when they caught the virus, many never know they have it, many who do know do not tell anyone as they lie dying. Africa can provide no treatment for those with AIDS. They will all die of tuberculosis, pneumonia, meningitis, diarrhea, or whatever overcomes their ruined immune systems first. And the statistics, grim as they are, may be too low. Without broad-scale AIDS testing, infection rates are calculated mainly from the presence of HIV in pregnant women. Death certificates in these countries do not record AIDS as the cause, making the statistics unreliable.

The region is caught in a double bind. Without treatment, those with HIV will sicken and die, but without prevention, the spread of infection cannot be checked. Southern Africa has no other means available to break the vicious cycle, except to change everyone's sexual behavior. The essential missing ingredient is adequate leadership. Neither the countries of Africa nor those of the wealthy world have been able or willing to really provide it. In South Africa, where one of every ten people has AIDS, President Thabo Mbeki has confounded many by opposing the use of AZT, one of the most successful AIDS drugs, and by appointing an AIDS council that lacks medical researchers or AIDS experts.[60] South Africa, comparatively well-off, and well-educated, has consequently blundered tragically for years. AIDS invaded just when apartheid ended, and a government absorbed in massive transition relegated the disease to a back page. An attempt at a national education campaign wasted millions on a farcical musical. The premature release of a local wonder drug ended in scandal when the drug turned out to be made of industrial solvent. Those fiascoes left the government skittish about embracing expensive programs, inspiring a 1998 decision not to provide AZT to HIV-positive pregnant women.

Even in Botswana, where the will to act is gathering strength, the resources to follow through have to come from foreign hands. AIDS' grip here is so pervasive and so complex that all societies must rally round to break it. The drugs that could begin to break the cycle will not be available in Africa until global pharmaceutical companies find ways to provide them inexpensively. The health-care systems required to prescribe and monitor complicated triple-cocktail regimens will not exist unless rich countries help foot the bill. If there is ever to be a vaccine, the West will have to finance its discovery and provide it to the poor. The cure for this epidemic is not national but international. The deep silence that makes African leaders and societies want to deny the problem, the corruption and incompetence that render them helpless, is something the West cannot fix. But the fact that they are poor is not. The wealthy world must help with its zeal and its cash if Africa is ever to be freed of the AIDS plague.

Unlike ebola or influenza, AIDS is a slow plague, gestating in individuals for five to ten years before killing them. Many people in Africa as well as the West shrug off this stark disparity, contending that it is also true for other diseases. But it is not. Drugs for the world's major infectious killers—tuberculosis, malaria, and diarrheal diseases—have been subsidized by the international community for years, as have vaccines for childhood illnesses such as polio and measles. However even at discounted prices, the annual cost of putting every African with HIV on triple combination therapy would exceed $150 billion, so the world is letting a leading infectious killer, for which treatment exists, mow down millions.

That might be more palatable if there were a Marshall Plan for AIDS prevention to slow the virus's spread. But a recent study by UNAIDS and Harvard shows that in 1997 international donor countries devoted $150 million to AIDS prevention in Africa. Meanwhile, the epidemic seeps into Central and West Africa. More than a tenth of adults in Côte d'Ivoire are believed to be infected. Frightening increases have been documented in Yaoundé and Douala, the largest cities in Cameroon. And in Nigeria, the continent's most populous country, past military dictatorships let the AIDS control program wither, even while the prevalence of HIV has climbed to almost one in every twenty adults. Quite simply, AIDS is on track to dwarf every catastrophe in Africa's recorded history. It is stunting development, threatening the economy, and transforming cultural traditions.

According to AVERT, tackling HIV/AIDS in Africa will not be an easy task. Many efforts are and will be needed. The long-term planning to slow the epidemic and reduce its impact needs be highlighted. One of the best ways to tackle HIV/AIDS is prevention. Those prevention efforts that work in Africa and individual countries need to be identified and sustained. This also means enabling more than 90 percent of Africans to protect themselves against infection. The other massive challenge is that of ensuring that the estimated 9 percent of African adults who are HIV-positive get the treatment and care they need.[61] More resources are needed in Africa for HIV/AIDS including money. However, if there are no resources to be used, innovative solutions need to be developed at lower cost. These efforts may be small but they will still play a role before sufficient resources are in place. Innovative and culturally specific approaches are needed to deal with any aspect of HIV/AIDS. They may not only be cheaper but more suitable for the people that they engage.[62]

It is also likely to be many years until ARVs are widely available in Africa. Therefore, it is important that anything feasible be done to provide care and support for people living with HIV/AIDS before the arrival of antiretroviral drugs. For example, many of the common HIV-related opportunistic infections are fairly easy to prevent and treat. The prevention and treatment of opportunistic infections can result in significant gains in life expectancy and quality of life among people living with HIV. It is vitally important that all aspects and means of prevention, treatment, and care be considered and used in Africa.[63]

Africa's response to AIDS is often depicted to be as dysfunctional as its economy, just another example of what some AIDS workers call "Afro-pessimism" arising from the stream of bad news coming out of Africa. Globally, HIV/AIDS has emerged as a threat to both human and national security. The epidemic threatens social cohesion in many countries and is increasingly recognized as a danger to social and political stability. Recognizing this, the UN Security Council has highlighted the epidemic's potential threat to international security, especially in conflict and peacekeeping situations. Increased access to comprehensive HIV care and support, including antiretroviral medicines and treatment for HIV-related opportunistic infections, is a global priority. As drug prices drop and health systems improve, significant progress is being made in these areas. But treatment and care are not yet reaching the vast majority of people in need.

A handful of African governments have mobilized a response remotely commensurate with the magnitude of the epidemic, which has already slashed life expectancy by as much as twenty years in some countries. Heroic as these efforts may be, they are tinged with poignancy and not just because the government, which could knit these isolated efforts into a powerful national response, has shirked its duty. Most community programs lack any but the most basic medicines. Certainly they cannot afford the expensive regimens that have reduced the AIDS death rate in wealthy countries. Without effective drugs, home-based care can seem like little more than home-based death.

According to the Secretary-General of the UN Economic Commission for Africa (ECA), economic output in Kenya will fall by 14.5 percent in the 1995–2005 period; 11 percent of all children in Uganda and 9 percent in Zambia have been orphaned as of today. AIDS treatment costs may account for more than one-third of total government health spending in Ethiopia, more than half in Kenya and almost two-thirds in Zimbabwe by the year 2005. Almost 15,000 teachers by the year 2010, and 27,000 teachers by the year 2020 will die in Tanzania.[64] With an infection rate of just over 4 percent (compared with Botswana, which, with a rate of thirty-six is the highest in Africa and in the world), such countries as Ghana, Togo, and Guinea, may have been spared the worst of this scourge. However, there should be no room for complacency because even 4 percent, the "turning point" figure for HIV / AIDS might be the point where either a country is going to roll back the tide or watch it cascade. In December 2002, ECA devoted its annual African Development Forum to the theme: "AIDS: Africa's Greatest Leadership Challenge," because any more time wasted could be the difference between victory and defeat. Defeat in this case could wipe out the flicker of hope that African leaders have.[65]

Deaths from AIDS now exceed those from the global influenza pandemic of 1918–1919 and the Bubonic Plague. Unlike influenza and plague, HIV/AIDS does not kill its victims for years, and most victims do not know they are infected. UNICEF estimates that only 5 percent of infected Africans are aware of their HIV-positive status, meaning millions of people unwittingly continue to transmit the disease. The effects on individuals, economies, social systems, and political stability surface slowly, hampering education and prevention efforts.

All over the continent, one can see sad pictures of the sick, the dead, the orphans, and hear appalling numbers of new infections, the number of the dead, the number who are sick without care, and the number walking around already fated to die. But the full horror of AIDS in Africa also encompasses the shame, stigma, ignorance, poverty, sexual violence, migrant labor, promiscuity, political paralysis, and the terrible silence that surrounds all the deaths. As AIDS migrated to man in Africa, it mutated into a complex plague with confounding social, economic, and political mechanics that locked together to accelerate the virus' progress. Until African leaders boldly tackle AIDS in its plenitude, there is very little hope for Africa and its so-called renaissance.

Conclusion

In many instances, conflict in Africa is a response to poor governance, unfair redistribution of wealth, and political exclusion. In recent years, most civil conflict in Africa has centered on the nature of the state and how power is exercised. At the same time, well-endowed states with weak security institutions have proven attractive to rebel movements. In many instances, violence has not been contained within national borders, but has spilled over into neighboring countries. In other cases, conflict has degenerated into lawlessness, or spawned multiple armed groups with changing allegiances. As a consequence, armed conflict became a major source of insecurity for populations throughout the continent and a fundamental constraint to development. According to Ayitteh, a new paradigm is needed:

> The new millennium calls for a paradigm shift: a new approach and a complete overhaul of how the international community deals with Africa's problems. The U.N. Security Council needs to deliver a blunt message to African leaders and governments: The international community is fed up with their silly antics and buffoonery. Africa cannot enter the new millennium preoccupied with violence, war and political instability. Sustainable development cannot occur in such an environment. Nor can control of the AIDS epidemic. Attempts by African leaders, governments and the Organization of African Unity (OAU) to resolve conflicts have been unimpressive. West African peacekeeping

troops sent to Liberia in 1990 to stop the mayhem even joined in the fighting and the looting. Guinean peacekeepers joined two rival factions in the shelling. Nigerian peacekeepers dismantled an entire iron ore processing plant and carted it off. The OAU was snoring when Somalia imploded in 1993, followed by Rwanda in 1994 and Congo in 1996. In the Congo conflict the neighboring countries that were supposed to stop the fighting joined in themselves. The solutions to Africa's numerous problems lie in Africa itself—not at the U.N. Security Council or at the World Bank. If African governments are unwilling to seek such internal solutions, the international community should not oblige them by giving in to their badgering and extortionary demands. That would only compound Africa's problems.[66]

Since independence, Africa has experienced all kinds of disasters, both man-made and natural: drought, flash floods, famine, genocide, and the spread of the AIDS pandemic racked the continent. While great strides toward peace were made in Angola and the Democratic Republic of Congo, and land mine removal is progressing up miles of Mozambique's rivers, the prospects for peace in Côte d'Ivoire or Sudan seem as grim as ever. Although democratization and elections have sometimes played multiple roles with relation to civil wars, peace implementation remains challenging. Despite multiparty elections and political reform on the continent, several countries continue to witness the eruption of long festering as well as new conflicts leading to brutal wars. Ultimately, improving governance and resolving conflicts remains the most basic requirement for faster development. Contrary to popular belief, Africa's conflicts do not stem from ethnic diversity, but rather from poverty, underdevelopment, and a lack of economic diversification, as well as political systems that marginalize large parts of the population. Widespread civil conflicts not only involve enormous costs, but also perpetuate poverty in a vicious circle on a continent plagued with AIDS.

Chapter 6

Required Shift of Paradigm

Despite their considerable natural resource endowments, most of Africa's nation-states have, over the last forty years, proved themselves to be economically unviable as independent sovereign entities. Their inability to integrate effectively has resulted in a record of economic and political performance . . . that has compares very unfavorably with the rest of the developing world.

Percy S. Mistry, "Africa's Record of Regional Co-operation and Integration."

After decades of reliance on the excuse of colonialism, Africa's "maldevelopment" clearly has more to do with its own leaders than centuries of colonial exploitation. The economic development of such former colonies as Malaysia or Indonesia in Asia falsifies the view that a colony cannot get out of underdevelopment. To their credit, some African leaders have attempted to deal with the development equation through socialism or misguided nationalism. Nyerere's *Ujamaa*, Kaunda's Humanism, Kenyatta's *Harambee*, or Mobutu's *Authenticité*, were all efforts to lift their countries out of misery. However, these leaders failed for lack of clear vision in the first three cases and because of an adamant will to loot in the last. Even countries such as Côte d'Ivoire or Gabon, which remained on a capitalist path of economic development, have very little success to show. The differences in economic progress cannot be explained by the ideological proclivities of African leaders, since capitalist, socialist, and nationalist leaders have all met with failure. On the eve of this new millennium, Africa's record on the economic and social development realms leaves much to be desired. An overhaul of the continent is in order if Africa is to have any chance to make up lost ground.

While democracy was thought to mark the beginning of a new era, the mere existence of free and fair elections will not alter politics on the continent. Even when they are transparent, elections in Africa do not necessarily bring a clear change of leadership. If the incumbent regime is not reelected, new administrations make little difference in the lives of Africans. More than a decade after the first wave of national conferences and subsequent political transfer in such African countries as Benin, Cape Verde, or Mali, the ordinary citizens have yet to notice any qualitative change in their lives. Democracy may have forced the venue and reminded players of the rules, but the game remains the same. Until there is a different set of rules, the game will hardly change. While a decade might be too short a span to evaluate democracy's progress in Africa, its travails are clear warnings of miscarriage. Without a clear paradigm shift, Africa will make no progress toward its goals of economic development and democratic governance.

Disappointing Results

Africa has felt the unfulfilled promises of global development strategies more sharply than the other continents of the world. Rather than resulting in an improvement in the economic situation of the continent, successive strategies have made Africa's economy stagnant and more susceptible than other regions to the economic and social crises suffered by the industrialized countries. Thus, Africa cannot point to any significant growth rate, or satisfactory index of general well-being, in the past twenty years. Faced with this situation, and determined to undertake measures for the basic restructuring of the economic base of their continent, African leaders have resolved to adopt a far-reaching regional approach based primarily on collective self-reliance. Clearly, the quest for unity in Africa has proved elusive. Unity in Africa has a deep historical resonance since it was the goal of the fathers of independence. Political and economic unity in Africa springs from the very roots of African identity, which has long resisted being arbitrarily divided into national citizenships. At the dawn of the twentieth century, Africa seems once again at a crossroads. After many false starts in the last few decades, Africa is trying to avoid being perceived as the land of broken promises, and of failed states that inevitably subvert the best intentions of their peoples and their development partners. Better governance, improved economic management, democratic rule, imposed by inescapable pressures, both internal and external, are really forcing African leaders to come to terms with the collective realities.

However, how Africans are to transform their expertise at coping with adversity into the capacity necessary to put Africa on the road to conquering poverty and division and achieving democracy and human rights, remains to be seen. There are high-level initiatives, including the AU and NEPAD. If history is any guide, these new institutions, by themselves, will not produce any result. Several initiatives in the past have only yielded disappointing results because of lack of political will and the deleterious effects of conflict. The growing culture of violence prevents any development from taking place. The establishment of an effective AU and regional economic integration requires peace and security along with good governance. In turn, developing the appropriate doctrines, institutions, and processes to underpin regional peace and security must precede peace and security.

Economic progress requires peace and order. Planning, saving, and investment become unprofitable without security. Strife may ruin a country or region. On the other hand, generalized poverty, especially sudden impoverishment, generates strife and disorder, so that a vicious circle traps a country in pitiful conditions. However, weak political structures complicate the relationship between economic conditions and ruinous strife. A gust of economic adversity that a strong system could withstand may break a weak political structure. The African states which have to cope with such tremendous economic difficulties are weakened by ethnic divisions, the lack of competent personnel, and above all the diversion of all the energy and resources into the struggle for power.

The greater and more widespread the poverty, the more important are the stakes of political contests. In an affluent country, a politician thrown out of office can usually find decent employment elsewhere, but in a poor country full of paupers a loss of office usually means financial ruin. In consequence, the fight for office becomes a matter of life and death for all the minor figures unable to place large funds in foreign banks, and assumes the form of a struggle for existence fought with every available means and without regard for law or convention. Under such circumstances, politics oscillates between despotism and anarchy because a constitutional democracy cannot function without a readiness to compromise and to observe the rules of the game.[1]

The causal relationship between parasitism and poverty is not unilateral but circular, and it exemplifies the principle of the least effort: all people seek the wealth necessary for the satisfaction of their basic needs, and wherever wealth can be conserved there are people who amass it in order to gain more power and glory. If the easiest or quickest road to minimal prosperity, and especially to riches, leads through participation in activities which add to the collective wealth, then people will put their energies into socially useful occupations. If, owing to circumstances among which general poverty usually occupies a prominent place, productive activities are unrewarding, then people will concentrate on devising ways of wresting from the others such wealth as already exists. In other words, the energies in an expanding economy will be applied to production, but in a stagnant or contracting economy they will be directed into open or veiled predation.[2]

A scrutiny of NEPAD throws doubt on its potentials for success. First the lack of consultation with the prime stakeholders is quite surprising. Given the importance of the new program and its demands on Africans, one would think that they should be informed. Much to their shock, Africans literally woke up with yet another scheme for the development of their continent in which they had no say. The real basis of African unity has been ignored because of African leaders' haste to deal with their development partners. Africa still lacks political unity, the prerequisite for any serious achievement on the continent. However, instead of devoting some time to resolving the numerous conflicts and disputes among leaders and peoples, both within and between individual countries, politicians decided to ignore the reality of African politics and move on with the creation of what is really a fictitious entity. African leaders placed great emphasis on Africa's cultural heritage and its contribution as the cradle of humankind, to remind the donor community of their obligation toward Africa. Right there is another false start.

As Professor Adedeji stressed, the full benefits of the regional integration can only be attained if the people of Africa are given ownership of the vision, and African governments shoulder the responsibilities of making that possible. In other words, all stakeholders must fully be engaged in policy formulation, implementation, and monitoring. Governments must learn to yield ample space to the private sector and organized labor. And, to maximize their effectiveness, governments must also play proactive roles at their respective national level as they have at the regional level. Adedeji underscored that the pursuit of economic integration must go hand in hand with the pursuit of political stability at the national level and dynamic political cooperation at sub regional and regional levels.[3] All successful efforts at regional integration have been underpinned by political will, not merely expressed in documents, but by practical commitment in carrying out obligations assumed by governments and political leaders. If the AU is to succeed this is a lesson that cannot be ignored.

In its first section called "Africa in Today's World: Between Poverty and Prosperity," the NEPAD document refers to Africa's "indispensable resource base that has served all humanity for so many centuries." This resource base, of which NEPAD boasts is fourfold: first, the rich complex of mineral, oil, and gas deposits, its flora and fauna, and its wide unspoiled natural habitat; second, the "ecological lung" provided by the continent's rain forests; third, the paleontological and archaeological sites containing evidence of the evolution of the earth, life and the human species; and, finally, the richness of Africa's culture and its contribution to the variety of the culture of the global community. However, this rich African heritage has been despoiled, looted, and plundered by, or with the complicity of, the same "development partners" to which NEPAD refers. This heritage, rather than becoming the basis for Africa's own development and transformation, became for NEPAD leaders, just a cheap bargaining chip.

To evaluate the chances of success of NEPAD, it is necessary to examine the promise it is making to the African people. While Africa must improve its position in the global economy, this has to be done by a concerted effort on the part of the leaders to deal with the very problems they want their "partners" to help resolve. First, NEPAD tries to address conflict among African states. Does such a solution require foreign partners to handle? Is not the key to minimizing such conflicts a political unity of the different territorial states that the colonialists created in their "divide and rule" policies? Second, Africa is already part of the global economy. Africa does not need to seek partners in order to join the global economy. The exploitation of Africa testifies to its economic openness. There is no one-to-one relationship between the need to be part of the globalization process and the need to accept global corporate dictatorship as a method through which Africa can transform its economy.

African countries will have trouble using regional economic integration, on the basis of free trade and regional customs unions in order to arrive at a continental union. The experience has been negative leading to unabated conflict between and within African states. NEPAD is to be implemented through national-state structures as well as regional and subregional ones. Indeed, the creation of the African Union in place of the old Organization of African Unity does not bring about any qualitative changes on continental political organization. If anything, the AU merely complicates the problem of regional integration by tying the implementation of the NEPAD to the institutions of the new continental body. By refusing to integrate the continent politically, these leaders open Africa for recolonization. African leaders, instead of choosing the path of political unity, have opted for the colonial division of Africa as the basis of its transformation. Political unity alone makes it possible for Africa's rich resource and cultural resources to be the basis of African development, rather than financial resources from outside. Indeed the fact that African leaders have opted for the latter shows that they are prepared to accept the dictates from rich countries in the implementation of the NEPAD, making them once again objects instead of subjects in the transformation of their region.

Africa in Troubled Waters: The Challenge of Globalization

Globalization spells confusion, confusion about what it really is, how the process unfolds, and where it is leading developed and developing countries to. Globalization can be described as a concept encompassing such tendencies as economic integration, technological developments in the field of communications, and the homogenization of culture, coupled with the expansion of consumer culture. However, globalization is not just the result of technological advancement and growing international trade, it is also the result of an increasing consensus about the need for countries or local communities to interact internationally.[4] The process is fed by dominant discourses imposing integration, global free trade and liberalization that have serious impact on Third World countries in general and on Africa in particular. The process of becoming global calls for a profound social transformation and clearly holds implications for states embarked on a democratization process. How Africa will fare vis-à-vis globalization remains to be seen.

At the end of the twentieth century, there is general agreement that major changes in the scope and organization of international economic activities are taking place, but there is considerable disagreement over their interpretation. Some argue that the interrelated economic and technological developments which are emerging as critical components of *globalization* will result in deep structural adjustments, perhaps leading to one of the major periods of change of this millennium.[5] French author and politician Jean-Marie Guehenno,[6] for example, links emerging global networks with the death of nation states and the state structure. Others claim that all that has ended is what Eric Hobsbawm[7] calls the "age of extremes," the economic dislocations and mass destruction—real or threatened—which characterized the twentieth century from 1914 to the end of the cold war in 1991. Martin Wolf believes that what has died is not the state, but the delusion of its omnipotence which existed from the 1950s through the 1990s.[8] Globalization, privatization, and liberalization have become dominant forces shaping societies and economies the world over. With the fall of communism and the decline of socialism in most parts of the world, these three interrelated phenomena accelerated in the 1990s. Globalized economies are likely to be more privatized and liberalized economies. At the same time, privatization and liberalization facilitate the process of globalization of a country or a region. Hence, it is essential that these processes be addressed collectively. Globalization, privatization, and liberalization are multidimensional phenomena that have implications not only for economic but also sociocultural and environmental aspects of countries and societies.

Two broad perspectives might be adopted to understand the significance of the cold war's end. The first regards the cold war's end as unleashing a new historical period predominantly characterized by fragmentation. The reasons for this are twofold. First, the end of the cold war signified the end of the systemic coherence which lay at the core of the cold war and, by definition, resulted in the dissipation of intra-systemic integration.[9] Second, the cold war acted as a structural control on preexisting ethnic and subnational aspirations that have now burst to the foreground. Cumulatively, observers felt that since "the Cold War was a stable system, they could envision only instability resulting from its end."[10] The other perspective is that the end of the cold war remains essentially irrelevant to the processes of globalization, particularly in its economic incarnation. Economic globalization continues apace, leading a life of its own now radically divorced from the international political framework which first nurtured it. In turn, these issues are tangled up with deep-seated disagreements as to whether the cold war period caused international integration or whether this integration reflects other, and deeper, changes in international relations.

Globalization can be defined as the unfolding resolution of the contradiction between ever expanding capital and its national political and social formation. Until the 1970s, the expansion of capital was always as national capital. With globalization, capital began to expand as the corporation. Ownership began to correspond less and less with national geographies. Just as capital once had to create a national state and a defined territory, in the form of the transnational corporation (TNC) it has had to remove or transform this shell to create institutions that will ensure and facilitate accumulation at the global level. These TNCs see markets in lieu of states. Globalization marks the end of national history of capital and the beginning of the history of the expansion of capital *sans* nationality. Globalization also represents the shift of the main venue of capital accumulation from the national to the supranational or global level. This is evidenced in the large number of TNCs that dominate world production and distribution, the pervasive transborder operations of these corporations, the preponderance of foreign direct investment.

Globalization promises humankind a borderless, peaceful, and harmonious world. Globalization conjures up images of communications flows, exchanges of goods and services, social interactions, and movements of people without regard to racial and territorial boundaries. Territorial and institutional boundaries no longer constrain economic activities. Lost in this framework, however, is the inability to account for the differential impacts of globalization and the new world order on different regions and countries. Market deregulation and economic policy liberalization, the new microelectronics-based information and communications technologies, and the globalization of financial markets all facilitate, even stimulate, a new wave of globalization.

Unquestionably, financial liberalization in developing countries and the ability of unfettered capital mobility can foster economic growth. The issue of financial liberalization in developing countries and the benefits and costs of private capital flows in economic development remain critical. Although investment may be necessary for growth, the content or composition of that investment varies. The volatility of short-term flows increases the vulnerability of developing economies in such a way that any gains that might have accrued from such capital inflows are more than offset by the losses in growth that occur with capital outflows. Although the IMF and the WB have embraced market reforms, they have paid insufficient attention to managing the systemic risks that accompany international capital flows. An institutional framework is thus required to shape the pattern as well as the composition of private capital flows, and to reconcile the trade-offs between the domestic and international dimensions of adjustment produced by increased capital mobility. While globalization might mean a closer integration of the world economy resulting from increasing flows of trade, ideas, and capital, it is vitally important for African leaders to understand the meaning and pervasive nature of globalization and its huge impact on the economies of their countries.[11]

Globalization, the most popular conceptual mantra of the 1990s, has been commonly invoked in virtually every discussion centering on the scale and direction of global transformation. The most prominent aspect of this transformation is the integration of the national economies into the global production system. Although globalization has opened possibilities for human life, various groups seek to co-opt the language of globalization for their own purposes. Opponents argue that many sponsors of globalization seek to create a global market freed from political and social control. Such a process would lead to great inequity without some architecture for global governance that could rein in corporate power. However, many states also need democratic reforms to make their participation in global governance viable.

Traditional investigations into world order have neglected the issue of inequality. They have confined themselves to questions such as: the ordering of relations among states, membership of the society of states, and the creation and enforcement of rules. In other words, they have eschewed investigating the role that equality and inequality have played in promulgating and influencing international order. Yet there are powerful reasons for investigating inequality in any discussion of order in international relations today. Traditionally great powers have provided stability and order through leadership or the balance of power, but today these rudimentary institutions will not suffice. Processes of globalization challenge the bases of order in profound ways by exacerbating inequalities both within and among states, and by eroding the capacity of traditional institutions to manage the new threats.

Concerns of social policy, traditionally the prerogative of sovereign states, have become global in scope. The management of economic activity, in a manner that also serves the purpose of social justice both within and among states, is now high on the agenda of global fora such as the G8, and international organizations such as the WB and the World Trade Organization. This epoch-making transformation has been characterized as a "geopolitical 'earthquake'."[12] The rapidity and intensity of this transformation could not have been predicted years ago. Many authors have used the terms globalization and the new world order as overarching conceptual roofs under which they subsume, for analytic convenience, the salient features of the trend-breaking changes in the world political economy. These changes have broader implications for both bilateral and multilateral relations.

Whether African leaders like it or not, globalization is an irreversible process and the possibility of developing a counter-hegemonic strategy to global neoliberalism is unthinkable. The right question is rather how to escape from the trap of marginalization, deepening impoverishment and state disintegration in the new era of globalization. That is why Cheru argues for a middle way beyond the simple state-led versus market-driven approaches to Africa's development.[13] This requires IFIs to discard their heavy-handed interventions in favor of allowing countries to decide their own development paths. It also requires African countries to renew democracy and improve governance, invest in education, revitalize agriculture, strengthen regional economic integration, and prevent yet more deadly conflicts. This means recognizing that there are no simple solutions. Leaders must also carry out concrete strategies, combine public management and private sector entrepreneurship, and commit to a new kind of politics. Globalization can best be navigated by African countries if they utilize the best of both state and market development approaches. That is why some are calling for "a guided embrace of globalization," a mixed approach that would work in the areas of renewing democracy, investing in education, revitalizing agricultural production, strengthening regional cooperation, and strengthening rural–urban interface. Only after these hurdles are overcome can Africans reap the benefits of globalization. A commitment to democracy and self-determination is necessary to resist the worst impacts of neoliberal globalization.[14]

The state of underdevelopment, poverty and declining share of world trade, make the continent's contribution to globalization almost negligible. Even NEPAD, as a means of consolidating the pride of Africa's people in their own humanity, and as a confirmation of the common humanity of the peoples of the world, faces a hard road ahead because of Africa's continued marginalization. With the challenges facing the continent, negotiating a new partnership with developed countries requires not only a coordinated approach but also a strong political will to mitigate decades of misfortune. The end of the cold war has created unprecedented convergence in priorities and values across the globe and eradication of poverty has become an accepted global priority. However, individual countries' leaders still need to find ways and means to tackle pressing needs of their populations. New leaders who have emerged in Africa seem committed to democracy, human rights, and good political and economic governance. However, this new generation of African leaders is accepting responsibility for creating conditions for sustainable development by ending conflicts, consolidating democracy, promoting good political and economic governance, increasing the pace of regional economic integration, and instituting peer review mechanism. This new generation of political leadership is calling on the industrialized countries to support the African regeneration program through a genuine partnership to overcome the legacy of underdevelopment and marginalization.

Sponsors of NEPAD believe that this organization will benefit not only Africa but also the global community as a whole. While a prosperous Africa, free of conflicts and diseases, might contribute to global prosperity, the evidence that Africans are truly benefiting from globalization is slim. One major criticism of the current economic recovery programs in Africa is that they pay inadequate attention to the needs of the average citizens, who are highly vulnerable to even the slightest economic crisis. The programs are aimed more at production recovery than at human recovery. Little attention is paid to raising the skills of the majority, and the basic facilities that would enable them to fully participate in their own economic ventures are not available. No significant attempt is made to reorient them to the new culture of private entrepreneurship, although it is the basis of the reform programs. Africa has a serious resource allocation problem that could, in the long run, explode into political instability. Since one of the key preconditions of sustainability of any economic development is a politically stable society, this resource allocation problem threatens to erode the little economic achievement that Africa has registered over the last decade.

Given the pace of globalization, Africa's reliance on developed countries for resolution of African economic problems seems misplaced. Rich and poor countries perceive themselves and their roles in world politics differently. These perceptions and the dynamics of location of the developed nations and the developing countries have been shaped by their power relations in the global system. The gap between North and South continues to grow due to the dominant political ideology and militarism in the North, coupled with their supportive local institutions and agencies in the South. As Claude Ake said:

> The disparity of means and power is stunning by any conventional measure of economic and technological distance and military capability. For instance, on a rough estimate, 75 percent of the world's population in the South accounts for less than 25 percent of the world's productive output and less than 15 percent of global trade. By all indications, the poor world's share of the world's population is still increasing, while its share of the world's output is diminishing. The ratio will approach 80 percent of world's population having less than 20 percent of its resources by year 2,000.[15]

Despite some common colonial heritage and similar economic, demographic, political, and technological characteristics among the countries in the developing world, some Third World countries as China, Brazil, India, and Indonesia are becoming productive parts of the global economy, while others are fragmented along the forces, definitions, and parameters of the old political geography and colonial political economy. African leaders should reevaluate the strengths and weaknesses of the economies of their countries in order to become true players of the global economy. In this respect, the past will prove instructive.

Digging in African History

The truth about Africa's heritage is as complex as it is elusive. Africa has witnessed the birth of many important developments in history. Human evolution, including the use of fire, food production via plant

cultivation and animal domestication, as well as the creation of sophisticated tools and hunting weapons from iron took place in Africa.
Other historical events such as the slave trade, the rise of Islam as a
world religion, colonization, and struggles for independence occurred
on African soil. For several centuries, distorted Western images of
Africa, as far back as the Greco-Roman period, have posed challenges
to understanding Africa's diverse societies. Recently, Harris has
uncovered the dynamic history and the relationship Africans have with
the rest of the world is revealed in *Africans and Their History*, exposing
and shattering ugly stereotypes that have dominated Western thought
for too long.[16]

Africa's contemporary problems create the impression that the
continent has always been miserable. However, Africa's history is
replete with instances where even autocratic leaders satisfied the needs
of their people. Subjects as Africans were to their monarchs, they still
commanded a minimum of human treatment that has vanished in
today's Africa. Having blamed Europeans for purposely denying
African history, African leaders likewise chose to ignore or to falsify
Africa's history to reach their selfish goals. The initial lie started with
the view that democracy did not exist on the continent and that early
days of independence did not allow any political pluralism since consensus was needed to build African nations.

European colonies in Africa acquired a new political order and an
administrative apparatus that essentially excluded Africans from effective participation. Government was paternalistic rather than participatory and it was founded on the superior wisdom of the governors
rather than on the consent of the governed. This authoritarian pattern
of colonial rule ensured that bureaucratic structures would predomi-
nate. All colonial governments were exploitative in the sense that they
extracted sufficient revenue from the peasantry to pay the costs of
administration, using forced labor, land expropriation, and military
conscription. The ideal colony was one which was economically self-
sufficient. Whether it produced much or little, whether its people
progressed fast or slowly, whether its economic development was
undertaken by the people themselves under the guidance of the colonial government or by European settlers or mining companies, all
these things mattered little in comparison with how nearly the budget
could be balanced and how small the grant-in-aid could be.

Clearly the first task of every colonial government was to establish
its authority over its own subjects. The touchstone of such an authority was the power to tax. For as long as a colonial administration
merely wished to live in the country at its own expense and without
getting too much in the way of the local inhabitants, fair words were

often sufficient and in some colonies this arrangement lasted for many years. It was when a colonial government wished to recover the costs of occupation that the real test came. What colonial governments tried to do was to establish a nucleus around the capital, and to extend its influence slowly outward as its resources increased. They learned from experience that the inhabitants of the peripheral areas did not wait peacefully until their turn to be brought under colonial administration arrived. Rather, these populations traded their ivory and built up their supplies of arms. They formed alliances against the colonial government and engaged in sabotage.

In many colonies, competition for political leadership led to the emergence of rival nationalist parties. However, a combination of legal restrictions, low levels of literacy, poor communications, and limited mobility rendered parties based more on ethnic, regional, and personal considerations than on ideological differences. The rhetoric of nationalism served quite well to disguise important ideological differences and, in their initial attempts to resist nationalist demands, the imperial powers often imprisoned those believed to be radicals. Given the stakes, Africans joined forces to defeat colonialism. Even together, the struggle was intense because of the superiority of the colonial powers' means, strategies, and their reliance on Africans to betray their own race or ethnic group. Ultimately though, independence was granted. However, while Africans hope to see a true new dawn of freedom, the new leaders presented a distorted view of Africa's history to highjack political power.

In the name of nation-building, almost all the new nationalist leaders used Africa's past to justify a single-party system. They maintained that pluralism was incompatible with traditional politics in their explanation of consensus. But the reality remains that even within kingdoms and empires, African traditional political systems found ways to allow the people to be heard. Consensus meant that the majority wins, not that the minority is prevented from speaking out. There must be a tradition that allows a multiplicity of parties, albeit of ethnic origin, at the beginning of the independence struggle. Of course, pluralism has always existed among Africans and to claim otherwise is a sheer travesty of Africa's history. There is debate neither around the fact that Europeans did not find written constitutions, nor around the fact that African monarchs ruled for life and could theoretically wield absolute powers. This might even explain why Europeans hastily dismissed the indigenous system of government as undemocratic, authoritarian, and primitive.[17]

Sadly, it is not solely Westerners who needed to be educated about African history and political culture. While they destroyed parliaments and characterized democracy as a colonialist invention and imperialist dogma, Africa's postindependent leaders abused this version of their indigenous heritage to justify the institution of cruel dictatorships, authoritarianism, one-party state systems, life-presidents, censorship, and flagrant violations of human rights. In reality:

> In [traditional] African society a person was born politically free and equal and his voice and counsel were heard and respected regardless of the economic wealth he possessed. Even where traditional leaders appeared to have greater wealth and hold disproportionate political influence over their tribal or clan community, there were traditional checks and balances including sanctions against any possible abuse of power. In fact, traditional leaders were regarded as trustees whose influence was circumscribed both in customary law and religion. In the traditional African society, an individual needed only to be a mature member of it to participate fully and equally in political affairs.[18]

The myth that democracy is alien to Africa has lasted too long and the time has come to debunk it. In her defense of democracy in Africa, Johnson-Sirleaf eloquently posits:

> They tell us that democracy is a luxury in Africa; that a multiparty political system is inappropriate to our traditions; that the electoral process is foreign to our heritage and that participatory politics is potentially exploitative of our masses. Such rubbish is repeated in one form or fashion by even some of our renowned continental leaders. But we know and can see clearly through their attempts to halt the development of political institutions merely to perpetuate themselves in power. This social African legacy has led to succession only through the barrel of a gun—a legacy which now threatens us with two political forces—the military and the civilian, the latter with no means to ensure full political choice or expression. Add to this a growing disguised military as a political force in the form of civilianized soldiers and we will realize how much behind Africans are falling in this important aspect of national development.[19]

Despite the timid return of democracy, the sense that one-party state is the most suitable system of African government persists. In several countries, either the former single party is split into peripheral allies, or a cluster of circumstantial bedfellows grants its support to the ruling party to create the impression of political pluralism. In his *Africa in Chaos*, Ayittey admirably describes African political systems from which contemporary African leaders could have borrowed to solve most of Africa's sociopolitical problems, but the new African leadership denounced these institutions as cultural throwbacks and borrowed alien ideologies inappropriate for African development.[20]

The other piece of history worth revisiting is the set of values Africa used to stand for: dignity and *ubuntu* (humaneness). Even at the height of hatred, exploitation, and abuse, Africans maintained a minimum of dignity. Although Africans are diverse and spread across a broad continent, Africans share important fundamental moral understandings. Herskovits argued that Africans possessed, then, a complex web of values that allowed them to resist some internal and external innovations.[21] These values include individual deference, loyalty and obligation to community, subordinating individualism to social cooperation, reverence for tradition, and above all, dignity and pride.

Ubuntu is about the essence of being human. It is based on the principle of caring for each other's well-being, and a spirit of mutual support. Each individual's humanity is ideally expressed through his or her relationship with others and theirs, in turn, through a recognition of the individual's humanity. *Ubuntu* means that "people are people through other people," people are socially constituted. It also acknowledges that each citizen possesses both the rights and the responsibilities of promoting individual and societal well-being. This vision of the world is expressed in the zulu maxim as *umuntu ngu-muntu ngabantu*, which means that to be human is to affirm one's humanity by recognizing the humanity of others in its infinite variety of content and form.[22] In traditional Africa, the solitary human being is a contradiction in terms. Therefore one seeks to work for the common good because one's humanity comes into its own in community. At root, this phrase communicates a basic respect, empathy and compassion for others. It describes a person as "being-with-others" and prescribes what "being-with-others" should be all about. The *ubuntu* philosophy on the community governing process is one of generating agreement or building consensus. African democracy is not simply majority rule. Traditional African democracy operates in the form of discussions. While there are leaders, everyone gets a chance to speak, building consensus.[23]

Ubuntu can also be understood as the essence of God's presence and manifestation among human beings, therefore, it is considered as a universal value. Africans believe that anyone who has *ubuntu* understands the values of human life. They would rather use their abilities for the good of the common cause. *Ubuntu* teaches them to love oneself, love others and their belongings, and help the community achieve what it has set out to achieve. The content of *ubuntu* sounds out the love and compassion of God. Unfortunately, a glance at recent events on the continent empties these concepts of their meaning. From becoming the perpetual beggar to inhumane behavior observed in Rwanda, Burundi, Democratic Republic of the Congo, Uganda, or elsewhere, to the continent's incapacity to tackle effectively AIDS, Africa seems to have lost both dignity and *ubuntu*. It is hard to credit contemporary Africa, its leaders, and even Africans themselves, with any of these values. Africa seems to be rapidly drifting away from its roots, desperate to become what it cannot be. In Ali Mazrui's view, the "triple heritage" combining indigenous, Islamic, and Western influences, risks being overwhelmed by foreign cultural incursions.[24]

While the end of the cold war has allowed opportunities for fostering human rights, governmental accountability, empowerment of the voluntary sector and improved efficiency, the important task for actors and institutions, both internal and external, is to create an enabling environment for the cultivation of democratic norms, structures, and practices. Given Africa's performance in the last decades, such an environment cannot be created within the old paradigm.

Charting a New Course: A Required Paradigm Shift

As a continent at the bottom of every socioeconomic indicator, Africa is not just the poorest, but is becoming poorer. A functionally redundant civil service continues to consume 60–80 percent of national budgets, resulting in fiscal paralysis, financial constraints on development, and little scope for political maneuverability.[25] Good governance required by the IFIs ensured the smooth implementation of structural adjustment. Creating an open and transparent bureaucracy, some degree of institutional capacity building, and some form of accountability was supposed to facilitate a new environment conducive to better economic and political conditions. Unfortunately, African politicians have used a series of techniques to maintain or enhance their political and economic power during adjustment. The politically powerful have managed to consolidate not only their political status, but also their socioeconomic position within society.[26] Ironically, the programs supposed to give Africans a say in the management of their continent actually granted more power to those already mighty. If political change happens at all, it occurs through the ruling elites.

If the "second independence" was meant to really liberate Africans, the news so far is not good. African politics seems to remain essentially chaotic, with the collapse of all things official working to reproduce forms of authority. Corruption, mismanagement, nepotism, civil war, disease, malnutrition, and drought, seem to represent hallmarks of a functioning African polity, not a collapsing one. Consequently, struggles for peace, democracy, and social progress are actually dysfunctional.[27] While multiparty elections have been held in many countries, these countries still lack the traditions of democratic culture and the institutions that support them. Whether through adequate voting systems, coalitions, separation of powers, or other constitutional means, a way must be found within democratic systems for opposition voices to be heard. In Africa, the gap between governments and citizens continues, despite the advent of democratization, to widen. A symbiotic relationship among the state, civil society, individual citizens, and democratic structures is missing, forcing Africans to put all their hope, once again in NEPAD. Given African leaders' records, only a genuine new paradigm can give a glimpse of hope to the continent. Browsing through NEPAD document, one gets the sense that the new leaders are, *in theory*, serious about transforming their continent.

NEPAD centers on African ownership and management. Through this program, African leaders are setting an agenda for the renewal of the continent. The agenda is based on national and regional priorities and development plans that must be prepared through participatory processes involving the people. African leaders acknowledged having derived their mandates from their people, and taking on themselves to articulate these plans as well as lead the processes of implementation on behalf of their people. The program is a new framework of interaction with the rest of the world, including the industrialized countries and multilateral organizations. It is based on the agenda set by African leaders through their own initiatives and of their own volition, to shape the destiny of their continent. Aware of the challenges facing their continent, African leaders have, once again, set up important objectives. To achieve them, African leaders will take joint responsibility for the following:

- Strengthening mechanisms for conflict prevention, management, and resolution at the regional and continental levels, and to ensure that these mechanisms are used to restore and maintain peace;
- Promoting and protecting democracy and human rights in their respective countries and regions, by developing clear standards of accountability, transparency, and participatory governance at the national and subnational levels;
- Restoring and maintaining macroeconomic stability, especially by developing appropriate standards and targets for fiscal and monetary policies, and introducing appropriate institutional frameworks to achieve these standards;
- Instituting transparent legal and regulatory frameworks for financial markets and auditing of private companies and the public sector;
- Revitalizing and extend the provision of education, technical training and health services, with high priority given to tackling HIV/AIDS, malaria and other communicable diseases;
- Promoting the role of women in social and economic development by reinforcing their capacity in the domains of education and

training; by the development of revenue-generating activities through facilitating access to credit; and by assuring their participation in the political and economic life of African countries;
- Building the capacity of the states in Africa to set and enforce the legal framework, as well as maintaining law and order; and
- Promoting the development of infrastructure, agriculture and its diversification into agro-industries and manufacturing to serve both domestic and export markets.

What seems to be an *African Renaissance* project, should allow Africa to take its rightful place in the world if a strong and competitive economy is built as the world moves toward greater liberalization and competition. Evidently, NEPAD will succeed only through proper management by diverse but unified African peoples. If Africa's enormous natural and human resources are properly harnessed and utilized, NEPAD could lead to equitable and sustainable growth of the continent and Africa's rapid integration into the world economy. While NEPAD might represent an expression of the commitment of Africa's leaders to translate the deep popular will into action, the struggle they would be waging will be successful only if Africans are the masters of their own destiny. Although African leaders are convinced that Africa's development process has been marked by false starts and failures, they deliberately chose to design a project by hiding the blueprints away from the stakeholders. The true genius of a people is measured by its capacity for bold and imaginative thinking, and determination in support of their development, and several voices are indeed challenging the new initiative.

African countries have remained mired in a disastrous economic, political, and social crisis, due mainly to dynamics internal to African state structures. As Wunsch posits,

> many of Africa's development problems have grown from a paradigm 'problem:' from the misunderstanding so powerful in the world today that governing is something done by governments rather than as a process carried on by citizens through diverse organizations empowered and limited by institutions or rules of law adopted and modified by a people.[28]

The sudden thaw of the cold war left a vacuum requiring a complete reassessment of national and continental purpose in the world. Although other continents might help tackle Africa's important issues, Africa and its leaders must confront Herculean tasks ahead.

the pursuit of development justified one-party states, authoritarian-ism, and an absence of meaningful electoral political accountability.[2] Those who held this position have become disenchanted and have joined the second camp, which holds that civil rights, democracy and a free-market economy are the preconditions to development, even if the hierarchy has yet to be established.[3] In spite of massive investment in development by Western nations and international organizations, Africa continues to show signs of dire poverty that only a true democ-racy can tackle.

Kratos to *Demos*: Getting Rid of Political Corruption

There is no denying the fact that most African countries have opened up politically in one way or another. This *abertura*[4] has taken the form of the introduction of multiparty constitutions. Consequently, multi-party politics led to a fairly strong literature on political transitions, institutions and elites, as opposed to the very process of democratiza-tion. Whether democratization has been implemented in an *undemoc-ratic* fashion did not seem to really matter.[5] In reality, as demonstrated by a handful of scholars,[6] democracy is only as good as people's capac-ity to struggle for and defend democracy. Assuming that democracy means the mere change of institutions is belied by various schemes and strategies developed in Africa by incumbents and their cronies to hold onto power. Across the continent, democracy is spreading, backed in theory by the new African Union, which has pledged a new resolve to deal with conflicts and censure deviation from the norm. These efforts are reinforced by voices in civil society, including associations of women, youth, and the independent media. In addition, African governments seem much more resolute about regional and continen-tal goals of economic cooperation and integration. However, a close look at the political scene reveals a democratic wave out of breath, in the throes of political corruption and elaborate network of thugs.

Political corruption, a general term for the misuse of a public posi-tion of trust for private gain varies with time, place, and culture. Many actions popularly described as corrupt may not be so defined in law, although they may constitute a departure from strict ethical standards. Electoral corruption the most common form of political corruption in Africa, involves purchasing of votes with money, promises of office or special favors, coercion, intimidation, and interference with free and fair elections. Corruption in office also includes sale of legislative votes, administrative or judicial decisions, or governmental appoint-ments. Corruption also includes disguised payment in the form of gifts, legal fees, employment, favors to relatives, social influence, or any relationship that sacrifices the public interest and welfare, with or without the implied payment of money.

The impact of corruption on Africa's political systems is quite grave. Corruption reflects deeper problems in effective governance, according to Charlick who argues that the transitions in Africa provide a unique opportunity to bring about positive change in policy pluralism, political accountability, and information openness. Nonetheless, corruption will be hard to eliminate since it is seen as a product of political competition and a drive among politicians to remain in office.[7]

It has become clear that economic liberalization, and its attendant reduction in public sector resources, has not contributed to decrease corruption. Given the African context, corruption poses special problems in the form of moral and social codes requiring that one help family and friends. Civil servants are expected to help their relations at significant cost to the government. A forced, periodic reassignment of civil servants to prevent favoritism to family members and friends might provide an initial solution. However, corruption and bribery will be difficult to wipe out in Africa if systemic poverty is not eliminated nor can stable democracy be guaranteed under the "dog eat dog" situation of poverty and want. Corruption as an abuse of power violates the new universal principle of humanitarian justice and hence is a concern of citizens of all countries of the world, their nationality, culture, level of development, and national sovereignty not withstanding.

Beneath commitment failures may lie, apart from the administrative and managerial incapacities, deeper political collective action problems. In Africa, predatory behavior by corrupt politicians distorts the composition of government expenditure. Besides reducing government spending on education and health, corruption directly influences the overall behavior of civil servants. The lack of example from the top echelon facilitates bribes and embezzlement at the bottom. In this respect accountability becomes critical, that is integral to the politics of participation and democracy. Nor is it accountability a voluntaristic affair, to be left to the good intentions of leaders who proclaim their determination and commitment to adhere, henceforth, to good governance. Instead, accountability becomes part of the structural imperatives of the political order, with clearly identifiable actors working within processes and structures that, in combination, serve as its guarantor within the public arena and at all levels of public life. For this reason, the proposal that African leaders introduce a peer review system to be backed by a code of conduct, while enticing, cannot really address the fundamental questions of political accountability.

NEPAD has designed such a peer review mechanism, to promote political accountability in Africa. However, many doubt the sincerity of African leaders based on the stealth with which NEPAD was set up in the first place. Such basic questions as who is to call whom to account, how, why and for what, and the issue of who determines the criteria for the *peer review system* only underscore the point that a voluntaristic approach to accountability in the exercise of power and public office will not take Africa away from bad governance. In any case, a peer-based approach is not, by definition, one that assures the integrity of the review process. All such review systems are subject to bias, abuse, problems of interpretation, and in the case of political leaders, strategic choices tied to the national interest. In the end, therefore, the *peer review* proposal might not only fail to live up to its promise but may also become the route by which some of the conditionalities of the adjustment years are locked into the fabric of the African economy and politics. Beyond this, the principle of reciprocity between Africa and the developed countries that underpins the NEPAD partnership itself could become a new source of conditionality in the relations between the donor community and the continent.

Although there is a political awakening in Africa, the movement seems to be marked by a shallow democracy, making little difference to ordinary people. There have been radical changes to constitutions and an expansion in party activity, but this seems accompanied by a sense of *plus ça change* among citizens. What is needed is a deeper democracy, one that requires more than merely a theatre of participation and accountability. Deep democracy requires more than two or three peaceful elections, it mandates a *process* of political organization and engagement with the state.[8] Eradicating political corruption requires political will that seems to be a rare currency in contemporary Africa. Politics as usual removes any incentive for born-again democrats to bring about necessary reforms to introduce genuine democracy.

Africa's *Perestroika*: Economic Restructuring

The governments that emerged out of democratization face the daunting tasks of consolidating pluralist institutions while undertaking urgent economic reform. In van de Walle's view, "for the fledgling democratic states, speedy stabilization of the economy is almost certainly a *sine qua non* of both sociopolitical stability and longer-term economic success."[9] Democracy cannot operate successfully amid abject poverty. African leaders need to devise a new paradigm for long-term sustainable growth. Okumu maintains that "the hope of Africa depends on its ability to raise the standard of living of its people through economic growth. In order to do so, Africa must choose an economic strategy suited to its particular situation and needs."[10]

It has become customary for Western creditors, including the WB and the IMF, to emphasize economic liberalization and "good governance." While human development and accountability require democratization, other vital issues factor into these reforms.[11] This is particularly the case since a country's political and economic transition is a function of its history, culture, tradition, and economic development. Most African countries rely on the production and export of raw materials and cash crops; they are also extremely susceptible to natural hazards and external shocks. They face unfavorable terms of trade and protectionist measures from industrialized countries. Many depend on foreign aid, and some on food handouts. Few countries attract foreign investment due to political instability.

African societies lack an economic safety net, in terms of state social security systems and political guarantees to protect themselves against ambitious politicians and warlords. The stridently vocal and pathologically ignorant can monopolize power. Moreover, the economic environment of insecurity, resource scarcity, and poverty creates a desperate search for resources in which economic decline and inequitable income distribution only worsen social tension. Surely, these are not propitious grounds for moderation and restraint. At the same time, the economic incapacity and vulnerability means that political actors—both the incumbent and those in opposition—have limited choice in terms of fresh proposals to economic policy changes. Since the existing strategic policies are already determined outside Africa by IFIs without the consent of the people, competition among parties has been reduced to the skill of each party in executing, rather than formulating, policy. This is another reality that constrains the process of democratization in Africa.

The economic reform measures imposed by IFIs do not take the proper account of social and political background of countries. Sometimes the intended political and economic reforms may conflict. For example, SAPs may work to weaken societies as they reduce the strength of associations such as trade unions. Moreover, privatization grants some regions and ethnic groups disproportionate benefits at the expense of others. They have no hard and fast rules to deal with emerging inequality and conflict. Moreover, they promote the least democratic practice in economic sphere at times requiring authoritarian dictatorship to impose measures that reduce people's chances to participate in economic and political life. Such programs render the state incapable of providing social services and they do so without creating adequate mechanism to deal with growing poverty and inequality, violence and conflicts, refugee flows, and so on. Their search for an enabling and lean state, that is nevertheless capable of maintaining law and order, translates to a search for state that is incapable of providing needed services but one licensed to terrorize and tax through coercion. IFIs seem to be promoting taxation without representation.

By the late 1980s, several African nations have negotiated SAPs with the WB and the IMF in order to get out economic crisis. Drawing from economic theories of monetarism and neoliberalism, SAPs imposed the following goals:

- *Rolling back the state*: Removing the state from many areas of the economy, including the dissolution of state marketing boards, the privatization of state-owned enterprises and measures to reduce budget deficits.
- *Liberalizing the economy*: Allowing prices to be determined more closely by supply and demand, comprising the removal of subsidies on consumer goods, the introduction of user charges for medical and education services.
- *Opening the national economy to the world*: Encouraging a closer integration into the world economy through the removal of barriers and the provision of incentives, including the removal of controls over foreign currency market, incentives to encourage foreign investment and the rewriting of investment codes in a more capital-friendly direction.[12]

Economic adjustment seems to have impeded rather than facilitated the institutionalization of democratic principles and procedures. Although economic liberalization may have earned democratically elected governments international claim and financial support in the initial stages of their new mandate, it simultaneously undermined their domestic base. In Abrahamsen's words:

> Adjustment imposed new hardships on a public that eagerly looked to democratic leaders to bring a reprieve from hunger and deprivation, and the resulting disappointment stimulated pervasive social unrest, widespread industrial strikes and fierce political opposition. Faced with such hostile conditions, democratic procedures and principles have been diluted or abandoned as governments have reverted to the tried and tested methods of the one-party state in order to contain civil disorder and silence critics. In most cases, the formal trappings of multiparty democracy (elections, constitutions, parliaments etc.) have survived, while the content of civil and political rights has been eroded.[13]

Indeed, the euphoria and optimism of the transition period seems to be giving way to disillusionment and discontent as democracy's promise of better days has failed to materialize.

Again while democracy in the West is about gradual change, the proposed SAPs require radical departure from the past. The conflicting approaches to economic reforms and the focus on the minimalist notion of democracy produce anomalous outcomes. We now have an impotent state with which to confront devastating health hazards such as the AIDS pandemic and an elite blemished by incredible corruption in the face of overwhelming poverty. We now have a democracy that is not about the needs of the people but about something else. Since the imposed policies are unpopular, the state and its institutions are rendered even more unpopular. To be credible, for example, economic decision-making institutions (mainly financial institutions such as the national banks) are expected to insulate themselves from the social and the political realm. Significant discussions over matters of importance take place among IFI officials and a handful of finance ministers or heads of banks without democratic input. When imposed policies fail, those who made the critical decisions are not accountable, yet that is not what democracy ought to entail. On the other hand, generations are asked to pay the national debt that dictators and autocrats were allowed to accumulate while purchasing the means of coercion against their own people. Still all these are part of the economic and political reform packages that the people bear, often unsuccessfully thus adding to popular cynicism and disillusion. The issues are many, and the following characteristics of postcolonial era contain important dilemmas in the discussion of multiparty democracy in Africa. Linkages between democratization and economic growth have become increasingly important. To remain viable, new democracies must improve the management of national economies and expand the provision of essential services. At the same time, sustainable economic growth requires not only economic restructuring but also governmental reforms to improve transparency and accountability.

Some nations, notably in Asia, have managed to enjoy the economic and social liberties necessary to encourage economic development, without the need to adopt the formal democratic institutions and cultural values of the West.[14] On the contrary, other Asian states have claimed that nondemocratic systems are better at bringing about economic development or even that democratic values are inconsistent with Asian values. The "Lee hypothesis," named for its advocate, Lee Kwan Yew, former leader of Singapore, draws on the fact that some disciplinarian states such as South Korea, China, and Singapore managed to have faster rates of economic growth than many less authoritarian ones such as India, Jamaica, and Costa Rica. However, there is no convincing general evidence that authoritarian governance and the suppression of political and civil rights are really beneficial to economic development. There is no clear relation between economic growth and democracy in *either* direction.[15] In Africa both authoritarian and democratic states have failed to produce economic development, largely because of the corruption that permeates regimes of all ideologies.

Until economic grievances became unbearable and Africans lost their patience, many governments managed to keep the lid on dissent. Popular demand for political change in Africa has as much to do with widespread and profound dissatisfaction with deterioration economic conditions as with deep commitment to democratic values and principles.[16] In other words, large-scale protests that swept the continent in the early 1990s were as much demands for better standards of living as for democracy. For a successful political transition in Africa, appropriate economic reforms need to be introduced since the viability and longevity of African political regimes will depend on the nature of economic assets, their distribution among individuals, and the balance of power among different social groups.[17]

Without an improvement in governance, sustained growth will not occur, because behind problems of economic mismanagement and corruption are political issues of leadership, interest group pressures, patronage politics, a lack of transparency and probity in government decision-making, and an absence of public accountability. However, the severity of economic problems is such that political reforms by themselves will not automatically correct decades of economic misfortune in Africa. The backbone of sustainable democracy on the continent lies in economic reforms, conducive not only to market economics but also to improving living conditions. Even under the wave of democratization, Western nations and the international financial institutions set up SAPs to reach these goals. However, the harsh conditions imposed by these very programs led to revolts and ultimately democracy. SAPs contributed to the emergence of democracy movements because most Africans opposed the negative social and economic effects of these programs. Even where it is slowly but surely becoming a reality, democracy has yet to answer basic questions that took Africans to the street in the first place: how to improve their living conditions.

The contention that democracy in development is desirable and that economic growth may be a windfall of democratic rule establishes a nexus between economic governance and political governance. Economic roads to political reform are of consequence because of their potential to engender groups with vested interests in the growth and sustainability of democracy. Sound economic policies can produce a growing economy that ultimately gives rise to a burgeoning middle class that might in turn become the seedbed of political governance. Good economic health of a state can also generate a window of opportunity for external donors to provide economic assistance. Because economic freedom might breed political freedom, whenever political leaders are unable to implement proper strategies of economic and social restructuring, the chances of sustainable democracy diminish. The miracle of democracy does not seem to be working in Africa, mainly because of the economic predicament. Endorsing Lipset's dictum that the "more well-to-do a country, the greater the chance that it will sustain democracy,"[18] Przeworski argues that poverty can prevent the democratic miracle from materializing.[19] Without reaching deterministic conclusions or establishing causal relationship between democratic breakdown and poverty, the evidence in Africa clearly suggests that only a clear recommitment to economic growth and redistribution can save Africa's democracy from another miscarriage. This might explain why all eyes are on NEPAD.

NEPAD as a framework for the sustainable development of the continent is based on the following basic principles:

- African ownership and leadership;
- anchoring the redevelopment of the continent on the resources and resourcefulness of the African people;
- accelerating and deepening of regional and continental economic integration;
- creation of conditions that make the African countries preferred destination by both domestic and foreign investors;
- new partnerships with the industrialized world;
- comprehensive, holistic and integrated development approach; and
- recognition of diversity of levels of development, capacity and resources of African countries, yet provides for the fast-tracking of programs by countries ready to do so.

African leaders deliberately chose the concept of "partnership" to emphasize that this must be a relationship of peoples who share a common future both positive and negative. There seems to be a renewed sense of trust in the developed world. This is at the heart of globalization. The principle of international responsibility in creating this world citizen underscores the partnership in NEPAD. However, past behavior and deeds do not seem to be in African leaders' favor. An overview of the very notion of partnership might reveal the difficulties ahead.

The NEPAD initiative incorporates two levels of partnership:

- Partnership between Africans and among Africans themselves, both as individuals, countries and Regional Economic Communities (RECs). It is also an invitation by African leaders to the led, to partner with them to crate the conditions and environment necessary for development. That is why the issue of integration, of improving intra-African trade and encouraging trans-border projects are central to NEPAD. Here the issues of trust and accountability become crucial.
- Partnership with the rest of the world: NEPAD provides the platform for Africa to bring to the table its contribution to the world—material and human resources, biodiversity, and markets—and partner with the rest of the world on terms it considers acceptable.

Clearly the initiative recognizes that partnership does not mean equality; rather it is a relationship, an association with common interests over a long period of time. Partnership implies a sharing of burden and rewards, and as in any partnership, the size of the investment is not as critical as the fact that the environment is conducive and stable for investment. Even if Africa were the junior partner, this does not in itself diminish the respectability that Africa gains as it redefines and redesigns its relationship with the rest of the world. By enhancing codes of conduct and values of governance for the continent, NEPAD places primacy on indigenous ownership of development. Notwithstanding these "commitments," it is clear that the road leading to the developed world's Plan of Action for NEPAD is not without potholes. No "development partner" can be expected to dispense investment or aid based on sentiments. Moreover aid and investment do not guarantee economic growth and development.

Ongoing environmental damage demonstrates the disconnect between African leaders and followers. For people close to nature, the human-environment relationship should be intimately cherished. However, the accelerated pace of environmental degradation is symptomatic of deep-seated political and economic problems, not least of all the neglect of agriculture and the rural sector. Available technology is adequate to solve many of Africa's environmental problems, but whether solutions are implemented largely depend on policymakers. Africa remains mired in poverty because its leaders fail to focus on grassroots development, foster indigenous knowledge and skills, and involve the farmer in political and economic decision-making, because of the very authoritarian nature of the state.

Reforming the African State

The much-lamented crisis of capacity building is not as much a crisis of technical ability as of institutional capacity. A structural and functional disconnect between informal, indigenous institutions rooted in the region's history and culture and formal institutions mostly transplanted from outside underlie most of Africa's problems. Addressing the challenges that Africa faces requires looking at the profligacy, fragility, and lack of performance of the African state and its managers. Although democracy can help provide the basis for sustainable development of Africa, the very nature of the new African state has been a barrier to such a development. The African state has allowed great plunders in policy and management, inefficient and ineffective but expanding bureaucracies, extermination or repression of the opposition, forced or voluntary exile of key leaders, mass cynicism and alienation of the people from governance. The overall effect has been counterproductive for development since resources have been wasted, lives have been destroyed, and existing institutions have decayed.[20] Development, whose ultimate goals are material improvement in the peoples' condition of life and political integration including the opportunities for popular participation, will not happen under current circumstances since democracy has yet to fundamentally alter attitudes on the continent.

A democratic political system seems to be the only system that allows greater freedom of choice and guarantees genuine civic rights to citizens, and its embrace by contemporary powers in the name of a new world order is not surprising. Since the advent of *Polis* (the city), human beings have been trying to craft some kind of political order on which humanity can agree to. Although the concrete meaning of democracy has varied considerably, even within the confines of scholarly debate, there seems to be a consensus that democracy is essential to progress in Africa. In fact, Ake asserts that "the problem of persistence of underdevelopment is related to lack of democracy in Africa . . . democracy is not just a consummatory value but also an instrumentalist one."[21] However, democracy has not managed to transform the state in Africa because new leaders are using the state to rather buttress their position.

Instead of trying to change the state on the continent, born-again-democrats seem to be using it to consolidate their grip on power. Describing the state in Africa, Olowu and Wunsch maintain that:

> The state, at least the way it is conceived and has developed in Africa, has tended to be one which designs institutions so the center dominates all other organizations. Whether they be markets, schools, universities,

local or regional governments, trade unions or political parties, the center seeks to control. Unity is confused with uniformity and all opinions contrary to those expressed by the state and its officials are regarded as threatening.[22]

Despite the rhetoric of democratization, the "center" seems intent on controlling not only the "periphery," but also any credible opposition within those peripheral states. New requirements such as citizenship or *ivoirité* in Côte d'Ivoire against the main opposition figure Alassane Ouattara, or in Zambia against the former founding father, Kenneth Kaunda, or in Tanzania seem more designed to eliminate serious opponents. Other countries such as Gabon, Guinea, or Togo have crafted such skillful measures as residence or tax filing requirements to keep challengers at bay.

The colonial conquest was a truly traumatic experience that perturbed the organic development of African societies because colonial states were the antithesis of national states capable of engineering appropriate policies to take Africa out its underdevelopment. The various patterns of colonial domination did not bode well for the continent. Potholm attributes the authoritarian and coercive nature of African state to Europeans:

> The indirect rule of the British; the Cartesian wholeness of the French; the sleepy repression of the Portuguese . . . all shared the following characteristics: (i) They were maintained by the use of force; (ii) they were authoritarian; (iii) they were disruptive of local economic systems; (iv) they were essentially exploitive in character (forced labor, extraction of primary products, captive markets for goods manufactured in Europe, etc.); (v) they imposed arbitrary boundaries all over Africa; and (vi) they 'colonized' the minds of Africans.[23]

These indelible marks constitute the root of patrimonialism in Africa. By the end of colonialism, the pluralism, the clear division between centralized and decentralized forms of political power, and the limitations on arbitrary use of power, have all disappeared. Consequently, postcolonial Africa has experimented with all kinds of authoritarianism and democracy was predicted to change the nature of the state in Africa.

What is missing in the current democratic debate is a call for the rebirth of a new state, an African developmental state that is also by definition democratic and whose economic foundations are built on policy heterodoxy. As long as old tactics and strategies to confiscate power persist, democracy will once again fail Africans. So far, most of the leaders who faced the street anger of the early 1990s, have found a way to maintain power, and even to be reelected "democratically," with implicit or tacit support of their outside sponsors. Even the new state envisaged in NEPAD remains until implementation a mere wish. NEPAD recognizes that there have been attempts in the past to set out continent-wide development programs. For a variety of reasons, including questionable leadership and ownership by Africans themselves, these have been less than successful. Today a new set of circumstances, which lend themselves to integrated practical implementation, allow some hope. The new phase of globalization, coincided with the reshaping of international relations in the aftermath of the cold war, is associated with the emergence of new concepts of security and self-interest, which encompass the right to development and the eradication of poverty. Democracy and state legitimacy have been redefined to include accountable government, a culture of human rights, and popular participation as central tenets.

The desired new conditions in Africa have already been recognized by governments across the world. The United Nations Millennium Declaration, adopted in September 2000, confirms the global community's readiness to support Africa's efforts to address the continent's underdevelopment and marginalization.[24] The Declaration emphasizes support for the prevention of conflict and the establishment of conditions of stability and democracy on the continent, as well as for the eradication of poverty and disease. The Declaration further points to the global community's commitment to enhance resource flows to Africa, by improving aid, trade, and debt relationships between Africa and the rest of the world, and by increasing private capital flows to the continent. It is now important to translate these commitments into reality but African leaders' actions do not give much room to hope because of their disregard for democracy and good governance.

The Democracy and Political Governance Initiative centers on the place of democracy and good political governance in Africa's quest for sustainable development. It incorporates a commitment by African leaders to create and consolidate basic processes and practices of governance that are in line with the principles of transparency, respect for human rights, promotion of the rule of law, accountability, and integrity; good governance; respect for the global standards of democracy, including political pluralism, multiparty politics, the right of workers to form unions, and fair and open elections organized periodically; institutionalization of all the commitments that ensure adherence to the political core values enshrined in the NEPAD; respect for the basic standards of democratic behavior; and identification and redress of existing institutional weaknesses. Sustainable development is considered inconceivable without appropriate framework. In NEPAD, African leaders have, perhaps for the first time, taken an open, collective commitment to promote and abide by the principles of good governance, complete with a peer review system and a code of conduct. This commitment is seen as inseparable from other related commitments to promote peace and security, carry out capacity building and institutional reforms, and improve economic governance.

The purported African ownership of the NEPAD has also been presented as part of the self-commitment of African leaders to universal democratic practice. However, democracy comes in many shapes and forms, adapted as it is to the specific historical context in which it has triumphed. The authors of the NEPAD seem to assume that there is a universal, ideal model of democracy and governance against which African and other experiences can be measured. What is more, it is assumed that this universal model can be abstracted from the current practices of the West, as though those practices themselves are not problematic and diverse. The consequence is that the kinds of creativity and originality that could have been brought to bear on the quest for a political framework that is at once liberating and empowering of the peoples of Africa are not explored. Instead emphasis is placed in the NEPAD document on good governance as opposed to democratic governance. And yet, the content of the governance framework that is espoused, borrowed as it is from the World Bank, seems too functionalist, managerial, and technocratic. It is a framework whose origins consist of an effort to subordinate politics to the dictates of neoliberal economic policies. In so doing, this framework facilitates the demobilization of political actors in the face of market orthodoxy. But, sustainable African development must proceed from a premise that treats politics as a legitimate arena that is integral to the developmental process and development itself as an equally legitimate terrain of politics. Viewed in this way, it becomes evident that the key issues in the creation of a political-governance framework for the development process consist not only of the promotion of a social bargain that links all key political actors to another and the state but also guarantees popular participation, assuming an educated citizenry, in the political and policy processes.

The Need for an Educational Revolution

With all the excitement about democracy in Africa, the reality remains that democracy will fail without proper education. Education holds tremendous significance to both the recipient and the entire society. Among the primary functions of education are the acquisition of knowledge, the preservation of culture, the transformation of intellectual traditions, and the facilitation of interethnic relations.[25] Because African societies did not develop the art of writing, their education was transmitted through informal and practical methods. However, the lack of writing did not inhibit the provision of education. Through oral education Africans passed down their civilization from generation to generation before either Muslims or Europeans set their foot on the continent. Education gradually became synonymous with foreign education at the expense of Africa's culture and history.

Because it was inextricably interwoven with culture and spirituality, African traditional education reflected, preserved, and transmitted the entire religio-cultural corpus of the peoples. According to Adekunle,

> African education was collectively provided for the benefit of the entire society. It was an education acquired for life in the community through a continuous and consistent process and for the continuity of the society. Education was both individual and community-oriented. The patterns of a child and the community conjoined in developing an intellectually and morally balanced person, as well as a vibrant, solid, and congenial society.[26]

Although different societies might have their own means of educating their children, the ideals of cooperation, societal development, and quality of life were common to traditional education in Africa. African education transcended mere acquisition of knowledge. A well-educated child demonstrated respectable behavior and maintained a good name, honesty, diligence at work, and willingness to help others.

Any educational system, whether informal or formal, grows out of relatively stable societies. Human societies and cultures have long been complex creations that took centuries to evolve, yet they must be replicated in new generations to survive. A major goal of society, aptly fulfilled by education, is to preserve and transmit the cultural heritage. Unfortunately, two main events altered profoundly traditional education in Africa: Islam and Colonialism. Although the former tried to accommodate to local cultures to some extent, the latter destroyed what was in place. Indeed, Europeans, who assumed that there was no history, culture, or civilization in Africa, spared no effort to fundamentally alter societies. Consistent with their premises, they imposed their culture on Africans in an attempt to "Europeanize" those who should help them reach their goals. Until it became important to have intermediaries or clerks, Europeans did very little to educate Africans. In the end, though, educating Africans turned out to be a double-edged sword, since education also helped Africans challenge Europeans and demand independence.

By the 1960s, Western education had taken its toll on African cultures. The transformation was so deep that those who went to European schools looked down on those who resented it. Western education became, sadly, the new yardstick by which to gauge intelligence and culture in Africa. Because the first nationalists were illiterate, the "intellectuals" who came much later, ended up "hijacking" the independence movement. Their familiarity with Western education seemed to have given them an edge that they exploited to the fullest extent. They served as "enlightened" leaders and managed to take the continent to independence. However, their knowledge of education and its power as a tool of resentment and revolt allowed them to despise intellectuals once they took over. All kinds of schemes were designed to eliminate, at the very early hours of independence, those who might pose a threat. Starting from the inner circle of the new leader, accusations of plot and rebellion reached powerful intellectuals who remained in opposite camps. Those who used Western education to their advantage also recognized it as a "danger."

A few years after independence, new leaders realized that they had to reverse centuries of European influence by changing the educational system. However, they faced a dilemma. Having come to power in the name of, and thanks to, Western education, turning against it that soon was impractical. Moreover, changing the educational system meant abandoning a world system they had embraced and they were not willing to make those sacrifices. Rather, what these new leaders chose to do was to remain in the educational system that profoundly altered their societies. Some found themselves at ease with the former colonial agents and improved Western educational systems, through agreements that only sought to perpetuate colonial ties. Even such countries as Benin or Guinea that wanted to change their educational systems crafted an ideology-driven system that destroyed rather than helped education. The new wave of democratization requires an educational revolution if the continent is to live up to new challenges. Not only is democracy itself a better and easier process when people are educated, but globalization and the digital divide require new tools and technologies that Africa has yet to master.

Some have rightly called for the teaching of more problem-solving and critical thinking throughout the African educational system.[27] However, in Africa such arguments seem to be isolated and generally unheard and unheeded. In Hokpins's view,

> The challenge to African cultures is to develop African versions of educational philosophies that teach thinking skills, problem-solving, and creative independence, not to become Western or even modern or

developed, but simply to deal effectively with the likelihood of constant societal change in the future. Educational systems that attempt merely to transmit culture, whether African or Western, will not accomplish this. The cultural conflict is deep, the challenge is great.[28]

Democracy without an educated citizenry is doomed to failure and the type of elections being held in Africa testifies to the level of democratization on the continent. Most political parties continue to be predominantly ethnic. There are hardly any political agendas for candidates running for political offices. Consequently, the elections are not based on ideology or a debate of ideas but rather on ethnicity and regionalism. Faced with dire economic conditions, voters are offered such basic needs as bread, soap, or even a T-shirt, in exchange for their votes. Obviously, the meaning of participatory democracy or a vote is lost in the process. Sadly, illiteracy becomes an advantage since most of the voting population fulfills its civic duty in the dark. Those in power, who should educate voters about their rights and duties, seem more comfortable with naïve and innocent citizens who they can exploit. Only a revolution within the educational system will allow informed citizens to be aware of the importance of the vote they are casting.

The technological and digital divide between developed countries and Africa has reached a critical point. Because the developed world has been investing in research and development while African leaders were looting their own countries, nothing has been done to bridge an earlier technological gap between the two camps. Rather, the gulf had widened to the point where going to some part of Africa reminds the visitor of a Jurassic Park. In Okumu's view:

> The only way that Africa can break away from reliance on primary commodity exports is to adopt a policy of science and technology-led development. Technological developments of this nature, accompanied by major transformation in the organization of production have taken place throughout the world apart from Africa. Knowledge-intensive rather than materials-intensive industries are setting the pace, with traditional raw materials being substituted on an increasing scale by synthetics, and even the production of raw materials being based to a greater extent on knowledge-intensive techniques.[29]

Development continues to be a fluid concept. However, regardless of how one defines development or progress, it is hard to credit any African country with true progress. Such countries as South Africa, Senegal, or Côte d'Ivoire have tried in vain to catch up technologically, while most seem to have given up. Concern that universities and colleges might be sanctuaries for rebels and antirevolution sentiment has forced leaders to neglect university campuses and libraries. Most Africans cannot afford a computer. Internet use is still at a primitive stage, and public administration functions with archaic equipment. Even electricity in most African countries continued to be "epileptic," giving up on you without warning.

Since independence, African countries have been variously involved in educational reform movements to institutionalize the teaching of thinking skills into education systems, mainly in mathematics and science education. However, such little money and effort have been put into these goals that they never materialized. Although in the past three decades many countries in Africa have made important inroads in expanding enrollment at all levels, some old problems persist and new emerge. Perhaps the most glaring case is that education has not been evenly distributed among the population nor has it always been inclusive of girls. Compounding these oversights is the fact that the poor in most African countries get considerably less than their fair share of government spending. Indeed statistics show that education spending is together with health spending, among the most regressive public policies. There is a clearer challenge today. African cultures need to develop African versions of educational philosophies that take into account the manners and customs of the continent, and yet can be flexible enough to interact with other cultures. Without having to reinvent the wheel, Africans should be conversant enough in other cultures and civilizations to learn from them. This has been done in other parts of the world, in Asia specifically, without too great damage to culture. To get to the information / digital highway, African leaders have to find short cuts to progress. Available technology is adequate to solve many of Africa's problems, but whether solutions are welcome and implemented is largely in the hands of the policymakers.

Conclusion

The worsening position of Africa in the world economy was the impetus for developing a program for African recovery by African governments. Both the African Union and NEPAD are designed to lift Africa out of its social, political and economic morass. Together, they aim to promote democracy and good governance, accelerate economic growth and development, combat poverty, human rights violations and environmental degradation, and bridge the gap between Africa and the developed world.

Since independence, the countries of sub-Saharan Africa have faced three central dilemmas of development. The first has been the challenge of state building. In the wake of colonial rule, governments have encountered the problems of establishing legitimate authority and constructing capable states. A second dilemma has been that of nation building and state–society relations. African countries have confronted the difficulties of managing ethnic diversity, forging national identities, and negotiating relations between citizens and rulers. The third challenge encompasses problems of economic development as the region has grappled with a legacy of poverty, slow growth, and external dependence. These are Herculean tasks that a genuine democracy, economic reforms, a new African state, and an educated citizenry might help tackle.

development may look for causes not only in the domestic sphere but also in the evolving contours of the international political and economic order.

Given the utter failures of the first moment of vision, hope, and expectation of the 1960s, the prospects, patterns, and problems of current political renewal in Africa deserve scrutiny. In considering the post–cold war international, political, and economic context as it bears upon Africa, some old, but still pertinent, questions have resurfaced. What is the role of Africa in the existing orbits of powers? Where does Africa fit in the current dynamics of the world political economy? In terms of societal projects and human progress, what are the policy implications of the new world order for the majority of Africans and for African states at the national and regional level?

After the end of the cold war, the demise of the stable bipolar world order made predicting the behavior of actors in international relations more difficult. After prevailing for decades, the major realist paradigm seems to be losing steam. In most cases, the dominant paradigms tend to be philosophically deterministic and ahistorical. However context and history can help explain how and why the actors in world politics pursue their interests as they do based on the realities of their regions or subregions in the dynamics of the global puzzle.

Just a few years after independence, Africa experienced a continuing and deepening crisis of democracy. A series of military coups in the mid-1960s followed visible signs of tension between civilian and military leaders in some African countries. Soldiers accused political leaders of corruption and economic mismanagement. Purporting to speak on behalf of the people, these soldiers promised to rid the system of such malpractices, and solemnly promised to return their countries to civilian rule as soon as they had completed their reforms. There was no immediate reason to doubt the sincerity of the then untainted men in uniform. Existentially, neither the leaders in khaki nor the public had had any prior knowledge of the evils of absolute power in the new African states. Very quickly, however, the soldiers discovered that military coups were the easiest and fastest route to state power, the only economic good left in Africa. Thus, all promises to turn over power to civilian rule at the earliest possible time evaporated into thin air as coups became a recurrent phenomenon. This made it impossible to distinguish between the corrupt civilian presidents for life and military dictators. In this context the belated cynical move by the OAU to deny recognition to coup-makers should be seen more as a ploy by the civilian wing of African dictatorships to out-flank their military rivals than as any concern for democratization on the continent. This is notwithstanding the fact that military regimes, compared to civilian governments, are prone to use force without prohibition. More relevant from the point of view of democracy is the fact that all dictatorships rely on illegitimate power and coercive methods. Therefore, depoliticization of the political process under presidents for life and militarization of politics under military dictators in Africa are tantamount to the same thing from the point of view of those who seek genuine democracy. Recent military takeovers in Central African Republic, in March 2003, in the tiny Democratic Republic of São Tomé and Príncipe, in July 2003, and in Guinea-Bissau, in September 2003, and the February 2005 ephemeral military coup in Togo, are evident signs of democracy's challenges on the continent.

Obviously, it is not enough to heap blame and opprobrium on acknowledged villains or culprits. Instead, we need to comprehend at the deepest level possible why these palpable aberrations have become endemic in this forsaken land. All kinds of explanations have been offered to account for autocratic tendencies, corruption, inefficiency, and mismanagement among African leaders. These range from personalization and arbitrariness of state institutions to power holders' unlimited access to public resources and to venality and lack of ethics among modern African leaders. These arguments might seem to overlook the fact that previously Europe was a land of corrupt absolute monarchs and predatory and callous feudal lords, yet, these institutions were superseded by liberal democracy in Europe. However, the situation in Africa has failed to parallel that of Europe. In contrast to Europe, Africa was unable to draw on its egalitarian traditional societies and representative political institutions, because Europeans destroyed the very foundation on which liberal democracies could be built. Attempts to adopt liberal democracy after independence succeeded only in producing one-party dictatorships under a veneer of European bureaucratic structures and procedures. Thus, the outcome was neither African nor European. This legacy has plagued virtually all African countries and accounts for a great deal of what went wrong in the postindependence period.

In Davidson's judgment, the transfer of political power in Africa failed to allow a genuine radical transformation that should take the continent out of its nightmare.[1] Like parrots captured in virgin forests, African leaders only reproduced their masters' voice and acted on cues, preventing them from realizing the true interests of their countries and continent. Democracy was "murdered" in its cradle by Europeans and their allies for selfish interests. Most contemporary African states might have been lineal descendants of the colonial conquest states imposed during colonial rule,[2] but beyond the similarities lie specific differences that cannot be reduced to that between an instrument for maintaining law and order, on the one hand, and an instrument for development on the other. The African states were not only objects of competition among competing factions of the emerging bourgeoisies, but they were also targeted by the former colonial powers to ensure that the colonial ties remained.

Once a region with bountiful stores of optimism and hope, Africa now teeters perilously on the brink of economic disintegration, political chaos, and institutional and social decay, with a revival in a quantum leap back to its own indigenous, political, and economic roots. Since independence, Africa has experienced violence, poverty, mismanagement, and corruption on an enormous scale. Steadily the pillars of government, law, and even economic life have been destroyed. Africa's democratic strides seem to be more cosmetic or temporary, failing to provide a true sense of relief that the people has been awaiting. Having constrained political choice in Africa on the premise that competitive politics is neither necessary nor suitable, African leaders were forced to engage in reforms. However the spread of democratic banner still faces enormous obstacles because neither autocrats in Africa nor their sponsors outside want genuine democracy that might take away their privileges.

According to some, the lessons of experience point to six factors in explaining Africa's stagnation: poor human, technological, and institutional capacities; policy "distortions"; external vulnerability derived from frail, un-diversified economic structures; political instability; poor governance; and failure to alleviate poverty.[3] In Clapham's view, the rulers of Africa are largely to blame for the economic crisis their countries experienced, through their pursuit of misguided development strategies and more or less incompetent and corrupt government. There was, of course, an alternative case that stressed the acute dependence of African states on volatile primary product markets, oil prices, and interest rate rises, and the fact that these "misguided" development strategies were the ones international institutions had previously advocated.[4] Concurring with Clapham, Mwaipaya asserts that "the source of underdevelopment, social and political instability in most African nations is essentially mediocre leadership."[5] He went on to suggest that quality leadership in Africa can only occur if a potential class of carefully screened leaders undergo rigorous training capable of providing them with intellectual sophistication, moral strength, farsightedness, courage, and determination. The acquisition of such values would help in instituting proper economic development and maintaining freedom and dignity.[6] However, the masses' pressure should not be discounted. The transformation of Africa also requires better organized masses, invigorated political parties, new and committed political leadership, and a more dedicated class of elites and intellectuals.

The African state has become weak, extensive, fragile, prebendal, and elitist, unable to function as a state should, and limited in its control over society. Although external circumstances and pressures are relevant, pathological patrimonialism diverts the resources, energy, capacity, and political will of African states away from the tasks of development and democratization into the enrichment of a rapacious horde of venal politicians. The crisis of the African state in postcolonial Africa results from the preoccupation of the authoritarian control structure with the political survival and material interests of those who control it. While some believe that disengagement or the withdrawal of society from state might force political leaders to alter their behavior,[7] others took the precarious balance between the state and society as a deliberate "de-linking" of certain social strata, a "weak yet exploitative" state engineered by people in positions of undisputed political and economic advantage.[8] Because the state's role is to set the stage rather than write the script, the failure of the state in Africa explains the elusiveness of development on the continent.

At the center of the failure of African states to chart viable paths for domestic accumulation and sustainable development is "the problem of accountability and the lack of democracy . . . *There is a definite correlation between the lack of democratic practices in African politics and the deteriorating socio-economic conditions* [italics in original]."[9] If political accountability, or rather democracy as political accountability, is the key to social and economic progress, Africans need to remain alert where democracy has burgeoned, and more demanding where it has yet to materialize, in order to prevent a "democratic" state from continuing to enrich the ruling elites. A vibrant civil society, dynamic political parties, and restructured civil–military relations will lead to a multiparty democracy in which voters choose between parties organized around socioeconomic issues rather than communal or regional demands. The dramatic penetration of African economies by outside agencies is best understood as the practical expression of the evolving normative structure of international society. The commitment to state sovereignty, still officially enshrined in the charters of the WB and the IMF, has become increasingly insignificant, as these institutions, and indeed almost all development agencies, have come to see African governments' claim to sovereignty and nonintervention as contingent upon their ability to improve the well-being of their society. Because states have failed in that task, they have become increasingly illegitimate in the eyes of many aid donors.[10]

What is currently being hammered out in much of Africa looks like a new democratic charter, but this time with constitutionally entrenched and externally guaranteed political space, human and civic freedoms, and political accountability, within broadly defined market economies. In many ways, Africa's political rebirth or renaissance returns to square one, decolonization, though this time states are being liberated from domestic autocrats rather than colonial powers. At the same time, the world community seeks to reimpose international tutelage on Africa by means of aid conditionality and disguised hegemony.[11] While the re-democratization of the continent is of crucial importance, unless it is accompanied by an economic new deal, African states, even democratic, will have to run faster to remain in the same place. In Randrianja's view, "the problem facing Africa is not so much having to choose between a collective conception of democracy and a representative conception based on individual choice, but rather how to harness democracy to economic development."[12]

Sustainable development must simultaneously satisfy economic, financial, social, political, and environmental criteria. It must insure that production and consumption remain in equilibrium over time, that international and external accounts are kept in balance, that income is distributed in a manner that is socially acceptable, that development policies are politically viable, and that the limits of the natural environment are respected. In other words, sustainable development will be served when Africans are freed from the exigencies of poverty and made to face relative prices that reflect social costs.

Africa's claim to the twentieth century requires strong and capable states. Stronger and better, not weaker and ineffective states, can effectively turn things around on the continent. The hallmarks of a capable state are strong institutions of governance, a sharp focus on the needs of the poor, a powerful watchdog in civil society, the rule of law, intolerance of corruption, transparency and accountability in the management of public affairs, respect for human rights, participation by all citizens in the decisions that affect their lives, and the creation of an enabling environment for the private sector and civil society. Capable states nurture all of these. Confident governments welcome the views of academics, civil society, the media, and even opposition parties. In the short term, there may be contradictions between the imperatives of political and economic reform. But in the long term, economic development and political stability cannot exist without pluralism. The bodies in our society charged with watchdog functions are increasing in number and maturity. Although there has been a significant proliferation of mass media organizations in both print and electronic media and a variety of civil society organizations have sprung up, these bodies have yet to be allowed to play their full civic role.

Corruption remains to be dealt with in a serious manner. Despite feeble efforts, a great deal remains to be done on this matter. Recently, an in-depth study that has just been conducted in Kenya entitled "The Link between Corruption and Poverty: Lessons from Kenya Case Studies," shows the tremendous impact corruption has on Africa and its people.[13] The study points out that corruption taxes the poor, increases transaction costs, and reduces the level of economic activity. Similarly, a study in Tanzania shows that corruption increases the cost of living by 25 percent. Corruption is one of the cancers that have preyed on Africa's misfortunes, driving the continent even further into economic mismanagement and despair. In Transparency International's 2003 Corruption Perception Index, a poll of polls reflecting the perceptions of business people, academics, and risk analysts, both resident and nonresident, several African countries were among the most corrupt countries in the world, with Nigeria claiming the second spot.[14] Ridding the continent of this cancer must be a key priority in the twenty-first century. Without some level of integrity and ethics within public administration and politics, Africa is doomed to further failures. That is why Transparency International calls on African leaders to sign, ratify, and implement the African Union Convention on Preventing and Combating Corruption and the United Nations Convention against Corruption.[15]

If public perception is a key barometer of governance, both new "democratic" leaders and their outside supports should be concerned about the disenchantment. For example, the Ghana Institute of Economic Affairs conducted two revealing studies—in 1995 and 1999. According to the Executive Secretary of the ECA, K.Y. Amoako, there are some positive signals including growing awareness of the constitution, recognition of the system of government, limitations to the president's power, the military's ceasing to be a source of fear, and freedom of expression taking root. However, there are also worrying signs such as the declining perception of political representation, the strong belief that political parties do not have an equal playing field and perhaps most worrying of all, the fact that two-thirds of Ghanaians feel that their quality of life has not improved. Although the trend is upward in a few countries, per capita income is lower than at independence, at a pitifully low $450 per annum.[16]

The other critical issue in Africa is the private sector response. It is shocking that several years after SAPs began, African leaders still look to plug Africa's financial gap with foreign aid rather than domestic savings or indigenous private entrepreneurs. This is not just because of the debt overhang, though that is a contributing factor. The accumulated loss of faith by Africans in the regimes that govern them is so profound that Africans either prefer immediate consumption to savings or export their savings through capital flight. Africans have transferred a staggering 37 percent of their wealth abroad, as compared to 29 percent in the Middle East, 17 percent in Latin America, 4 percent in South Asia, and 3 percent in East Asia.[17] Africa is also a net exporter of its most talented human capital: several hundreds highly educated Africans live and work abroad, while over 100,000 experts from developed countries are currently employed in Africa. The lack of foreign direct investment (FDI), another measure of confidence in an economy, displays Africa's contradictions. The rate of return on FDI to Africa is 29 percent per year, higher than in any other region of the world. Yet only 4 percent of the total investment pouring into developing countries is going to Africa. It is no good bemoaning the fact that investors are not coming to Africa. If Africans don't have the confidence to come back, if politicians continue to steal and invest stolen funds into the economies of other continents, and if African entrepreneurs do not have the confidence to invest, why should foreign investors, who have the whole globe to choose from, act any differently?[18]

Africa's economic performance has been dismal, and although the failure to live up to expectations can be attributed to many causes, most significantly bad governance in general and internal conflicts in particular. Economic growth is impossible where war, insurgency, and terrorism destroy lives and property at random, prevent agricultural production, create multitudes of refugees and displaced persons, and divert precious resources into massive arms purchase and military buildups.[19] Extreme poverty and its corollaries continue to characterize broad swaths of Africa. The most congenial type of agency for African countries would seem to be autonomous regional institutions that avoid any impression of dependence on the former colonial powers or the West. But Africa is not there yet.

Some believe that "dynamic" and new leaders who came to power in Ethiopia, Eritrea, Uganda, and Rwanda will offer the chance for real progress in the struggle against poverty, misrule, corruption, and state erosion. Their regimes are supposed to pave the way for a more democratic future. Indeed, Museveni, Isaias, and Meles, compared to the "big men" of the independence era, "have been innovative leaders capable of charting a new course for their countries."[20] Unfortunately, put to a test, the theory of strong and capable leadership in Ethiopia and Eritrea yielded a disappointing outcome. Despite the huge economic and social challenges their countries face, these "enlightened leaders" chose to launch their countries in a futile war over a barren land that lasted nevertheless two years, and diverted important scarce resources. In Uganda, a "no-party" democracy continues to be the only new game in town, challenging the very definition of democracy or political pluralism. In Rwanda, the Tutsi-controlled regime seems to be taking steps to consolidate its hold on power, and recent municipal and presidential elections confirmed Kagame's desire to keep Hutu out of Rwandan politics for a while. The "winner-take-all" political arrangement does not seem to work in Africa and only genuine reconciliation, rooted in sound economic and social policies, can bridge the gap between apparently irreconcilable contenders. As Dia rightly contends, "majority rule, winner-take-all, or other forms of zero-sum games were not acceptable alternatives to consensus decisionmaking."[21]

According to NEPAD's own documents, Africa's place in the global community is defined by the fact that the continent is an indispensable resource base that has served all humanity for so many centuries. This is a depressingly narrow perspective on how Africa serves humanity: merely as a resource base. At this critical juncture, one would like to believe that African leaders see the potential of Africa as more than an indispensable resource base. That statement, as naïve as it might sound, exposes the very nature of the new leadership and conveys the difficulty of the road ahead. Even an optimistic view of contemporary conditions of the continent reminds any observer that it is going to take more than new acronyms and slogans to fix centuries of misguided policies and misfortune. While democracy is a necessary condition in redressing Africa's problems, it is not a sufficient one and its travails on the continent is a good indication that a new road map is needed in order to allow Africa to see brighter days, and to finally put an end to what has become fatalism.

In the absence of such credible restraints as constitutional checks and balances, independent and public-spirited information media, ruling elites have abused political power to accumulate wealth and more power.[22] Pathological patrimonialism has allowed a dramatic increase in state revenues that the ruling elites could tap in at will, raising considerably the potential for corruption. Such agricultural exports as coffee, cocoa, tea, and groundnuts, and mineral resources such as copper, cobalt, uranium, diamonds, bauxite, and coltane, continue to enrich the power-holders at the expense of the hard-working populations.[23] Instead of trying to meet the basic human needs of their citizens and establish a national or regional framework for sustained and self-reliant development, African leaders seem more preoccupied with power for power's sake and self-aggrandizement.

As Ake observed candidly:

> The tragedy in Africa is that power, to a very large extent, is applied arbitrarily: courts may be ordered to convict innocent people, public treasuries may be expropriated almost at will, and laws may be changed by simple executive decree. Basic democratic principles such as the separation of powers, checks and balances, representative government, alternance in power, freedom of the press, etc., do not really exist in Africa. As a result, the state does not, as a rule, operate in such a way that is conducive to the promotion and preservation of the public good or interest, which is the primary *raison d'être* of a democratic system.[24]

Because of its fits and starts, democratization has yet to make serious strides in African politics. Ake's observation remains pertinent despite the sense of renewal on the continent. Contrary to their rhetoric, democracy seems to be threatening interests of both African leaders and their outside supporters. The political rebirth heralded as a new beginning that should usher in freedom, welfare, and prosperity for Africans seems out of steam, with democratization abandoned, aborted, or subverted in country after country. In his valedictory statements to the OAU as ECA's Chief Executive, Adedeji conveyed his distinct opinion on what is needed for Africa to prepare for the twenty-first century:

> New African transformation ethic based on a human-centred development paradigm which puts the people at the centre of the development process, on the driving seat as it were and is predicated, above all, on the rational proposition that development has to be engineered and sustained by the people themselves through their full and active participation. In other words, the new African transformation ethic rests on the firm belief that development should not be undertaken on behalf of a people; rather, that it should be the organic outcome of a society's value system, its perceptions, its concerns and its endeavours.[25]

A decade of democracy has yet to transform Africa because a true new dawn will not come from current leadership, but from the ordinary citizens who, armed with determination and education, will force a genuine renaissance on the continent. Looking at various stratagems developed by newly "democratic" leaders intent on keeping political and economic power in Africa, democracy's road will surely be bumpy on the continent. Africans who took to the street for genuine reforms are realizing that the *Beautyful Ones Are Not Yet Born*,[26] since, in lieu of a visionary reconstruction, the continent continues to be exposed to a vivid impression of corruption and moral decay.

Tordoff is no romantic in his assessment of the third wave of democratization that has fitfully flowed over the African political scene in the 1990s. He argues that democracy and authoritarianism overlap in many African countries: "they are not so much alternatives as uncomfortable bedfellows."[27] Ihonbvere also maintains that current democratic "transitions" are largely dominated by the very same elite who subverted the early democratic experiments, collaborated with military juntas, and ruined African economies. Their new conversion to democracy may be no more than a strategic retreat to allow them to remain politically relevant and to strengthen their hold on the state, which is in reality a means to rapid primitive accumulation.[28]

To Africans' chagrin, several obstacles stand in the way of genuine democratization on their continent: weak and underdeveloped economies, traditions of military interventionism, cheap and easy access to small arms in the post-cold war era, widespread and growing acceptance of graft and other forms of corruption, and the potential for class conflict. Combined with individual politicians' egos and thirst for power, these hurdles pose a tremendous challenge to a true new dawn on the African continent.

Notes

Introduction

1. Colin Legum, "The Coming of Africa's Second Independence," *Washington Quarterly*, no. 1 (Winter 1990), pp. 129–140.
2. Samuel Decalo, "Back to Square One: The Re-Democratization of Africa," *Africa Insight*, vol. 21, no. 3 (1991), p. 157.
3. Douglas G. Anglin, "Southern African Responses to Eastern European Developments," *Journal of Modern African Studies*, vol. 28, no. 3 (1990), p. 448.
4. Marina Ottaway, *Africa's New Leaders: Democracy or State Reconstruction* (Washington, DC: Carnegie Endowment for International Peace, 1999), p. 6.
5. Jean-François Bayart, "L'Afro-pessimisme par le Bas," *Politique Africaine*, no. 40 (décembre 1990), pp. 12–23.
6. Saul B. Cohen, *Geopolitics of the World System* (Lanham, MD: Rowman & Littlefield Publishers, 2003), p. 373.
7. OECD, *African Economic Outlook 2001–2002* (Paris: OECD Publications, 2002), p. 13.
8. Athanase Bessala, "L'Économie du Continent Menacée," *Cameroon Tribune*, Yaoundé, septembre 23, 2003.
9. UNDP, *Human Development Report 2002* (Oxford, UK: Oxford University Press, 2002), pp. 16–65.
10. Victor Chesnault, "Que Faire de l'Afrique Noire?" *Le Monde*, février 28, 1990, p. 1.
11. Philippe Leymarie, "Une Afrique Appauvrie dans la Spirale des Conflits," in *Manière de Voir*, no. 25, février 1995.
12. Stephen Ellis, "Introduction: Africa Now," in Stephen Ellis, ed. *Africa Now: Peoples, Policies, Institutions* (Portsmouth: Heinemann and Currey, 1996), p. xiii.
13. See James Coleman and Gabriel Almond, eds. *The Politics of Developing Areas* (Princeton, NJ: Princeton University Press, 1960); Douglas Rimmer, ed. *Africa, Thirty Years On: The Record and Outlook after Thirty Years of Independence* (London, UK: James Currey, Ltd., 1996); Forbes J. Munro, *Africa and the International Economy* (London, UK: J. M. Dent & Sons, 1976); and Colin Leys

and B. Berman, eds. *African Capitalists in African Development* (Boulder, CO: Lynne Rienner Publishers, 1994).

14. See Samir Amin, *La Faillite du Développement en Afrique et dans le Tiers-Monde* (Paris: L'Harmattan, 1989); Claude Ake, *Democracy and Development in Africa* (Washington, DC: Brookings Institution, 1996); and Walter Rodney, *How Europe Underdeveloped Africa* (Washington, DC: Howard University Press, 1974).

15. Samir Amin, *La Faillite du Développement en Afrique et dans le Tiers-Monde* (Paris: L'Harmattan, 1989), p. 5.

16. See e.g., Guy Hunter, *The Best of Both Worlds? A Challenge on Development Policies in Africa* (Oxford, UK: Oxford University Press, 1967).

17. Serge Michailof, ed. *La France et l'Afrique: Vade-Mecum pour un Nouveau Voyage* (Paris: Karthala, 1993).

18. Walter Rodney, *How Europe Underdeveloped Africa* (Washington, DC: Howard University Press, 1974); and W. E. Burghardt Du Bois, *The World and Africa* (New York, NY: International Publishers, 1965).

19. Basil Davidson, "Conclusion" in Prosser Gifford and William R. Louis, eds. *Decolonization and African Independence: The Transfers of Power, 1960–1980* (New Haven, CT: Yale University Press, 1988), p. 506.

20. Claude Ake, *Democracy and Development in Africa* (Washington, DC: Brookings Institution, 1996), pp. 8–9.

21. See e.g., George Ayittey, *Africa Betrayed* (New York, NY: St. Martin Press, 1992); Susan Rose-Ackerman, *Corruption and Government: Causes, Consequences, and Reform* (Cambridge, UK: Cambridge University Press, 1999); Kempe Ronald Hope, Sr., *From Crisis to Renewal: Development Policy and Management in Africa* (Leiden: Brill Academic Publishers, 2002); and Peter Schwabe, *Africa: A Continent Self-Destructs* (New York, NY: Palgrave, 2001).

22. Quoted in Peter Hitchcock, "Postcolonial Africa? Problems of Theory," *Women's Studies Quarterly*, nos. 3 and 4 (1997), p. 234.

23. Robert D. Putnam, *Making Democracy Work: Civic Traditions in Modern Italy* (Princeton, NJ: Princeton University Press, 1993), pp. 121–162.

24. Quoted in Francis M. Deng and I. William Zartman, *A Strategy Vision for Africa: The Kampala Movement* (Washington, DC: Brookings Institution Press, 2002), p. 106.

25. Ellis, "Introduction: Africa Now."

26. Ahmad Aly, *Economic Cooperation in Africa: In Search of Direction* (Boulder, CO: Lynne Rienner Publishers, 1994).

27. Keith Somerville, "Africa: Is there a Silver Lining?" *The World Today*, vol. 50, no. 11 (November 1994), p. 215.

28. Marina Ottaway, *Africa's New Leaders*, p. 1.

29. Ibid., p. 6.

30. Peter VonDoepp, "Political Transition and Civil Society: The Cases of Kenya and Zambia," *Studies in Comparative International Development*, vol. 31 (1996), p. 26.

31. Colin Legum, *Africa since Independence* (Bloomington, IL: Indiana University Press, 1999), p. 72.
32. Boutros Boutros-Ghali, *Agenda for Democratization*, paragraph 15, U.N. Doc. A/51/761 (New York, NY: UN, 1996).
33. Juan J. Linz, "Transitions to Democracy," *Washington Quarterly*, vol. 13, no. 3 (Summer 1990), p. 158.
34. Samuel Huntington, *The Third Wave: Democratization in the Late Twentieth Century* (Norman, OK: University of Oklahoma Press, 1991).
35. Steve Friedman, "Agreeing to Differ: African Democracy, Its Obstacles and Prospects," *Social Research*, vol. 66 (1999), p. 826.
36. Francis M. Deng, "African Policy Agenda: A Framework for Global Partnership," in F. Deng, ed. *African Reckoning: A Quest for Good Governance* (Washington, DC: Brookings Institution Press, 1998), p. 136.
37. Ghislain C. Kabwit, "Zaire: The Roots of the Continuing Crisis," *Journal of Modern African Studies*, vol. 17, no. 3 (1979), p. 397.
38. According to Thomas Kuhn, a paradigm is the perspective of the world including beliefs and commitments to theory, methodology, method, and concept that should change to reflect new circumstances. See *The Structure of Scientific Revolution* (Chicago, IL: University of Chicago Press, 1970).
39. William Reno, *Warlord Politics and African States* (Boulder, CO: Lynne Rienner Publishers, 1998), p. 1.

Chapter 1   A Synopsis of Africa's Plight

1. Alice L. Conklin, *A Mission to Civilize* (Stanford, CA: Stanford University Press, 1997).
2. Richard Sandbrook with Judith Barker, *The Politics of Africa's Economic Stagnation* (Cambridge, UK: Cambridge University Press, 1985).
3. Gwendolen M. Carter and Patrick O'Meara, eds. *African Independence: The First Twenty-Five Years* (Bloomington, IN: Indiana University Press, 1985), p. iv.
4. Roland Oliver and John. D. Fage, *A Short History of Africa* (Harmondsworth, UK: Penguin Books Ltd., 1962), pp. 229–274.
5. Christopher Clapham, "Discerning the New Africa," *International Affairs*, vol. 74, no. 2 (1998), p. 263.
6. Sandbrook, *The Politics of Africa's Economic Stagnation*, p. 62.
7. John Hatch, *Africa Emergent: Africa's Problems since Independence* (London, UK: Secker & Warburg, 1974), pp. 60–61.
8. Richard Hull, *Modern Africa: Change and Continuity* (Englewood Cliffs, NJ: Prentice-Hall, 1980), p. 88.
9. R. R. Palmer and Joel Colton, *A History of The Modern World*, 4th ed. (New York, NY: Alfred A. Knopf, 1971), p. 5.
10. Toyin Falola, "Africa in Perspective," in Stephen Ellis, ed. *Africa Now: Peoples, Policies, Institutions* (Portsmouth, UK: Heinemann and Currey, 1996), pp. 3–4.

11. Anne Phillips, *The Enigma of Colonialism: British Policy in West Africa* (Bloomington, IN: Indiana University Press, 1989).
12. Kenneth E. Boulding and Tapan Mukerjee, eds. *Economic Imperialism* (Ann Arbor, MI: The University of Michigan Press, 1972), p. 2.
13. James S. Wunsch, "Foundations of Centralization: The Colonial Experience and The African Context," in James S. Wunsch and Dele Olowu, eds. *The Failure of the Centralized State: Institutions and Self-Governance in Africa* (Boulder, CO: Westview Press, 1990), p. 23.
14. Stewart C. Easton, *The Rise and Fall of Western Colonialism* (New York, NY: Praeger, 1964).
15. Harry H. Johnston, *A History of the Colonization of Africa by Alien Races* (Cambridge, UK: Cambridge University Press, 1899), pp. 151–152.
16. Wyatt Macgaffey, "Concepts of Race in the Historiography of Northeast Africa," *Journal of African History*, vol. 7, no. 1 (1966), pp. 1–2.
17. Irving L. Markovitz, *Power and Class in Africa: An Introduction to Change and Conflict in African Politics* (Englewood Cliffs, NY: Prentice-Hall, Inc., 1977), p. 26.
18. Marc Bloch, *Feudal Society* (Chicago, IL: University of Chicago Press, 1961), p. xix.
19. In his book *Things Fall Apart* (London, UK: Heinemann, 1962), Chinua Achebe portrays a functioning and viable African society that disintegrates in the face of white missionary and administrative intrusion.
20. A. Adu Boahen, "The Colonial Era: conquest to independence," in L. H. Gann and Peter Duigan, eds. *The History and Politics of Colonialism, 1914–1960* (Cambridge, UK: Cambridge University Press, 1965), pp. 523–524.
21. Ladun Anice, "Descent into Sociopolitical Decay: Legacies of Maldevelopment in Africa," in Mulugeta Agonafer, ed. *Africa in the Contemporary International Disorder: Crises and Possibilities* (New York, NY: University Press of America, Inc., 1996), p. 345.
22. Gavin Williams, "Reforming Africa: Continuities and Changes," in *Europa Encyclopedia* (London, UK: Europa, 2003), pp. 3–11.
23. Falola, "Africa in Perspective," pp. 10–11.
24. Thandika Mkandawire, "Shifting Commitments and National Cohesion in African Countries," in Lennart Wohlgemuth et al., ed. *Common Security and Civil Society in Africa* (Uppsalla: Nordic Institute of African Studies, 1999), p. 19.
25. Kwame Nkrumah, *Autobiography of Kwame Nkrumah* (London, UK: Panaf Books Ltd, 1973), p. 135.
26. Williams, "Reforming Africa."
27. Robert H. Jackson and Carl G. Rosberg, *Personal Rule in Black Africa: Prince, Autocrat, Prophet, Tyrant* (Berkeley, CA: University of California Press, 1982).

28. Elizabeth Riddell-Dixon, "Individual Leadership and Structural Power," *Canadian Journal of Political Science*, vol. 30, no. 2 (June 1997), p. 260.
29. See Kenneth N. Waltz, "Realist Thought and Neorealist Theory," in Robert L. Rothstein, ed. *The Evolution of Theory in International Relations* (Columbia, SC: University of South Carolina Press, 1991), pp. 21–37.
30. G. John Ikenberry and Charles A. Kupchan, "Socialization and Hegemonic Power," *International Organization*, vol. 44, no. 3 (1990), p. 283.
31. Ibid., p. 315.
32. Joseph S. Nye, Jr., "The Changing Nature of World Power," *Political Science Quarterly*, vol. 105 (1990), p. 186.
33. Monte Palmer, "Development: Political, Economic, Social—An Overview," in Monte Palmer, ed. *The Human Factor in Political Development* (Waltham, MA: Ginn & Cie, 1970), p. 9.
34. Robert C. Tucker, *Politics as Leadership* (Columbia, MO: University of Missouri Press, 1995), p. iii.
35. See Patrick Chabal and Jean-Pascal Daloz, *Africa Works: Disorder as Political Instrument* (London, UK: James Currey/Bloomington, IN: Indiana University Press, 1999).
36. Falola, "Africa in Perspective," p. 14.
37. Samuel E. Finer, "Political Regimes in Tropical Africa," *Government and Opposition* (Winter 1969), vol. 4, no. 1, p. 14.
38. David K. Leonard and Scott Strauss, *Africa's Stalled Development* (Boulder, CO: Lynne Rienner Publishers, 2003).
39. Anice, "Descent into Sociopolitical Decay," p. 342.
40. Ibid., p. 345.
41. Leonard Barnes, *African Renaissance* (London, UK: Victor Gollancz Ltd., 1971).
42. René Dumont, *L'Afrique Noire est Mal Partie* (Paris: Éditions du Seuil, 1962).
43. Pierre-François Gonidec, *Les Systèmes Politiques Africains* (Paris: Librairie Générale de Droit et de Jurisprudence, 1978), p. 287.
44. Aderanti Adepoju, ed. *The Impact of Structural Adjustment on the Population of Africa* (London, UK: UNFPA, 1993), p. 6.
45. George B. N. Ayittey, *Africa in Chaos* (New York, NY: St. Martin's Press, 1998), p. 7.
46. Claude Ake, *Democracy and Development in Africa* (Washington, DC: The Brookings Institution, 1996).
47. Axelle Kabou, *Et Si l'Afrique Refusait le Développement* (Paris: L'Harmattan, 1991).
48. Kofi Buenor Hadjor, *On Transforming Africa: Discourse with Africa's Leaders* (Trenton, NJ: Africa World Press, Inc., 1987), p. 6.
49. Quoted in Barnes, *African Renaissance*, p. 152.
50. Larry Diamond, *Class, Ethnicity and Democracy in Nigeria: The Failure of the First Republic* (London, UK: Macmillian, 1988), p. 283.

51. See Richard Joseph, *Democracy and Prebendal Politics in Nigeria: The Rise and Fall of the Second Republic* (Cambridge, UK: Cambridge University Press, 1987), p. 67.
52. According to Machiavelli, leaders will be forced by necessity (*necessità*) to take necessary actions.
53. Sandbrook, *The Politics of Africa's Economic Stagnation*, p. 95.
54. J. P. Olivier de Sardan, "A Moral Economy of Corruption in Africa?" *Journal of Modern African Studies*, vol. 37, no. 1 (1999), p.25.
55. Michael Bratton and Nicholas van de Walle, "Towards Good Governance in Africa: Popular Demands and State Responses," in G. Hyden and M. Bratton, eds. *Governance and Politics in Africa* (Boulder, CO: Lynne Rienner Publishers, 1992), pp. 27–55; and Michael Bratton and Nicolas van de Walle, *Democratic Experiments in Africa: Regime Transitions in Comparative Perspective* (Cambridge, UK: Cambridge University Press, 1997).

Chapter 2   Democracy's Travails in Africa

1. Ben Turok, *Africa: What Can Be Done?* (London, UK: Zed Books Ltd, 1987), p. 11.
2. David Held, *Democracy and Global Order: From Modern State to Cosmopolitan Governance* (Stanford, CA: Stanford University Press, 1995).
3. Ian Shapiro and Casiano Hacker-Gordon, "Promises and Disappointments: Reconsidering Democracy's Values," in Ian Shapiro and Casiano Hacker-Gordon, eds. *Democracy's Value* (Cambridge, UK: Cambridge University Press, 1999), p. 1.
4. Peter Anyang, "Political Instability and the Prospects for Democracy in Africa," *Africa Development*, vol. 13, no. 1 (1988), pp. 71–86.
5. Claude Ake, *Democracy and Development in Africa* (Washington, DC: Brookings Institute, 1996).
6. David A. Lake, "Powerful Pacifists: Democratic States and War," *American Political Science Review*, vol. 86, no. 1 (March 1992), pp. 24–37.
7. Seymour M Lipset, "Some Social Requisites of Democracy," *American Political Science Review*, vol. 53, no. 1 (March 1959), pp. 69–105.
8. Samuel Huntington, *The Third Wave: Democratization in the Late Twentieth Century* (Norman, OK: University of Oklahoma Press, 1991).
9. That theory assumes that democracy is a "near-perfect sufficient condition for peace." See Nils P. Gleditsch, "Geography, Democratic, and Peace," *International Interactions*, vol. 20, no. 4 (1995), p. 318.
10. Alex Hadenius and Fredrik Uggla, "Making Civil Society Work, Promoting Democratic Development: What Can States and Donors Do?" *World Development*, vol. 24, no. 1 (1996), pp. 1621–1639.

11. David K. Fieldhouse, *The West and the Third World* (Oxford, UK: Blackwell Publishers, 1999), p. 227.
12. Samuel Huntington, "Will More Countries Become Democratic?" *Political Science Quarterly*, vol. 99, no. 2 (Summer 1984), p. 218.
13. Decalo, "Back to Square One," p. 154.
14. *Uhuru* is freedom in Kiswahili.
15. Jean-François Bayart, "Civil Society in Africa," in P. Chabal, ed. *Political Domination in Africa* (Cambridge, UK: Cambridge University Press, 1986), pp. 109–125; Naomi Chazan, "Africa's Democratic Challenge: Strengthening Civil Society and the State," *World Policy Journal*, vol. 9, no. 2 (Spring 1992), pp. 279–307; and Robert Fatton, Jr., *The State and Civil Society* (Boulder, CO: Lynne Rienner Publishers, 1992).
16. James S. Wunsch and Dele Olowu, "The Failure of the Centralized African State," in James S. Wunsch and Dele Olowu, eds. *The Failure of the Centralized State: Institutions and Self-Governance in Africa* (Boulder, CO: Westview Press, 1990), p. 1.
17. Falola, "Africa in Perspective," p. 13.
18. Rita Abrahamsen, "The Victory of Popular Forces or Passive Revolution? A Neo-Gramscian Perspective on Democratisation." *Journal of Modern African Studies*, vol. 35, no. 1 (1997), pp. 129–152; also Michael Bratton and Nicholas van de Walle, *Democratic Experiments in Africa* (Cambridge, UK: Cambridge University Press, 1998).
19. Bayart, "Civil Society in Africa;" also Achille Mbembe, "Democratization and Social Movements in Africa," *Africa Demos*, vol. 1, no. 1 (November 1990), pp. 4–18.
20. Colin Legum, "The Coming of Africa's Second Independence," *Washington Quarterly*, vol. 13, no. 1 (Winter 1990), p. 129.
21. Peter Anyang' Nyong'o, ed. *Popular Struggles for Democracy in Africa* (New Jersey, NJ: Zed Books Ltd, 1987).
22. Larry Diamond, Juan Linz, and Seymour M. Lipset, *Democracy in Developing Countries: Vol. 2: Africa* (Boulder, CO: Lynne Rienner Publishers, 1988); Robert Fatton, Jr., "Democracy and Civil Society in Africa," *Mediterranean Quarterly*, vol. 2, no. 4 (1991), pp. 83–95; Richard Sandbrook, "Taming the African Leviathan," *World Policy Journal*, vol. 7, no. 4 (1990), pp. 673–701; and John A. Wiseman, *The New Struggle for Democracy in Africa* (Brookfield, VT: Avebury, 1996).
23. Larry Diamond, "Towards Democratic Consolidation," *Journal of Democracy*, vol. 5, no. 3 (1994), p. 4.
24. Wiseman, *The New Struggle*, pp. 35–69.
25. Michael Bratton, "Beyond the State: Civil Society and Associational Life in Africa," *World Politics*, vol. 41, no. 3 (1989), p. 407.
26. Amy Patterson, "A Reappraisal of Democracy in Civil Society: Evidence from Rural Senegal," *Journal of Modern African Studies*, vol. 36, no. 3 (1998), p. 423.

27. Gideon Baker, "Civil Society and Democracy: The Gap between Theory and Possibility," *Politics*, vol. 18, no. 2 (1998), p. 81.

28. Dwayne Woods, "Civil Society in Europe and Africa: Limiting State Power Through a Public Sphere," *African Studies Review*, vol. 35, no. 2 (1992), p. 94.

29. Jurgen Habermas, *The Structural Transformation of the Public Sphere* (Cambridge, UK: Polity, 1989), p. 234.

30. Luis Roniger, "Civil Society, Patronage, and Democracy," *International Journal of Comparative Sociology*, vol. 35, nos. 3–4 (1994), pp. 214–215.

31. John M. Mbaku and Julius O. Ihonvbere, eds. *Multiparty Democracy and Political Change: Constraints to Democratization in Africa* (Brookfield, VT: Ashgate, 1998).

32. Morris Janowitz, *The Military in the Political Development of New Nations* (Chicago, IL: University of Chicago Press, 1964); also Samuel Decalo, *Coups and Army Rule in Africa*, 2nd ed. (New Haven, CT: Yale University Press, 1990).

33. Samuel E. Finer, *The Man on Horseback: The Role of the Military in Politics* (London, UK: Penguin Books Ltd, 1962); Samuel P. Huntington, *Political Order in Changing Societies* (New Haven, CT: Yale University Press, 1968); and Bayo Ogunjimi, "The Military and Literature in Africa," *Journal of Political and Military Sociology*, vol. 18 (Winter 1990), pp. 327–341.

34. Dennis Austin, "The Underlying Problem of the Army Coup d'État in Africa," *Optima*, vol. 16, no. 2 (June 1966), pp. 65–72; William F. Gutteridge, *The Military in African Politics* (London, UK: Methuen, 1969); and J. M. Lee, *African Armies and Civil Order* (New York, NY: Praeger, 1969).

35. Robin A. Luckham and Gordon White, eds. 1996. *Democratization in the South: The Jagged Wave* (Manchester, UK: Manchester University Press, 1996), p. 119.

36. Claude Ake, "A Plausible Transition," *Tell*, no. 39 (September 25, 1995), p. 34.

37. René Lemarchand, "Uncivil States and Civil Societies: How Illusion Became Reality," *Journal of Modern African Studies*, vol. 30, no. 2 (1990), p. 190.

38. Robert M. Press, *The New Africa: Dispatches from A Changing Continent* (Gainesville, FL: University Press of Florida, 1999), p. 47.

39. Jean-Germain Gros, ed. *Democratization in Late Twentieth-Century Africa: Coping with Uncertainty* (Westport, CT: Greenwood Press, 1998).

40. Earl Conteh-Morgan, *Democratization in Africa: The Theory and Dynamics of Political Transitions* (Westport, CT: Praeger, 1997).

41. The French Revolution of 1789 and the revolutions of 1848 allowed democracy to become a universal goal.

42. Dipak K. Gupta, *The Economics of Political Violence: The Effects of Political Instability on Economic Growth* (New York, NY: Praeger, 1990), p. 254.

43. M. V. Naidu, " 'Initial Development:' An Attempt at Conceptualization for Comparative Analyses of Models of Development," *Peace Research*, vol. 26, no. 1 (February 1994), p. 3.

44. René Dumont, *L'Afrique Noire est Mal Partie* (Paris: Éditions du Seuil, 1962).

45. The Democratic Peace theory assumes that democracy is a "near-perfect sufficient condition for peace." See Nils P. Gleditsch, "Geography, Democratic, and Peace," *International Interactions*, vol. 20, no. 4 (1995), p. 318.

46. Thomas Hobbes, *Leviathan* (New York, NY: E. P. Dutton & Cie, Inc., 1950), p. 103.

47. Francis Fukuyama, *The End of History and the Last Man* (London, UK: Penguin Books, 1992).

48. See Ronald J. Glossop, "Democratic Politics: Alternative to War within Nation-States and for Planet Earth," *Peace Research*, vol. 29, no. 3 (August 1997), pp. 13–29.

49. M. V. Naidu, *Dimensions of Peace* (Oakville, Ontario, Canada: MITA, 1996), p. i.

50. Niel D. Karunaratne, "Growth Euphoria, Academia and the Development Paradigm," *Third World Quarterly*, vol. 4, no. 2 (April 1982), p. 268.

51. Simon Kuznets, "Economic Growth and Income Inequality," *American Economic Review*, vol. 45, no. 1 (March 1995), pp. 1–28.

52. Dudley Seers, "The New Meaning of Development," in David Lehmann, ed. *Development Theory: Four Critical Studies* (London, UK: Frank Cass, 1979), p. 26.

53. Seymour M. Lipset, *Political Man* (Garden City, NY: Doubleday Anchor, 1960), and Seymour M. Lipset, "Some Social Requisites of Democracy," pp. 69–105, Phillips Curtright, "National Political Development: Measurement and Analysis," *American Sociological Review*, vol. 28, no. 2 (April 1963), pp. 253–264; and Walt Rostow, *Stages of Economic Growth* (Cambridge, UK: Cambridge University Press, 1960).

54. Seymour M. Lipset, "Economic Development," *The Encyclopedia of Democracy*, vol. II (Washington, DC: Congressional Quarterly Inc., 1995), p. 350.

55. Carol Lancaster, "Democratisation in Sub-Saharan Africa," *Survival*, vol. 35, no. 3 (Autumn 1993), p. 40.

56. Michael Bratton and Nicolas van de Walle, "Popular Protest and Political Reform in Africa," *Comparative Politics*, vol. 24, no. 4 (July 1992), p. 422.

57. Christopher Clapham, *Africa and the International System: The Politics of State Survival* (Cambridge, UK: Cambridge University Press, 1996), p. 173.

58. See David E. Sahn, Paul A. Dorosh, and Stephen D. Younger, *Structural Adjustment Reconsidered: Economy Policy and Poverty in Africa* (Cambridge, UK: Cambridge University Press, 1997).

59. Quoted in Thandika Mkandawire, "Shifting Commitments and National Cohesion in African Countries," in Lennart Wohlgemuth et al., eds. *Common Security and Civil Society in Africa* (Uppsala, Sweden: Nordic Institute of African Studies, 1999), p. 31.

60. Naidu, *Dimensions of Peace*.

61. Ibid.

62. Kempe Ronald Hope, "From Crisis to Renewal: Towards A Successful Implementation of the New Partnership for Africa's Development," *African Affairs*, vol. 101, no. 404 (2002), p. 387.

63. Lipset, "Economic Development."

64. Andrea Brown, "Democratization in Tanzania: Stability Concerns during Transition and Consolidation," *Peace Research*, vol. 30, no. 3 (August 1998), p. 94.

65. Richard Cornwell, "Africa's Watershed?" *Africa Insight*, vol. 22, no. 1 (1992), p. 2.

66. Jean-François Bayart, "La Revanche des Sociétés Africaines," *Politique Africaine*, vol. 11 (Septembre 1983), pp. 99–100.

67. Mahmood Mamdani, "A Critique of the State and Civil Society Paradigm in Africanist Studies," in Mahmood Mamdani and Ernest Wamba-Dia-Wamba, eds. *African Studies in Social Movements and Democracy* (Dakar, Senegal: CODESRIA, 1995), p. 611.

68. Mark Neocleous, *Administering Civil Society: Towards a Theory of State Power* (London, UK: MacMillan Press, 1996), p. 22.

69. Uma O. Eleazu, "The Role of the Army in African Politics: A Reconsideration of Existing Theories and Practices," *Journal of Developing Areas*, vol. 7, no. 2 (April 1973), pp. 265–286.

70. John Hatch, *Africa Emergent: Africa's Problems since Independence* (London, UK: Secker & Warburg, 1974), p. 23.

71. Robin A. Luckham, "The Military, Militarization, and Democratization in Africa: A Survey of Literature and Issues," *African Studies Review*, vol. 37, no. 2 (September 1994), pp. 13–76.

72. Richard W. Hull, *Modern Africa: Change and Continuity* (Englewood Cliffs, NJ: Prentice-Hall, Inc., 1980), p. 26.

73. See Edward Feit, "Military Coups and Political Development," *World Politics*, vol. 20, no. 2 (January 1968), pp. 179–193.

74. Lucian W. Pye, "Armies in the Process of Political Modernization," in John J. Johnson, ed. *The Role of the Military in Underdeveloped Countries* (Princeton, NJ: Princeton University Press, 1962), p. 86.

75. See Edward Shils, "The Military in the Political Development of the New States," in John J. Johnson, ed. *The Role of the Military in Underdeveloped Countries* (Princeton, NJ: Princeton University Press, 1962).

76. Charles M. Gaile, "The Military in Developing System: A Brief Overview," in Monte Palmer, ed. *The Human Factor in Political Development* (Waltham, MA: Ginn and Co., 1970), p. 342.

77. See Finer, *The Man on Horseback*; Gutteridge, *Military in African Politics*; and Janowitz, *The Military in the Political Development*.

78. Isaac J. Mowoe, The Performance of Soldiers as Governors: African Politics and the African Military (Washington, DC: University Press of America, 1980), p. 15.
79. Zakis Ergas, ed. The African State in Transition (New York, NY: St. Martin's Press, 1987), p. 314.
80. See Henry S. Bienen, Armies and Parties in Africa (New York: Africana Publishing, 1978); Claude E. Welch, Jr., ed. Soldier and State in Africa: A Comparative Analysis of Military Intervention and Political Change (Evanston, IL: Northwestern University Press, 1970); and Robin A. Luckham, "A Comparative Typology of Civil-Military Relations," Government and Opposition, vol. 6, no. 1 (1971), pp. 5–35.
81. See Abdul K. Bangura, "Explaining and Predicting the Causes of Military Coups d'État in Africa: A Meta-Analysis," in A. K. Bangura, ed. Research Methodology and African Studies, vol. 1 (Lanham, MD: University Press of America, 1994).
82. Thomas H. Johnson, R. O. Slater, and Patrick McGowan. 1984. "Explaining African Military Coups d'État, 1960–1982," American Political Science Review, vol. 78, no. 3 (1984), pp. 622–640; and Robin A. Luckham, "The Military, Militarization, and Democratization in Africa: A Survey of Literature and Issues," African Studies Review, vol. 37, no. 2 (September 1994), pp. 13–76.
83. Claude E. Welch, Jr., "Changing Civil-Military Relations," in Robert O. Slater, Barry M. Schutz, and Steven R. Dorr, eds. Global Transformations and the Third World (Boulder, CO: Lynne Rienner Publishers, 1993), p. 71.
84. Chuka Onwumechili, Chuka. 1998. African Democratization and Military Coups (Westport, CT: Praeger, 1998), pp. 75–89.
85. Larry Diamond and Marc F. Plattner, Civil-Military and Democracy (Baltimore, MD: John Hopkins University Press, 1996), pp. xx–xxi.
86. Douglas L. Bland, "A Unified Theory of Civil-Military Relations," Armed Forces and Society, vol. 26, no. 1 (1999), p. 10.
87. Huntington, Political Order, pp. 59–79.
88. Peter D. Feaver, "The Civil-Military Problematique: Huntington, Janowitz, and the Question of Civilian Control," Armed Forces and Society, vol. 23, no. 2 (Winter 1996), p. 149.
89. Samuel Huntington, The Third Wave: Democratization in the Late Twentieth Century (Norman, OK: University of Oklahoma Press, 1991), p. 231.
90. Douglas L. Bland, "A Unified Theory of Civil-Military Relations," Armed Forces and Society, vol. 26, no. 1 (1999), p. 13.
91. James Burk, "Theories of Democratic Civil-Military Relations," Armed Forces and Society, vol. 29, no. 1 (Fall 2002), p. 7.
92. Sam C. Sarkesian, "Military Professionalism and Civil-Military Relations in West Africa," International Political Science Review, vol. 2, no. 3 (1981), p. 291.
93. George Ayittey, Africa in Chaos (New York, NY: St. Martin Press, 1998).

94. See, e.g., George Ayittey, *Africa Betrayed* (New York, NY: St. Martin Press, 1992); Susan Rose-Ackerman, *Corruption and Government: Causes, Consequences, and Reform* (Cambridge, UK: Cambridge University Press, 1999); Kempe Ronald Hope, Sr., *From Crisis to Renewal: Development Policy and Management in Africa* (Leiden: Brill Academic Publishers, 2002); and Peter Schwabe, *Africa: A Continent Self-Destructs* (New York, NY: Palgrave, 2001).

Chapter 3   The Contemporary African State:
Res Publica or *Res Privata*?

1. Chuka Onwumechili, *African Democratization and Military Coups* (Westport, CT: Praeger, 1998), p. 2.
2. William Tordoff, *Government and Politics in Africa*, 3rd ed. (Bloomington: Indiana University Press, 1997), p. 82.
3. Earl Conteh-Morgan, Democratization in Africa: The Theory and Dynamics of Political Transitions (Westport, CT: Praeger, 1997), p. 37.
4. Janine Aron, "The Institutional Foundations of Growth," in Stephen Ellis, ed. *Africa Now: Peoples, Policies, Institutions* (Portsmouth, UK: Heinemann and Currey, 1996), p. 96.
5. See Alexander Passerin d'Entreves, *The Notion of the State* (Oxford, UK: Clarendon Press, 1967); J. P. Nettl, "The State as a Conceptual Variable," *World Politics*, vol. 20, no. 4 (1968), pp. 509–592; Ralph Miliband, *The State in Capitalist Society* (London, UK: Camelot Press, 1969); Perry Anderson, *The Lineages of the Absolute State* (London, UK: NLB, 1974); Charles Tilly, ed. *The Formation of National States in Western Europe* (Princeton, NJ: Princeton University Press, 1975); Gianfranco Poggi, *The Development of the Modern State* (Stanford, CA: Stanford University Press, 1978); and also *Daedalus*, "The State," vol. 108, no. 4 (Special Issue, 1979).
6. Neera Chandhoke, *State and Civil Society: Explorations in Political Theory* (New Delhi, India: Sage Publications, 1995), p. 46.
7. Harry Redner, "Beyond Marx-Weber: A Diversified and International Approach to the State," *Political Studies*, vol. 38, no. 4 (1990), pp. 638–653.
8. David Easton, "The Political System Besieged by the State," *Political Theory*, vol. 9, no. 3 (1981), pp. 303–325.
9. J. Hoffman, *Power, State and Democracy* (Sussex, UK: Wheatsheaf, 1988).
10. Okwudiba Nnoli, *Introduction to Politics* (Harlow, UK: Longman, 1986), p. 16.
11. Ibid., p. 37.
12. Chandoke, *State and Civil Society*, p. 47.
13. M. Harrington, "What Exactly is Wrong with the Liberal State as an Agent of Change?" in Petersons, ed. *Gendered States Feminist*

(Re/Visions of International Relations Theory (Boulder, CO: Lynne Rienner Publishers, 1992), p. 66.

14. Eric J. Hobsbawm, "The Future of the State," *Development and Change,* vol. 27, no. 2 (1996), p. 276.

15. See Adam Smith, *An Inquiry into the Nature and Causes of the Wealth of Nations* (Dent, UK: Everyman, 1977).

16. Nnoli, *Introduction to Politics,* p. 188.

17. Chandoke, *State and Civil Society,* p. 20.

18. Ibid., pp. 20–21.

19. Laurent Zecchini, "Le Double Langage de l'Afrique?" *Le Monde,* Octobre 23, 2001, p. 1.

20. Christian P. Potholm, *The Theory and Practice of African Politics* (Englewood Cliffs, NJ: Prentice-Hall, 1979), p. 8.

21. Lucy Mair, *African Kingdoms* (Oxford, UK: Oxford University Press, 1977).

22. Dorothy Dodge, *African Politics in Perspective* (New York, NY: D. van Nostrand Co., Inc., 1966), p. 23.

23. Franz A. Kunz, "Liberalization in Africa: Some Preliminary Reflections," *African Affairs,* vol. 90, no. 359 (1991), p. 227.

24. Kofi A. Busia, *Africa in Search of Democracy* (London, UK: Routledge & Kegan Paul, 1967), p. 30.

25. Kunz, "Liberalization in Africa," pp. 226–227.

26. John A. A. Ayoade, "The African Search for Democracy," in Dov Ronen, ed. *Democracy and Pluralism in Africa* (Boulder, CO: Lynne Rienner Publishers, 1986), p. 25.

27. Alice Conklin, *A Mission to Civilize* (Stanford, CA: Stanford University Press), p. 188.

28. Catherine Coquery-Vidrovitch, "Trente Années Perdues ou Étapes d'une Longue Évolution?" *Afrique Contemporaine,* vol. 164, no. 4 (1992), p. 6.

29. Rupert Emerson, *From Empire to Nation; the Rise to Self-Assertion of Asian and African Peoples* (Cambridge, MA: Harvard University Press, 1960), p. 113.

30. William Pfaff, "A New Colonialism? Europe Must Go back into Africa," *Foreign Affairs,* vol. 74, no. 1 (1995), pp. 3–4.

31. Dodge, *African Politics in Perspective,* p. 24.

32. Crawford Young, "The Colonial State and its Political Legacy," in Donald Rothchild and Naomi Chazan, eds. *The Precarious Balance: State and Society in Africa* (Boulder, CO: Westview, 1988), p. 41.

33. A. I. Asiwaju, "The Concept of Frontier in the Setting of States in Pre-Colonial Africa," *Présence Africaine,* nos. 127/128 (1983), pp. 44–45.

34. Richard W. Hull, *Modern Africa: Change and Continuity* (Englewood Cliffs, NJ: Prentice-Hall, Inc., 1980), pp. 92–111.

35. Lucy Mair, "African Chiefs Today: The Lugard Memorial Lecture for 1958," *African Affairs,* vol. 28, no. 3 (July 1958), p. 197.

36. Raymond Duvall and John R. Freeman, "The State and Dependent Capitalism," *International Studies Quarterly*, vol. 25, no. 1 (1981), p. 106.
37. Peter J. Schraeder, *African Politics and Society: A Mosaic in Transformation* (New York, NY: Bedford/St. Martin's Press, 2000), p. 103.
38. Tordoff, *Government and Politics*, p. 2.
39. Nelson Kasfir, "Designs and Dilemmas: An Overview." In *Local Government in the Third World: The Experience of Tropical Africa* (New York, NY: John Wiley, 1983), p. 34.
40. Falola, *Africa in Perspective*, p. 13.
41. Lanciné Sylla, "La Gestion Démocratique du Pluralisme Socio-Politique en Afrique: Démocratie Concurrentielle et Démocratie Consociationnelle," *Civilisations*, vol. 33, no. 1 (1982), p. 26.
42. Both Frantz Fanon (*The Wretched of the Earth*, New York, NY: Grove Press, 1968) and Albert Memmi (*The Colonizer and the Colonized*, Boston, MA: Beacon Press, 1967) described the impact of colonialism on African societies.
43. Ike E. Udogu, "Incomplete Metamorphic Democracy as a Conceptual Framework in the Analysis of African Politics: An Explanatory Investigation," *Journal of African and Asian Studies*, vol. 31, nos. 1–2 (1996), p. 9.
44. Quoted in Robert M. Press, *The New Africa: Dispatches from A Changing Continent* (Gainesville, FL: University Press of Florida, 1999), p. 29.
45. Christopher Clapham, "Democratization in Africa: Obstacles and Prospects," *Third World Quarterly*, vol. 14, no. 3 (1993), p. 428.
46. Donald L. Gordon, "African Politics," in A. April and Donald L. Gordon, eds. *Understanding Contemporary Africa* (Boulder, CO: Lynne Rienner Publishers, 1996), pp. 71–72.
47. Naomi Chazan et al., *Politics and Society in Contemporary Africa*, 3rd ed. (Boulder, CO: Lynne Rienner Publishers, 1999), p. 113.
48. René Lemarchand, "Political Clientelism and Ethnicity in Tropical Africa : Competing Solidarities in Nation-Building," *American Political Science Review*, vol. 64, no. 1 (March 1972), p. 86.
49. In his March 1998 tour of Africa, the US President William J. Clinton made a similar suggestion when he declared that there is no blueprint for democracy, and that each country can have its own version of democracy.
50. Ruth S. Morgenthau, "Single-Party Systems in West Africa," *American Political Science Review*, vol. 55, no. 2 (1961), pp. 978–993.
51. Frantz Fanon, *Les Damnés de la Terre* (Paris: Éditions Maspero, 1968), p. 165.
52. Schraeder, *African Politics and Society*, p. 218.
53. Ibid., pp. 219–227.
54. Leonardo A. Villalón and Phillip A. Huxtable, eds. *The African State at a Critical Juncture: Between Distinction and Reconfiguration* (Boulder, CO: Lynne Rienner Publishers, 1998).

NOTES 189

55. Robert Fatton, Jr., *Predatory Rule: State and Civil Society in Africa* (Boulder, CO: Lynne Rienner Publishers, 1992).
56. Thomas Callaghy, "Absolutism, Bonapartism, and the Formation of Ruling Classes: Zaire in Comparative Perspective," in Irving L. Markowvitz, ed. *Studies in Power and Class in Africa* (New York, NY: Oxford University Press, 1987).
57. William Reno, *Corruption and State Politics in Sierra Leone* (Cambridge, UK: Cambridge University Press, 1995).
58. Larry Diamond, "Class Formation in the Swollen African State," *Journal of Modern African Studies*, vol. 25, no. 4 (December 1987), pp. 567–596; Donald Rothchild and Naomi Chazan, eds., *The Precarious Balance: State and Society in Africa* (Boulder, CO: Westview Press, 1988); Michael Bratton, "Beyond the State: Civil Society and Associational Life in Africa," *World Politics*, vol. 41, no. 3 (April 1989), pp. 407–430; and The Carter Center, *Beyond Autocracy* (Atlanta, GA: The Carter Center, 1989).
59. Adigun Agbaje, "A Quarantine for the African State," *Journal of Modern African Studies*, vol. 29, no. 4 (1991), p. 723.
60. William I. Zartman, ed. *Collapsed States: The Disintegration and Restoration of Legitimate Authority* (Boulder, CO: Lynne Rienner Publishers, 1995); Gerald B. Helman and Steven R. Ratner, "Saving Failed States," *Foreign Policy*, vol. 89 (1992–1993), pp. 3–20; and Robert H. Jackson, *Quasi-States: Sovereignty, International Relations, and the Third World* (New York, NY: Cambridge University Press, 1990).
61. Villalón and Huxtable, *The African State*.
62. Robert H. Jackson and Carl G. Rosberg, "The Political Economy of African Personal Rule," in David E. Apter and Carl G. Rosberg, eds. *Political Development and the New Realism in Sub-Saharan Africa* (Charlottesville, VA: University Press of Virginia, 1994).
63. Angelique Haugerud, *The Culture of Politics in Modern Kenya* (Cambridge, UK: Cambridge University Press, 1995), pp. 180–191.
64. Bruce J. Berman, "Ethnicity, Patronage and the African State: The Politics of Uncivil Nationalism," *African Affairs*, vol. 97, no. 388 (1998), pp. 334–335.
65. Schraeder, *African Politics and Society*, p. 229.
66. See Jean-François Bayart, *The State in Africa: The Politics of the Belly* (London, UK: Longman, 1996).
67. Berman, "Ethnicity, Patronage and the African State," p. 338.
68. Robert H. Jackson and Carl G. Rosberg, "Personal Rule Theory and Practice in Africa," *Comparative Politics*, vol. 16, no. 4 (July 1984), p. 425.
69. See Larry Diamond, "Class Formation in the Swollen African State," *The Journal of Modern African Studies*, vol. 25, no. 4 (1987), pp. 567–596.
70. Otwin Marenin, "The Managerial State in Africa: A Conflict Coalition Perspective," in Zaki Ergas, ed. *The African State in Transition* (New York, NY: St. Martin's Press, 1987), p. 61.

71. Villalón and Huxtable, *The African State*.
72. Richard Joseph, "Class, State and Prebendal Politics in Nigeria," *The Journal of Commonwealth and Comparative Politics*, vol. 21, no. 3 (1983), p. 22.
73. Marenin, "The Managerial State," pp. 65–69.
74. Zaki Ergas, "Introduction," in Z. Ergas, ed. *The African State in Transition* (New York, NY: St. Martin's Press, 1987), p. 2.
75. Crawford Young, "Patterns of Social Conflict: State, Class and Ethnicity," *Daedalus*, vol. 111, no. 2 (1982), p. 75.
76. See Jonathan H. Frimpong-Ansah, *The Vampire State in Africa: The Political Economy of Decline in Ghana* (Trenton, NJ: Africa World Press, 1992).

Chapter 4   Corruption in Africa

1. Alan Doig and Robin Theobald, "Introduction: Why Corruption," *Commonwealth and Comparative Politics*, vol. 37, no. 1 (March 1999), p. 1.
2. Quoted in Ibid.
3. UNGA Declaration, New York, NY, December 1996.
4. United Nations, *United Nations Human Development Report 1998* (New York, NY: Oxford University Press, 1998), p. 11.
5. Anne O. Krueger, "The Political Economy of the Rent-Seeking Society," *American Economic Review*, vol. 3, no. 64 (June 1974), pp. 291–303.
6. Paolo Mauro, "Why Worry About Corruption?" *Economic Issues Series*, no. 6, International Monetary Fund, Washington, DC, 1997.
7. Paul Heywood, ed., *Political Corruption* (Oxford, UK: Blackwell Publishers, 1997).
8. Arvind K. Jain, ed., *Economics of Corruption* (Norwell, MA: Kluwer Academic Publishers, 1998).
9. Rose-Ackerman, *Corruption and Government*.
10. Ibid., p. 9.
11. Brian Cooksey, "Corruption and Poverty: What are the Linkages?" Paper presented at the 9th *International Anti-Corruption Conference*, Durban, 10–15 October 1999a.
12. Raúl Carvajal, "Large-scale Corruption: Definition, Causes, and Cures," *Systemic Practice and Action Research*, vol. 12, no. 4 (1999), pp. 335–353.
13. Mark P. Hampton, "Where Current Meets: The Offshore Interface between Corruption, Offshore Finance Centres and Economic Development," *IDS Bulletin*, vol. 27, no. 2 (April 1996), pp. 78–87.
14. Abhijit V. Banerjee, "A Theory of Misgovernance," *Quarterly Journal of Economics*, vol. 112, no. 4 (1997), pp. 1289–1332.
15. Jean Cartier-Bresson, "Corruption Networks, Transaction Security and Illegal Social Exchange," *Political Studies*, no. 65 (1997), pp. 463–476.

16. Edgardo J. Campos and Donald Line, "The Impact of Corruption on Investment: Predictability Matters," *World Development*, vol. 27, no. 6 (1999), pp. 1059–1067.

17. W. Ofusu-Amaah, Raj Soopramanien Paatii, and Kishor Uprety, *Combating Corruption: A Comparative Review of Selected Legal Aspects of State Practice and Major International Initiatives*, (Washington, DC: The World Bank, 1999).

18. Ibid.

19. Quoted in Ibid.

20. Ibid.

21. Ibid.

22. Shang-Jin Wei, "Corruption in Economic Development: Beneficial Grease, Minor Annoyance, or Major Obstacle?" *Policy Research Working Paper*, no. 2048 (Washington, DC: World Bank, 1999).

23. Robert Klitgaard, *Controlling Corruption* (Berkeley, CA: University of California Press, 1988).

24. Donatella Della Porta and Ives Mény, eds. *Democracy and Corruption in Europe* (London, UK: Pinter, 1997)

25. Ema Ateba, "Growth and Development in Africa: Potential Role of Institutions," *Canadian Journal of Development*, vol. 20, no. 2 (1999), pp. 277–306.

26. Stanislav Andreski, *The African Predicament: A Study in the Pathology of Modernisation* (London, UK: Michael Joseph Ltd., 1968).

27. Ibid., p. 95.

28. Ibid., p. 96.

29. Ibid.

30. Jean-François Médard, "La corruption internationale et l'Afrique," *Revue Internationale de Politique Comparée*, vol. 4, no. 2 (1997), pp. 12–31.

31. ———, "Public Corruption in Africa: A Comparative Perspective," *Corruption and Reform*, no. 1 (1986), pp. 115–131.

32. Jean-Pierre Olivier de Sardan, "A Moral Economy of Corruption in Africa?" *The Journal of Modern African Studies*, vol. 37, no. 1 (1999), pp. 25–52.

33. Patrick Chabal and Jean-Pascal Daloz, *Africa Works: Disorder as Political Instrument* (London, UK: James Currey/Indiana University Press, 1999).

34. Ibid., p. 102.

35. Oskar Kurer, "The Political Foundations of Economic Development Policies," *Journal of Development Studies*, vol. 32, no. 5 (1996), pp. 645–668.

36. Global Witness, *Time for Transparency* (London, UK: Global Witness Ltd, 2004).

37. Ibid.

38. Ibid.

39. Ibid.

40. Global Witness, *Time for Transparency*.
41. Roger Charlton, "Exploring the Byways of African of African Political Corruption: Botswana and Deviant Case Analysis," *Corruption and Reform*, no. 5 (1990), pp. 1–27.
42. Kenneth Good, "Corruption and Mismanagement in Botswana— A Best-Case Example?" *Journal of Modern African Studies*, vol. 32, no. 3 (1994), pp. 499–521.
43. Arne Bigsten and Karl O. Moene, "Growth and Rent Dissipation: The Case of Kenya," *Journal of African Economies*, vol. 5, no. 2 (June 1997), pp. 177–198.
44. Kivutha Kibwana, Smokin Wanjala, and Okeh-Owiti, *The Anatomy of Corruption in Kenya: Legal, Political and Socio-Economic Perspectives* (Nairobi, Kenya: Claripress Ltd., 1996).
45. J. M. Kaunda, "The State and Society in Malawi," *Journal of Commonwealth & Comparative Politics*, vol. 36, no. 1 (1998), pp. 48–67.
46. Jakob Svensson, "The Cost of Doing Business: Ugandan Firms' Experiences with Corruption," *Development Research Group* (Washington, DC: World Bank, 1999).
47. Stephen Ouma, "Corruption in Public Policy and Its Impact on Development: The Case of Uganda since 1979," *Public Administration and Development*, vol. 11, no. 5 (1991), pp. 473–489.
48. Bornwell C. Chikoulo, "Corruption and Accumulation in Zambia," in Kempe Ronald Hope, Sr. and Bornwell C. Chikulo, eds. *Corruption and Development in Africa* (London, UK: MacMillan Press, 2000), pp. 161–182.
49. Andreski, *The African Predicament*, p. 109.
50. Rose-Ackerman, *Corruption and Government*, p. 117.
51. Jean-François Bayart, *The State in Africa : The Politics of the Belly* (London, UK: Longman, 1993).
52. Vito Tanzi, "Corruption around the World: Causes, Consequences, Scope and Cures," *International Monetary Fund Staff Papers*, vol. 45, no. 4 (1998), pp. 559–594.
53. Sahr J. Kpundeh, "Political Will in Fighting Corruption," *Corruption & Integrity Improvement Initiatives in Developing Countries*, Seminar Paper, UNDP (New York, NY: UN, October 1997).
54. Ndiva Kofele-Kale, "Partimonicide: The International Economic Crime of Indigenous Spoliation," *Vanderbilt Journal of Transnational Law*, vol. 28, no. 45 (1995), pp. 45–118.
55. See Ronald Kempe Hope, Sr. and Bornwell C. Chikulu, eds. *Corruption and Development in Africa: Lessons From Country Experiences* (London, UK: MacMillan Press, 2000).
56. See Ernest Harsch, "Accumulators and Democrats: Challenging State Corruption in Africa," *Journal of Modern African Studies*, vol. 31, no. 1 (1993), pp. 31–48.
57. Chabal and Daloz, *Africa Works*, p. 81.
58. Ibid., p. 103.

59. Jacqueline Coolidge and Susan Rose-Ackerman, "High-Level Rent-Seeking and Corruption in African Regimes," *World Bank Policy Research Working Paper* 1780 (Washington, DC: World Bank, 1997).

60. Jean-François Bayart, *The State in Africa*, Stephen Ellis and Béatrice Hibou, *La Criminalisation de l'État en Afrique*, (Paris : Éditions Complexe, 1997).

61. Ibid., p. 102.

62. Ibid., p. 115.

63. Charles Hauss, *Comparative Politics: Domestic Responses to Global Challenges*, 2nd ed. (New York, NY: West Publishing Company, 1997), p. 445.

64. Daniel O. Edevbaro, *The Political Economy of Corruption and Underdevelopment in Nigeria* (Helsinki, Finland: University of Helsinki, Department of Political Science, 1998).

65. Oluwole Adejare, "Clinton, Debt and Nigeria's Paradise of Paupers," *The Post Express* (Lagos), August 25, 2000.

66. Ibid.

67. Jean-Claude Willame, *L'automne d'un despotisme. Pouvoir, argent et obéissance dans le Zaïre des années quatre-vingt* (Paris: Éditions Karthala, 1992).

68. John M. Mbaku, "Africa after More than Thirty Years of Independence: Still Poor and Deprived," *Journal of Third World Studies*, vol. 11, pp. 13–58.

69. Rose-Ackerman, *Corruption and Government*, p. 116.

70. Andrew Wedeman, "Looters, Rent-Scrapers, and Dividend-Collectors: The Political Economy of Corruption in Zaire, South Korea, and the Philippines," *The Journal of Developing Areas*, vol. 31, no. 4 (Summer 1997), pp. 457–478.

71. *Global Witness*, "A Crude Awakening."

72. *West Africa*, May 9, 1983, p. 1142.

73. Kodjo M. Agbéyomè, *Il est Temps d'Espérer* (Lomé, Togo, June 27, 2002).

74. Bayart, Ellis, and Hibou, *Criminilization of the State in Africa*, p. 107.

75. Peter M. Ward, *Corruption, Development and Inequality* (London, UK: Routledge, 1989).

76. Gary S. Becker, "Crime and Punishment: An Economic Approach," *Journal of Political Economy*, vol. 76, no. 2 (March–April 1968), pp. 169–217.

77. Ateba, "Growth and Development."

78. UNDP, "Corruption and Good Governance," *Discussion Paper* 3, Management Development and Governance Division (New York, NY: UNDP, July 1997).

79. Brian Cooksey, "Does Aid Cause Corruption?" *East African Alternatives*, no. 2, January–February 1999 (Nairobi, Kenya).

80. Brian Cooksey, "Do Aid Agencies have a Comparative Advantage in Fighting Corruption in Africa?" Paper presented at the 9th Inter-national Anti-Corruption Conference, Durban, 10–15 October 1999.

81. Robert Klitgaard, "International Cooperation Against Corruption," Paper presented at the International Conference "*Democracy, Market Economy and Development*," 26–27 February 1999, (Seoul, South Korea).
82. Mark Robinson, ed. *Corruption and Development* (London, UK: Frank Cass, 1998).
83. Robin Theobald, ed. *Corruption, Development and Inequality: Soft touch or hard graft?* (London, UK: 1990, MacMillan).
84. Andreas Schedler, Larry Diamond, and Marc F. Plattner, eds. *The Self-restraining State. Power and Accountability in New Democracies* (London, UK: Lynne Rienner Publishers, 1999).
85. J. Pope, ed. *National Integrity Systems: The TI Source Book*, 2nd ed. Transparency International & EDI/World Bank (Washington, DC, 1997).
86. Morris Szeftel, "Misunderstanding African Politics: Corruption & the Governance Agenda," *Review of African Political Economy*, no. 76 (1998), pp. 221–240.
87. M. K. I. Obadan, *The State, Leadership, Governance and Economic Development*, Nigerian Economic Society (Ibadan, Nigeria 1998), pp. 9–14.
88. Chabal and Daloz, *Africa Works*, p. 105.

Chapter 5   Africa at its Nadir

1. Mathurin C. Houngnikpo, *L'Afrique au Passé Recomposé* (Paris: l'Harmattan, 2001), p. 239.
2. A. Thompson, *An Introduction to African Politics* (London, UK: Routledge, 2000), pp. 58–59.
3. Ibid.
4. Breytenbach, "Resource Wars," p. 12.
5. Quoted in Ieuan Ll. Griffiths, *The African Inheritance* (London, UK: Routledge, 1995), p. 84.
6. William Cyrus Reed, "The New International Order: State, Society and African International Relations," *Africa Insight*, vol. 25, no. 3, p. 142.
7. Griffiths, *The African Inheritance*, p. 123.
8. Jean-François Bayart, Stephen Ellis, and Béatrice Hibou, *The Criminalization of the State in Africa* (Bloomington, IN: Indiana University Press, 1999).
9. William Reno, *Warlord Politics and African Politics* (Boulder, CO: Lynne Rienner Publishers, 1998).
10. Breytenbach, "Resource Wars," p. 4.
11. Hugh McCullum, *The Angels Have Left Us: The Rwanda Tragedy and the Chruches* (Geneva: WCC Publications, 1995), p. 2.
12. Ibid.
13. Ibid., p. 3.

14. Peter Uvin, *Aiding Violence: The Development Enterprise in Rwanda* (West Harford, CT: Kumarian Press, 1998), p. 17.
15. McCullum, pp. 5–6.
16. Wayne Madsen, *Genocide and Covert Operations in Africa, 1993–1999* (Lewiston, NY: The Edwin Mellen Press, 1999), pp. 107–109.
17. Timothy Longman, "State, Civil Society, and Genocide in Rwanda," in Richard Joseph, ed. *State, Conflict, and Democracy in Africa* (Boulder, CO: Lynne Rienner Publishers, 1999), pp. 339–340.
18. McCullum, *The Angles Have Left Us*, p. 35.
19. Rukiya Omaar and Alex de Waal, *Rwanda: Death, Despair and Defiance* (London, UK: African Rights, 1995), pp. 59–60.
20. <http://www.usinfo.state.gov/regional/af/prestrip/w980325a. htm>.
21. U.N. Department of Public Information, May 7, 1998, p. 13.
22. McCullum, *The Angles Have Left Us*, pp. 24–26.
23. See Philippe Gourevitch, *We Wish to Inform You That Tomorrow We Will Be Killed with Our Families* (New York, NY: Farrar, Straus, and Giroux, 1998).
24. PBS Frontline, *The Triumph of Evil: How the West Ignored the Warnings of the 1994 Rwanda Genocide and Turned Its Back on the Victims* (Alexandria, VA, 1999).
25. <http://www.pbs.org/wgbh/pages/frontline/shows/evil/ etc/slaughter.html>.
26. Ibid.
27. Ibid.
28. Madsen, *Genocide*, p. 119.
29. <http://www.pbs.org/wgbh/pages/frontline/shows/evil/ interviews/ gourevitch.html>.
30. <http://www.hrw.org/reports/1999/rwanda/Geno15-8-01. htm#p67_18615>.
31. McCullum, *The Angles Have Left Us*, pp. 27–29.
32. <http://www.hrw.org/reports/1999/rwanda/Geno15-8-01. htm#p71_19996>.
33. Linda Melvern and Paul Williams, "Britannia Waived the Rules: The Major Government and the 1994 Rwandan Genocide," *Africa Affairs*, vol. 103, no. 410 (2004), pp. 1–22.
34. McCullum, *The Angles Have Left Us*, pp. 24–26.
35. <http://www.hrw.org/reports/1999/rwanda/Geno15-8-01. htm#P78_21914>.
36. <http://www.hrw.org/reports/1999/rwanda/Geno15-8-01. htm#P80_22680>.
37. McCullum, *The Angles Have Left Us*, pp. 29–30.
38. Ibid.
39. <http://www.hrw.org/reports/1999/rwanda/Geno15-8-01. htm#P83_23783>.
40. Michael Barnett, *Eyewitness to a Genocide: The United Nations and Rwanda* (Ithaca, NY: Cornell University Press, 2002), p. 156.

41. McCullum, *The Angles Have Left Us.*
42. This section draws on the works of AVERT, an international AIDS Charity Organization.
43. John Christensen, "AIDS in Africa: Dying by the numbers," *CNN Interactive*, CNN.com accessed on 03/23/05.
44. <http://www.avert.org/aidsimpact.htm>.
45. Ibid.
46. Ibid.
47. Ibid.
48. Ibid.
49. Ibid.
50. Ibid.
51. <http://www.avert.org/aidsimpact.htm>.
52. Ibid.
53. Joint United Nations Programme on HIV/AIDS (UNAIDS), *Press Release: AIDS in Africa: Three Scenarios to 2025*, Addis-Ababa, March 04, 2005.
54. Ibid.
55. Ibid.
56. Ibid.
57. Ibid.
58. Ibid.
59. K. A. Stanecki, "The AIDS Pandemic in the 21st century," Draft Report, July 2002, XIV International Conference on AIDS, Barcelona, US Census Bureau.
60. Christensen, "AIDS in Africa."
61. <http://www.avert.org/aidsimpact.htm>.
62. Ibid.
63. Ibid.
64. Kingsley Y. Amoako in a speech at Legon University, Accra, Ghana.
65. Ibid.
66. George Ayittey, "Time for a Blunt Message to Africa," Opinion, *CNN Interactive*, CNN.com accessed on 03/21/05.

Chapter 6 Required Shift of Paradigm

1. Stanislav Andreski, *The African Predicament: A Study in the Pathology of Modernisation* (London, UK: Joseph, 1968), pp. 31–32.
2. Ibid., p. 34.
3. Quoted in "African Integration Process Must Involve All Stakeholders," *The Daily Monitor*, Addis-Ababa, March 6, 2002.
4. Petrus de Kock, "*Globalisation and Dominant Discourses,*" in Hussein Solomon and Ian Liebenberg, eds. *Consolidation of Democracy in Africa: A View from the South* (Aldershot, UK: Ashgate, 2000), pp. 203–204.
5. Richard G. Lipsey and C. Bekar, "A Structuralist View of Technical Change and Economic Growth," *Bell Canada Papers on Economic*

and Public Policy, vol. 3, Proceedings of the Bell Canada Conference at Queen's University (Kingston: John Deutsch Institute) 1995, pp. 9–75.

6. Jean-Marie Guehenno, The End of the Nation-State. Trans. Victoria Elliott (Minneapolis, MN: University of Minnesota Press, 1995).

7. Eric J. Hobsbawm, *The Age of Extremes: The Short Twentieth Century 1914–1991* (London, UK: Penguin, 1994).

8. Martin Wolf, "Cooperation or Conflict? The EU Liberal Global Economy," *International Affairs*, vol. 71, no. 2, (April 1995), pp. 325–337.

9. Andrew Wyatt-Walter, "Regionalism, Globalization, and the World Economic Order," in Louise Fawcett and Andrew Hurrell, eds. *Regionalism in World Politics: Regional Organization and International Order* (Oxford, UK: Oxford University Press, 1995), p. 92.

10. Richard Crockatt, *The Fifty Years War: The United States and the Soviet Union in World Politics, 1941–1991* (New York, NY: Routledge, 1995), p. 372.

11. Washington A. J. Okumu, *The African Renaissance: History, Significance and Strategy* (Trenton, NJ: Africa World Press, Inc., 2002), p. 251.

12. Roland Robertson, *Globalization: Social Theory and Global Culture* (London, UK: Sage Publications, 1992), p. 50.

13. Fantu Cheru, *African Renaissance: Roadmaps to the Challenge of Globalization* (London, UK: Zed Books, 2002).

14. Ibid.

15. Claude Ake, *The New World Order: A View from the South* (London, UK: Malthouse Press, 1992), p. 14.

16. Joseph E. Harris, *Africans and Their History* (New York, NY: Penguin, 1998).

17. George Ayittey, *Africa Betrayed* (New York: St. Martin's Press, 1992), p. 62.

18. Quoted in Ayittey, *Africa Betrayed*, p. 63.

19. *Index on Censorship*, May 1987, p. 14.

20. See George B. N. Ayittey, *Africa in Chaos* (New York: St. Martin's Press, 1998), chap. 3.

21. Melville Herkovits, *The Human Factor in Changing Africa* (New York, NY: Vintage Books, 1958), p. 472.

22. Michael J. Battle, *Reconciliation: The Ubuntu Theology of Desmond Tutu* (Pretoria, South Africa: Pilgrim Press, 1997).

23. Ibid.

24. Ali A. Mazrui, *The Africans : A Triple Heritage* (London, UK: BBC Publications, 1986).

25. Decalo, "Back to Square One," p. 154.

26. Graham Harrison, *Issues in the Contemporary Politics of Sub-Saharan Africa: The Dynamics of Struggle and Resistance* (New York: Palgrave MacMillan, 2002), p. 72.

27. Ibid., p. 158.

28. James S. Wunsch, "Beyond the Failure of the Centralized State: Toward Self-Governance and an Alternative Institutional Paradigm," in J. S. Wunsch and D. Olowu, eds. *The Failure of the Centralized State: Institutions and Self-Governance in Africa* (Boulder, CO: Westview Press, 1990), p. 259.

Chapter 7   Herculean Tasks Ahead

1. Patrick Chabal, "The Socialist Ideal In Africa" (Review Article), *Africa*, vol. 60, no. 2 (1990), p. 296; Samir Amin, *La Faillite du Développement en Afrique et dans le Tiers-Monde* (Paris : l'Harmattan, 1989); also Claude Ake, *Democracy and Development in Africa*, (Washington, DC : The Brookings Institute, 1996).
2. See Aristide Zolberg, *Creating Political Order: The Party States of West Africa* (Chicago, IL: Rand McNally & Co., 1966).
3. See Peter Anyang' Nyongo'o, "Africa: The Failure of One-Party Rule," *Journal of Democracy*, vol. 3, no. 1 (1992), pp. 90–96.
4. Richard Joseph, "Africa, 1990–1997: From *Abertura* to Closure," *Journal of Democracy*, vol. 9, no. 2 (1998), pp. 3–17.
5. Harrison, *Issues in Contemporary Politics*, p. 78.
6. D. Ruschmeyer, E. Stephens, and J. Stephens, *Capitalist Development and Democracy* (Oxford, UK: Polity, 1992); E. M. Wood, *Democracy against Capitalism* (Cambridge, UK: Cambridge University Press, 1995); G. Therborn, "The Rule of Capital and the Rise of Democracy," *New Left Review*, vol. 2, no. 10 (1977), pp. 3–41; and also Barrington Moore, Jr., *Social Origins of Dictatorship and Democracy* (London, UK: Penguin, 1966).
7. Robert B. Charlick, "Corruption in Political Transition: A Governance Perspective," *Corruption and Reform*, vol. 7, no. 3 (1993), pp. 177–187.
8. Harrison, *Issues in Contemporary Politics*, pp. 81–82.
9. Nicolas van de Walle, "Economic Reform and the Consolidation of Democracy in Africa," in Marina Ottaway, ed. *Democracy in Africa: The Hard Road Ahead* (Boulder, CO: Lynne Rienner Publishers, 1997), p. 17.
10. Washington A. J. Okumu, *The African Renaissance: History, Significance and Strategy* (Trenton, NJ: Africa World Press, Inc., 2002), p. 165.
11. Seyoum Hameso, "Issues and Dilemmas of Multiparty Democracy in Africa," *West Africa Review*, vol. 3, no. 2 (2002), pp. 10–25.
12. Harrison, *Issues in Contemporary Politics*, p. 57.
13. Rita Abrahamsen, *Disciplining Democracy: Development Discourse and Good Governance in Africa* (London, UK: Zed Books, 2000), pp. 112–113.
14. Sylvia Chan, *Liberalism, Democracy and Development: The Relevance of Liberal Democracy for Developing Countries* (Cambridge, UK: Cambridge University Press, 2002).

NOTES 199

15. Amartya Sen, "Democracy as a Universal Value," *Journal of Democracy*, vol. 10, no. 3 (1999), p. 7.
16. Abrahamsen, *Disciplining Democracy*, p. 87.
17. Carles Boix, *Democracy and Redistribution* (Cambridge, UK: Cambridge University Press, 2003).
18. Seymour M. Lipset, *Political Man: The Social Bases of Politics* (London, UK: Heinemann, 1960), p. 31.
19. Adam Przeworski, "Minimalist Conception of Democracy: A Defense," in I. Shapiro and C. Hacker-Gordon, eds. *Democracy's Value* (Cambridge, UK: Cambridge University Press, 1999), p. 49.
20. Dele Olowu and James S. Wunsch, "Conclusion: Self-Governance and African Development," in J. S. Wunsch and D. Olowu, eds. *The Failure of the Centralized State: Institutions and Self-Governance in Africa* (Boulder, CO: Westview Press, 1990), p. 296.
21. Claude Ake, "The Case for Democracy," in Richard Joseph, ed. *African Governance in the 1990s: Objectives, Resources, and Constraints* (Atlanta, GA: Carter Center, 1990), p. 2.
22. Dele and Wunsch, "Conclusion," p. 297.
23. Christian P. Potholm, *The Theory and Practice of African Politics* (Englewood Cliffs, NJ: Prentice-Hall, 1979), p. 35.
24. UN Millennium Declaration (New York, NY: UN, 2002).
25. Julius O. Adekunle, "Education," in Toyin Falola ed. *Africa Vol. 2: African Cultures and Societies Before 1885* (Durham, NC: Carolina Academic Press, 2000), p. 59.
26. Ibid., p. 60.
27. Zaccharus A. Ademuwagua, "Education for Social Change," *Ghana Journal of Education*, vol. 2 (October 1971), pp. 36–46; also Richard L. Hopkins, "An Education to Fit a Changing World: A Challenge for African Cultures," *Africa Insight*, vol. 22, no. 3 (1992), pp. 199–205.
28. Hopkins, "An Education to Fit a Changing World," p. 204.
29. Okumu, *The African Renaissance*, p. 166.

Conclusion

1. Basil Davidson, "Conclusion" in Prosser Gifford and William Roger Louis, eds. *Decolonization and African Independence: The Transfers of Power, 1960–1980* (New Haven, CT: Yale University Press, 1988), p. 506.
2. Michael Schatzberg, *The Dialectics of Oppression in Zaire* (Bloomington, IN: Indiana University Press, 1988), p. 19.
3. Ndulu Benno and Nicolas van de Walle et al., *Agenda for Africa's Economic Renewal* (Washington, DC: Overseas Development Council, 1996).
4. Christopher Clapham, *Africa and the International System: The Politics of State Survival* (Cambridge, UK: Cambridge University Press, 1996), p. 168.

5. Paul A. Mwaipaya, *The Importance of Quality Leadership in National Development, with Special Reference to Africa* (New York, NY: Vantage Press, 1980), p. 1.

6. Ibid.

7. Donald Rothchild and Naomi Chazan, *The Precarious Balance: State and Society in Africa* (Boulder, CO: Westview Press, 1988).

8. Kwame Ninsin, "Three Levels of State Reordering: The Structural Aspects," in Rothchild and Chazan, eds. The Precarious Balance: State and Society in Africa (Boulder, CO: Westview Press, 1988), pp. 265–281.

9. Peter Anyang' Nyong'o, ed. *Popular Struggles for Democracy in Africa* (London, UK: Zed Books, 1987), p. 19.

10. Francis Deng, "Reconciling Sovereignty with Responsibility: A Basis for International Humanitarian Action," in John Harbeson and Donald Rothchild, eds. *Africa in World Politics: Post–Cold War Challenges* (Boulder, CO: Westview Press, 1995), p. 298.

11. Decalo, Back to Square One, p. 158.

12. Solofo Randrianja, "Nationalism, Ethnicity and Democracy," in Stephen Ellis, ed. *Africa Now: Peoples, Policies, Institutions* (Porstmouth, UK: Heinemann, 1996), p. 41.

13. K. Y. Amoako, "Economic Development and Reform Issues in Africa," Speech at the University of Ghana, Accra Legon, September 21, 2000; <www.africaresource.com/scholar/amoako.htm>.

14. Transparency International, *2003 Corruption Perception Index* (Berlin, Germany: TI, 2004).

15. ———, "Transparency International urges African leaders to sign and ratify AU and UN Anti-Corruption Conventions," Berlin, Germany, February 25, 2004.

16. Amoako, "Economic Development."

17. Ibid.

18. Ibid.

19. Deng, "Reconciling Sovereignty," p. 137.

20. Marina Ottaway, *Africa's New Leaders: Democracy or State Reconstruction* (Washington, DC: Carnegie Endowment for International Peace, 1999), p. 11.

21. Mamadou Dia, *Africa's Management in the 1990s and Beyond: Reconciling Indigenous and Transplanted Institutions* (Washington, DC: World Bank, 1996), p. 41.

22. Zaki Ergas, "Introduction," in Z. Ergas, ed. *The African State in Transition* (New York, NY: St. Martin's Press, 1987), p. 11.

23. Ibid., p. 10.

24. Quoted in Ergas, "Introduction," p. 11.

25. Adebayo Adedeji, Preparing Africa for the Twenty-first Century: Agenda for the 1990s (Addis Ababa, Ethiopia: UNECA, May 1991), p. 49.

26. In his book, *The Beautyful Ones Are Not Yet Born* (London, UK: Heinemann, 1967), Ghanaian Ayi Kwei Armah offers a visionary

reconstruction of the past, and at the same time, a vivid impression of corruption and moral decay in independent Africa.

27. William Tordoff, *Government and Politics in Africa*. 4th ed., revised and updated (Bloomington, IN: Indiana University Press, 2002), p. 224.

28. Julius O. Ihonbvere, "Democratization in Africa: Challenges and Prospects," in George A. Agbango, ed. *Issues and Trends in Contemporary African Politics* (New York, NY: Peter Lang, 1997), p. 300.

Bibliography

Abrahamsen, Rita. 1997. "The Victory of Popular Forces or Passive Revolution? A Neo-Gramscian Perspective on Democratisation." *Journal of Modern African Studies*, vol. 35, no. 1, pp. 129–152.

———. 2000. *Disciplining Democracy: Development Discourse and Good Governance in Africa*. London, UK: Zed Books.

Achebe, Chinua. 1962. *Things Fall Apart*. London, UK: Heinemann.

———. 1966. *A Man of the People*. London, UK: Heinemann.

Adedeji, Adebayo. 1991. *Preparing Africa for the Twenty-first Century: Agenda for the 1990s*. Addis Ababa, Ethiopia: ECA.

———, ed. 1993. *Africa within the World: Beyond Dispossession and Dependence*. London, UK: Zed Books.

———. 2002. U.N. Economic Commission for Africa, NEPAD forum 2002, *Nairobi, Kenya, 26–29 April*.

Adekunle, Julius O. 2000. "Education." In Toyin Falola, ed. *Africa Vol. 2: African Cultures and Societies Before 1885*. Durham, NC: Carolina Academic Press.

Ademuwagua, Zaccharus A. 1971. "Education for Social Change." *Ghana Journal of Education*, vol. 2 (October), pp. 36–46.

Adepoju, Aderanti, ed. 1993. *The Impact of Structural Adjustment on the Population of Africa*. London, UK: UNFPA.

Agbaje, Adigun. 1991. "A Quarantine for the African State." *Journal of Modern African Studies*, vol. 29, no. 4, pp. 723–727.

Agbese, Pita Ogaba. 1992. "With Fingers on the Trigger: The Military as Custodian of Democracy in Nigeria." *Journal of Third World Studies*, vol. 9, no. 2, pp. 220–253.

Agbéyomè, Kodjo M. 2002. *Il est Temps d'Espérer*, Lomé, Togo, June 27.

Agyeman-Duah, Baffour. 1990. "Military Coups, Regime Change and Interstate Conflicts in Africa." *Armed Forces and Society*, vol. 16, no. 4, pp. 547–570.

Ake, Claude. 1990. "The Case for Democracy." In Richard Joseph, ed. *African Governance in the 1990s: Objectives, Resources, and Constraints*. Atlanta, GA: Carter Center.

———. 1991. "Rethinking African Democracy." *Journal of Democracy*, vol. 2, no. 1 (Winter), pp. 33–44.

Ake, Claude. 1992. *The New World Order: A View from the South.* London, UK: Malthouse Press.
———. 1993. "The Unique Case of African Democracy." *International Affairs,* vol. 69, pp. 239–244.
———. 1996. *Democracy and Development in Africa.* Washington, DC: The Brookings Institute.
Albright, David E. 1980. "A Comparative Conceptualization of Civil-Military Relations." *World Politics,* vol. 32, no. 4 (July), pp. 553–576.
Allen, Chris, Carolyn Baylies, and Morris Szaftel. 1992. "Surviving Democracy?" *Review of African Political Economy,* vol. 54, pp. 3–10.
Allison, Lincoln. 1994. "On the Gap between Theories of Democracy and Theories of Democratization." *Democratization,* vol. 1, no. 1 (Spring), pp. 8–26.
Almond, Gabriel and Sydney Verba. 1963. *The Civic Culture.* Princeton: Princeton University Press.
Aly, Ahmad. 1994. *Economic Cooperation in Africa: In Search of Direction.* Boulder, CO: Lynne Rienner Publishers.
Amin, Samir. 1989. *La Faillite du Développement en Afrique et dans le Tiers-Monde.* Paris: L'Harmattan.
Amin, Samir. 1991. "The Issue of Democracy in the Contemporary Third World." *Socialism and Democracy,* vol. 12 (January), pp. 83–104.
Amundsen, Inge. 1999. "Political Corruption: An Introduction to the Issues," Bergen: Christian Michelsen Institute, *Working Paper,* no. 7.
Anderson, Perry. 1974. *The Lineages of the Absolute State.* London, UK: NLB.
Andreski, Stanislav. 1968. *The African Predicament: A Study in the Pathology of Modernisation.* London, UK: Michael Joseph Ltd.
Anglin, Douglas G. 1990. "Southern African Responses to Eastern European Developments." *Journal of Modern African Studies,* vol. 28, no. 3, p. 448.
Anice, Ladun. 1996. "Descent into Sociopolitical Decay: Legacies of Maldevelopment in Africa." In Mulugeta Agonafer, ed. *Africa in the Contemporary International Disorder: Crises and Possibilities.* New York, NY: University Press of America, Inc.
Anyang' Nyong'o, Peter, ed. 1987. *Popular Struggles for Democracy in Africa.* New Jersey, NJ: Zed Books Ltd.
———. 1988. "Political Instability and the Prospects for Democracy in Africa." *Africa Development,* vol. 13, no. 1, pp. 71–86.
———. 1991. "Democratization Processes in Africa." *CODESRIA Bulletin,* vol. 2, no. 3, pp. 13–17.
———. 1992. "Africa: The Failure of One-Party Rule." *Journal of Democracy,* vol. 3, no. 1, pp. 90–96.
Armah, Ayi Kwei. 1967. *The Beautyful Ones Are Not Yet Born.* London, UK: Heinemann.
Aron, Janine. 1996. "The Institutional Foundations of Growth." In Stephen Ellis, ed. *Africa Now: Peoples, Policies, Institutions.* Portsmouth, UK: Heinemann and Currey.
Asiwaju, A. I. 1983. "The Concept of Frontier in the Setting of States in Pre-Colonial Africa." *Presence Africaine,* nos. 127–128, pp. 44–45.

Ateba, Ema. 1999. "Growth and Development in Africa: Potential Role of Institutions." *Canadian Journal of Development*, vol. 20, no. 2, pp. 277–306.

Austin, Dennis. 1966. "The Underlying Problem of the Army Coup d'État in Africa." *Optima*, vol. 16, no. 2 (June), pp. 65–72.

Ayittey, George B. N. 1990. "La Démocratie en Afrique Précoloniale." *Afrique 2000*, no. 2, pp. 39–75.

———. 1992. *Africa Betrayed*. New York, NY: St. Martin's Press.

———. 1998. *Africa in Chaos*. New York, NY: St. Martin's Press.

———. 2005. "Time for a Blunt Message to Africa," Opinion, *CNN Interactive*.

Ayoade, John A. A. 1986. "The African Search for Democracy." In Dov Ronen. Boulder, ed. *Democracy and Pluralism in Africa*. Boulder, CO: Lynne Rienner Publishers.

Azarya, Victor. 1988. "Reordering State-Society Relations: Incorporation and Disengagement." In Donald Rothchild and Naomi Chazan, eds. *The Precarious Balance: State and Society in Africa*. Boulder, CO: Westview Press.

Azevedo, Mario. 1995. "Ethnicity and Democratization: Cameroon and Gabon." In Harvey Glickman, ed. *Ethnic Conflict and Democratization in Africa*. Atlanta, GA: ASA Press.

Bakary, Tessy. 1992. "Une Autre Forme de Putsch: La Conférence Nationale Souveraine." *Géopolitique Africaine*, no. 15 (September–October), pp. 25–32.

Baker, Gideon. 1998. "Civil Society and Democracy: The Gap between Theory and Possibility. *Politics*, vol. 18, no. 2, pp. 81–87.

Ball, Nicole. 1981. "The Military in Politics: Who Benefits and How." *World Development*, vol. 9, no. 6, pp. 569–582.

Banerjee, Abhijit V. 1997. "A Theory of Misgovernance." *Quarterly Journal of Economics*, vol. 112, no. 4, pp. 1289–1332.

Bangura, Abdul K. 1994. "Explaining and Predicting the Causes of Military Coups d'État in Africa: A Meta-Analysis." In Abdul K. Bangura, ed. *Research Methodology and African Studies*, vol. 1. Lanham, MD: University Press of America.

Barber, Benjamin R. 1993. "Global Democracy or Global law: Which Comes First?" *Indiana Journal of Global Legal Studies*, vol. 1, no. 1 (September), pp. 119–137.

Barkey, Henry J. 1990. "Why Military Regimes Fail: The Perils of Transition." *Armed Forces and Society*, vol. 16, no. 2, pp. 169–192.

Barnes, Leonard. 1971. *African Renaissance*. London, UK: Victor Gollancz Ltd.

Barnett, Michael. 2002. *Eyewitness to a Genocide: The United Nations and Rwanda*. Ithaca, NY: Cornell University Press.

Barrows, Walter L. 1967. "Ethnic Diversity and Political instability in Black Africa." *Comparative Political Studies*, vol. 9, no. 2, pp. 139–170.

Bates, Robert H. 1994. "The Impulse to Reform in Africa." In Jennifer Widner, ed. *Economic Change and Political Liberalization in Sub-Saharan Africa*. Baltimore, MD: The John Hopkins University Press.

Bates, Robert H. 1995. *Democratic Transition in Africa: A First Report on an Empirical Project*. Development Discussion Paper, no. 514. Cambridge, MA: Harvard Institute for International Development.

Battle, Michael J. 1997. *Reconciliation: The Ubuntu Theology of Desmond Tutu*. Pretoria, South Africa: Pilgrim Press.

Bayart, Jean-François. 1983. "La Revandre des Sociétés Africaines." *Politique Africaine*, vol. 11 (Septembre), pp. 99–100.

———. 1986. "Civil Society in Africa." In Patrick Chabal, ed. *Political Domination in Africa*. Cambridge, UK: Cambridge University Press.

———. 1989. *L'État en Afrique: La Politique du Ventre*. Paris: Fayard.

———. 1990. "L'Afro-pessimisme par le Bas," *Politique Africaine*, no. 40 (Décembre), pp. 53–82.

———. 1991. "La Problématique de la Démocratie en Afrique Noire: La Baule et puis après?" *Politique Africaine*, no. 43 (Octobre), pp. 5–20.

———. 1993. *The State in Africa: The Politics of the Belly*. London, UK: Longman.

Bayart, Jean-François, Stephen Ellis, and Béatrice Hibou. 1997. *La Criminalisation de l'État en Afrique*. Paris: Éditions Complexe.

———. 1999. *The Criminalization of the State in Africa*. Bloomington, IN: Indiana University Press.

Baynham, Simon, ed. 1986. *Military Power and Politics in Black Africa*. London, UK: Croom Helm.

———. 1991a. "Geopolitics, Glasnost and Africa's Second Liberation: Political and Security Implications for the Continent." *Africa Insight*, vol. 21, no. 4, pp. 263–268.

———. 1991b. "Security Issues in Africa: The Imperial Legacy, Domestic Violence and the Military." *Africa Insight*, vol. 21, no. 3, pp. 180–189.

Becker, Gary S. 1968. "Crime and Punishment: An Economic Approach." *Journal of Political Economy*, vol. 76, no. 2 (March–April), pp. 169–217.

Beckman, Bjorn. 1989. "Whose Democracy? Bourgeois versus Popular Democracy." *Review of African Political Economy*, no. 45, pp. 84–97.

———. 1993. "The Liberation of Civil Society: Neoliberal Ideology and Political Theory." *Review of African Political Economy*, no. 58, pp. 20–33.

Beetham, David. 1994. "Conditions for Democratic Consolidation." *Review of African Political Economy*, no. 60, pp. 157–172.

Benno, Ndulu, Nicolas van de Walle, Simon Appleton, Christopher L. Delgado, and Ibrahim A. Elbadawi, eds. 1996. *Agenda for Africa's Economic Renewal*. Washington, DC: Overseas Development Council.

Berg-Schlosser, Dirk. 1984. "African Political Systems: Typology and Performance." *Comparative Political Studies*, vol. 17, no. 1, pp. 121–151.

Berman, Bruce J. 1998. "Ethnicity, Patronage and the African State: The Politics of Uncivil Nationalism." *African Affairs*, vol. 97, no. 388, pp. 305–341.

Bermeo, Nancy. 1990. "Rethinking Regime Change." *Comparative Politics*, vol. 22, no. 3 (April), pp. 359–377.

———. 1993. "Democracy and the Lessons of Dictatorship." *Comparative Politics*, vol. 24, no. 3 (April), pp. 273–291.

Berton, Georges. 1992. "Afrique: L'État de la Démocratisation." *Croissance* (October), pp. 25–28.

Bessala, Athanase. 2003. "L'Économie du Continent Menacée." *Cameroon Tribune*, Yaounde, Septembre 23.

Bienen, Henry S. 1978. *Armies and Parties in Africa.* New York, NY: Africana Publishing.

———. 1984. "Military Rule and Military Order in Africa." In Richard E. Bissell and Michael S. Radu, eds. *Africa in the Post-Decolonization Era.* New Brunswick, NJ: Transaction Books.

———. 1985. "Populist Military Regimes in West Africa." *Armed Forces and Society*, vol. 11, no. 3, pp. 357–377.

———. 1989. *Armed Forces, Conflict, and Change in Africa.* Boulder, CO: Westview Press.

———. 1993. "Leaders, Violence, and the Absence of Change in Africa." *Political Science Quarterly*, vol. 108, no. 2 (Summer), pp. 271–282.

Bienen, Henry S. and Jeffrey Herbst. 1991. "Authoritarianism and Democracy in Africa." In Dankwart A. Rustow and Kenneth P. Erickson, eds. *Comparative Political Dynamics: Global Research Perspectives.* New York, NY: HarperCollins.

Bienen, Henry S. and William J. Foltz. 1985. *Arms and the African: Military Influences's International Relations.* New Haven, CT: Yale University Press.

Bigsten, Arne and Karl O. Moene. 1997. "Growth and Rent Dissipation: The Case of Kenya," *Journal of African Economies*, vol. 5, no. 2 (June), pp. 177–198.

Binnendijk, Hans. 1987. "Authoritarian Regimes in Transition." *Washington Quarterly*, vol. 10, no. 2, pp. 153–164.

Bland, Douglas L. 1999. "A Unified Theory of Civil–Military Relations." *Armed Forces and Society*, vol. 26, no. 1, pp. 7–25.

Blaney, David L. and Mustapha K. Pasha. 1993. "Civil Society and Democracy in the Third World: Ambiguities and Historical Possibilities." *Studies in Comparative International Development*, vol. 28, no. 1 (Spring), pp. 3–24.

Bloch, Marc. 1961. *Feudal Society.* Chicago, IL: University of Chicago Press.

Boahen, Adu. 1986. *Topics in West African History*, 2nd ed. London, UK: Longman.

———. "The Colonial Era: Conquest to Independence." In L. H. Gann and Peter Duigan, eds. *The History and Politics of Colonialism, 1914–1960*, vol. II of *Colonialism in Africa*. London, UK: MacMillan.

———. 1991. "Military Rule and Multi-Party Democracy: The Case of Ghana." *Africa Demos*, vol. 1, no. 2, pp. 5–9.

Boggio, Philippe. 1992. "Soleil Noir sur Gorée." *Le Monde*, March 21.

Boix, Carles. 2003. *Democracy and Redistribution.* Cambridge, UK: Cambridge University Press.

Boulding, Kenneth E. and Tapan Mukerjee, eds. 1972. *Economic Imperialism*, Ann Arbor, MI: The University of Michigan Press.

Boutros-Ghali, Boutros. 1996. *Agenda for Democratization*, paragraph 15, U.N. Doc. A/51/761. New York, NY: United Nations.

Bratton, Michael. 1989. "Beyond the State: Civil Society and Associational Life in Africa." *World Politics*, vol. 41, no. 3, pp. 407–430.

———. 1995. "Are Competitive Elections Enough? *Africa Demos*, vol. 3, no. 4, pp. 7–8.

——— and Nicolas van de Walle. 1992. "Popular Protest and Political Transition in Africa." *Comparative Politics*, vol. 24, no. 4 (July), pp. 419–442.

———. 1992. "Toward Governance in Africa: Popular Demands and State Response." In Goran Hyden and Michael Bratton, eds. *Governance and Politics in Africa*. Boulder, CO: Lynne Rienner.

———. 1994. "Neopatrimonial Regimes and Political Transitions in Africa." *World Politics*, vol. 46 (July), pp. 453–489.

———. 1998. *Democratic Experiments in Africa*. Cambridge, UK: Cambridge University Press.

Breytenbach, W. J. 2002. "Is there an Easy Explanation for the Continent's 'Resource Wars?': Rulers, Rebels and Mercantilists" *Africa Insight*, vol. 32, no. 2, pp. 1–3.

Brown, Andrea. 1998. "Democratization in Tanzania: Stability Concerns during Transition and Consolidation," *Peace Research*, vol. 30, no. 3 (August), pp. 91–103.

Brown, Michael B. 1996. *Africa's Choices: After Thirty Years of the World Bank*. Boulder, CO: Westview Press.

Buijtenhuijs, Rob and Elly Rijnierse. 1993. *Democratisation in Sub-Saharan Africa, 1989–1992: An Overview of the Literature*. Leiden, The Netherlands: African Studies Center.

Buijtenhuijs, Rob and Céline Thiriot. 1995. *Democratization in Sub-Saharan Africa, 1992–1995: An Overview of the Literature*. Leiden, The Netherlands: African Studies Center.

Burk, James. 2002. "Theories of Democratic Civil–Military Relations." *Armed Forces and Society*, vol. 29, no. 1 (Fall), pp. 7–29.

Busia, Kofi A. 1967. *Africa in Search of Democracy*. London, UK: Routledge & Kegan Paul.

Buzan, Barry, Charles Jones, and Richard Little. 1993. *The Logic of Anarchy: From Neorealism to Structural Realism*. New York, NY: Columbia University Press.

Callaghy, Thomas M. 1987. "Abolutism, Bonapartism, and the Formation of Ruling Classes: Zaire in Comparative Perspective." In Irving L. Markowvitz, ed. *Studies in Power and Class in Africa*. New York, NY: Oxford University Press.

———. 1994. "Africa: Back to the Future." *Journal of Democracy*, vol. 5, no. 4, pp. 133–145.

Callaghy, Thomas M and John Ravenhill, eds. 1993. *Hemmed In: Responses to Africa's Economic Decline*. New York, NY: Columbia University Press.

Campos, Edgardo J. and Donald Line. 1999. "The Impact of Corruption on Investment: Predictability Matters." *World Development*, vol. 27, no. 6, pp. 1059–1067.

Carlton, Eric. 1997. *The State against the State: The Theory and Practice of the Coup d'État*. Hants, UK: Scolar Press.

Caron, B., A. Gboyega, and E. Osaghae, eds. 1992. *Democratic Transition in Africa.* Ibadan: CREDU.

Carter, Gwendolen M. and Patrick O'Meara, eds. 1985. *African Independence: The First Twenty-Five Years.* Bloomington, IN: Indiana University Press.

Carter Center. 1989. *Beyond Autocracy in Africa.* Atlanta: Emory University.

———. 1990. "African Governance in the 1990s," Working Papers from the Second Annual Seminar of the African Governance Program. Atlanta, GA: Emory University.

Cartier-Bresson, Jean. 1997. "Corruption Networks, Transaction Security and Illegal Social Exchange." *Political Studies,* no. 65, pp. 463–476.

Cartwright, John R. 1983. *Political Leadership in Africa.* Cambridge, UK: Cambridge University Press.

Carvajal, Raúl. 1999. "Large-scale Corruption: Definition, Causes, and Cures." *Systemic Practice and Action Research,* vol. 12, no. 4, pp. 335–353.

Catt, Helena. 1999. *Democracy in Practice.* London, UK: Routledge.

Chabal, Patrick, ed. 1986. *Political Domination in Africa.* Cambridge, UK: Cambridge University Press.

———. 1990. "The Socialist Ideal in Africa." (Review Article) *Africa,* vol. 60, no. 2, pp. 295–297.

———. 1991. "Pouvoir et Violence en Afrique Post-Coloniale." *Politique Africaine,* no. 42 (Juin): 51–64.

———. 1994a. *Power in Africa: An Essay in Political Interpretation.* New York, NY: St. Martin's Press.

———. 1994b. "Democracy and Daily Life in Black Africa." *International Affairs,* vol. 70, no. 1, pp. 83–91.

———. 1998. "A Few Considerations on Democracy in Africa." *International Affairs,* vol. 74, no. 2, pp. 289–303.

Chabal, Patrick and Jean-Pascal Daloz. 1999. *Africa Works: Disorder as Political Instrument,* London, UK: James Currey/Bloomington, IN: Indiana University Press.

Chan, Steve. 1994. "Mirror, Mirror on the Wall . . . Are the Freer Countries more Pacific?" *Journal of Conflict Resolution,* vol. 28, no. 4, pp. 617–648.

Chan, Sylvia. 2002. *Liberalism, Democracy and Development: The Relevance of Liberal Democracy for Developing Countries.* Cambridge, UK: Cambridge University Press.

Chandhoke, Neera. 1995. *State and Civil Society: Explorations in Political Theory.* New Delhi, India: Sage Publications.

Charlick, Robert B. 1991. *Niger: Personal Rule and Survival in the Sahel.* Boulder, CO: Westview Press.

———. 1993. "Corruption in Political Transition: A Governance Perspective." *Corruption and Reform,* vol. 7, no. 3, pp. 177–187.

Charlton, Roger. 1983. "Dehomogenizing the Study of African Politics: The Case of Interstate Influence on Regime Formation and Change." *Plural Societies,* vol. 14, nos. 1–2, pp. 32–48.

———. 1990. "Exploring the Byways of African Political Corruption: Botswana and Deviant Case Analysis." *Corruption and Reform,* no. 5, pp. 1–27.

Chazan, Naomi. 1982. "The New Politics of Participation in Tropical Africa."
    Comparative Politics, vol. 14, no. 2, pp. 169–189.
———. 1989. "Planning Democracy in Africa: A Comparative Perspective on
    Ghana and Nigeria." *Policy Sciences*, vol. 22, nos. 3–4, pp. 325–357.
———. 1992. "Africa's Democratic Challenge: Strengthening Civil Society
    and the State." *World Policy Journal* (Spring), pp. 279–307.
———. 1994. "Between Liberalism and Statism: African Political Cultures
    and Democracy." In Larry Diamond, ed. *Political Culture and Democracy
    in Developing Countries.* Boulder, CO: Lynne Rienner Publishers.
Chazan, Naomi, P. Lewis, R. Mortimer, J. Ravenhill, D. Rothchild, and
    S. J. Stedman. 1999. *Politics and Society in Contemporary Africa*, 3rd ed.
    Boulder, CO: Lynne Rienner Publishers.
Chege, Michael. 1995a. "Between Africa's Extremes." *Journal of Democracy*,
    vol. 6, no. 1, pp. 44–51.
———. 1995b. "The Military in the Transition to Democracy in Africa: Some
    Preliminary Observations." *CODESRIA Bulletin*, vol. 3, no. 13, pp. 7–9.
Cheru, Fanta. 1989. *The Silent Revolution in Africa.* London, UK: Zed Books.
———. 2002. *African Renaissance: Roadmaps to the Challenge of
    Globalization.* London, UK: Zed Books.
Chesnault, Victor. 1990. "Que Faire de l'Afrique Noire?" *Le Monde*,
    Février 28.
Chikoulo, Bornwell C. 2000. "Corruption and Accumulation in Zambia." In
    Kempe Ronald Hope, Sr. and Bornwell C. Chikulo, eds. *Corruption and
    Development in Africa*, London, UK: MacMillan Press, pp. 161–182.
Chimutengwende, Chen. 1997. "Pan-Africanism and the Second Liberation
    of Africa." *Race and Class*, vol. 38, no. 3, pp. 25–33.
Christensen John. 2005. "AIDS in Africa: Dying by the numbers," *CNN
    Interactive.*
Clapham, Christopher. 1985. *Third World Politics: An Introduction.*
    Madison, WI: University of Wisconsin Press.
———. 1993. "Democratization in Africa: Obstacles and Prospects." *Third
    World Quarterly*, vol. 14, no. 3, pp. 423–438.
———. 1996. *Africa and the International System: The Politics of State
    Survival.* Cambridge, UK: Cambridge University Press.
———. 1998. "Discerning the New Africa," *International Affairs*, vol. 74,
    no. 2, pp. 263–284.
——— and George Philip, eds. 1985. *The Political Dilemmas of Military
    Regimes.* London, UK: Croom Helm.
Clark, John F. 1993. "Theoretical Disarray and the Study of Democratisation
    in Africa." *Journal of Modern African Studies*, vol. 31, no. 3, pp. 529–534.
———. 1997. "The Challenges of Political Reform in Sub-Saharan Africa:
    A Theoretical Overview." In John F. Clark and David E. Gardinier, eds.
    Political Reform in Francophone Africa. Boulder, CO: Westview Press.
———. 1998. "National Conferences and Democratization in *Francophone*
    Africa." In J. M. Mbaku and J. O. Ihonvbere, eds. *Multiparty Democracy
    and Political Change: Constraints to Democratization in Africa.* Bookfield,
    VT: Ashgate.

Clark, John C. and David Gardinier, eds. 1997. *Political Reform in Francophone Africa*. Boulder, CO: Westview Press.

Clarke, Walter S. 1995. "The National Conference Phenomenon and the Management of Political Conflict in Sub-Saharan Africa." In Harvey Glickman, ed. *Ethnic Conflict and Democratization in Africa*. Atlanta: ASA Press.

Cohen, Saul B. 2003. *Geopolitics of the World System*, Lanham, MD: Rowman & Littlefield Publishers.

Coleman, James S. and Belmont Brice, Jr. 1962. "The Role of the Military in Sub-Saharan Africa." In John J. Johnson, ed. *The Role of the Military in Underdeveloped Countries*. Princeton, NJ: Princeton University Press, pp. 359–405.

Collier, Paul. 1955. "The Marginalization of Africa," *International Labour Review*, vol. 134, nos. 4–5, pp. 23–45.

Collier, Ruth B. 1978. "Parties, Coups, and Authoritarianism Rule: Patterns of Political Change in Tropical Africa." *Comparative Political Studies*, vol. 11, no. 1, pp. 62–93.

————. 1982. *Regimes in Tropical Africa: Changing Forms of Supremacy, 1945–1975*. Berkeley, CA: University of California Press.

Conac, Gérard. 1993. *L'Afrique en Transition vers le Pluralisme Politique*. Paris: Economica.

Conklin, Alice L. 1997. *A Mission to Civilize*. Stanford, CA: Stanford University Press.

Conteh-Morgan, Earl. 1997. *Democratization in Africa: The Theory and Dynamics of Political Transitions*. Westport, CT: Praeger.

Cooksey, Brian. 1999a. "Corruption and Poverty: What are the Linkages?" Paper presented at the 9th *International Anti-Corruption Conference*, Durban, 10–15 October.

————. 1999b. "Do Aid Agencies have a Comparative Advantage in Fighting Corruption in Africa?" Paper presented at the 9th *International Anti-Corruption Conference*, Durban, 10–15 October.

————. 1999c. "Does Aid Cause Corruption?" *East African Alternatives*, no. 2 (January–February), pp. 3–9.

Coolidge, Jacqueline and Susan Rose-Ackerman. 1997. "High-Level Rent-Seeking and Corruption in African Regimes." *World Bank Policy Research Working Paper*, no. 1780, Washington, DC: The World Bank.

Coquery-Vidrovitch, Catherine. 1976. "L'Afrique Coloniale Française et la Crise de 1930: Crise Structurelle et Genèse du Sous-Développement." *Revue Française d'Histoire d'Outre-Mer*, vol. 63, nos. 232–233, pp. 386–424.

————. 1979. "Colonialisme ou Impérialisme: La Politique Africaine de la France Entre les Deux Guerres." *Mouvement Social*, no. 107 (Avril–Juin), pp. 51–76.

————. 1992a. "History and Historiography of Politics in Africa: The Need for a Critical Re-reading Regarding Democracy." *Politique Africaine*, no. 46 (June), pp. 31–40.

————. 1992b. "Trente Années Perdues ou Étapes d'une Longue Évolution?" *Afrique Contemporaine*, vol. 164, no. 4 (Numéro Spécial), pp. 5–17.

Cornwell, Richard. 1992. "Africa's Watershed?" *Africa Insight*, vol. 22, no. 1, pp. 1–3.

Cox, Robert W. 1999. "Civil Society at the Turn of the Millenium: Prospects for an Alternative World Order." *Review of International Studies*, vol. 25, pp. 3–28.

Crocker, Chester A. 1974. "Military Dependence: The Colonial Legacy in Africa." *Journal of Modern African Studies*, vol. 12, pp. 265–286.

Crowder, Michael. 1987. "Whose Dreams Was It Anyway? Twenty-Five Years of African Independence." *African Affairs*, vol. 86, no. 342, pp. 7–24.

Crummell, Alexander. 1860. *Africa and America: Missionary for Twenty Years in Africa*. Atlanta, GA: Gammon Theological Seminary.

Cumming, Gorden. 1995. "French Development Assistance to Africa: Towards a New Agenda?" *African Affairs*, vol. 94, no. 376, pp. 383–398.

Curtright, Phillips. 1963. "National Political Development: Measurement and Analysis," *American Sociological Review*, vol. 28, no. 2 (April), pp. 253–264.

Dabezies, Pierre. 1992. "Vers la Démocratisation de l'Afrique." *Défense Nationale* (Mai), pp. 21–33.

Daedalus. 1974. "The State," vol. 108, no. 4 (Special Issue), pp. 3–112.

Dahl, Robert A. 1970. *Polyarchy: Participation and Opposition*. New Haven, CT: Yale University Press.

———. 1989. *Democracy and Its Critics*. New Haven, CT: Yale University Press.

———. 1992. "The Problem of Civic Competence." *Journal of Democracy*, vol. 3, no. 4, pp. 45–59.

———. 1998. *On Democracy*. New Haven, CT: Yale University Press.

Daloz, Jean-Pascal et Patrick Quantin. 1997. *Transitions Démocratiques Africaines: Dynamiques et Contraintes (1990–1994)*. Paris: Karthala.

Danopoulos, Constantine P., ed. 1992. *From Military to Civilian Rule*. London, UK: Routledge.

———. ed. 1992. *Civilian Rule in the Developing World: Democracy on the March?* Boulder, CO: Westview Press.

Davidson, Basil. 1992. *The Black Man's Burden: The Curse of the Nation-State in Africa*. London, UK: James Currey.

———. 1998. "Conclusion." In Prosser Gifford and William Roger Louis, eds. *Decolonization and African Independence: The Transfers of Power, 1960–1980*. New Haven, CT: Yale University Press.

Decalo, Samuel. 1974. "The Military Takeovers in Africa." *International Problems* (September), pp. 80–90.

———. 1985. "The Morphology of Radical Military Rule in Africa." *Journal of Communist Studies* (December), pp. 23–35.

———. 1986a. "Socio-Economic Constraints on Radical Action in the People's Republic of Congo." In John Markakis and Michael Waller, eds. *Military Marxist Regimes in Africa*. London, UK: Frank Cass.

———. 1986b. "The Morphology of Radical Military Rule in Africa." In John Markakis and Michael Waller, eds. *Military Marxist Regimes in Africa*. London, UK: Frank Cass.

———. 1989. "Modalities of Civil–Military Stability in Africa." *Journal of Modern African Studies*, vol. 27, no. 4, pp. 547–578.

————. 1990. *Coups and Army Rule in Africa*, 2nd Edition. New Haven, CT: Yale University Press.

————. 1991a. "Towards Understanding the Sources of Stable Civilian Rule in Africa: 1960–1990." *Journal of Contemporary African Studies*, vol. 10, no. 1, pp. 66–83.

————. 1991b. "Back to Square One: The Re-Democratization of Africa." *Africa Insight*, vol. 21, no. 3, pp. 153–161.

————. 1992. "The Process, Prospects and Constraints of Democratization in Africa." *African Affairs*, vol. 91, no. 2, pp. 7–35.

————. 1994. "The Future of Participatory Democracy in Africa." *Futures*, vol. 26, no. 9, pp. 987–992.

————. 1997. "Benin: First of the New Democracies." In John F. Clark and David E. Gardinier, eds. *Political Reform in Francophone Africa*. Boulder, CO: Westview Press.

————. 1998. *The Stable Minority: Civilian Rule in Africa, 1960–1990*. Gainesville, FL: FAP Books.

De Kock, Petrus. 2000. *"Globalisation and Dominant Discourses."* In Hussein Solomon and Ian Liebenberg, eds. *Consolidation of Democracy in Africa: A View from the South*, Aldershot, UK: Ashgate, pp. 203–228.

Della Porta, Donatella and Ives Mény, eds. 1997. *Democracy and Corruption in Europe*, London, UK: Pinter.

Deng, Francis M. 1995. "Reconciling Sovereignty with responsibility: A Basis for International Humanitarian Action." In John Harbeson and Donald Rothchild, eds. *Africa in World Politics: Post-Cold War Challenges*. Boulder, CO: Westview Press.

————. 1998. "African Policy Agenda: A Framework for Global Partnership." In *African Reckoning: A Quest for Good Governance*, Washington, DC: Brookings Institution Press.

Deng, Francis M. and I. William Zartman. 2002. *A Strategy Vision for Africa: The Kampala Movement*, Washington, DC: Brookings Institution Press.

Di Palma, Guiseppi. 1990. *To Craft Democracies*. Berkeley, CA: University of California Press.

Dia, Mamadou. 1996. *Africa's Management in the 1990s and Beyond: Reconciliating Indigenous and Transplanted Institutions*. Washington, DC: The World Bank.

Diagne, Pathé. 1986. "Pluralism and Plurality in Africa." In Dov Ronen ed. *Democracy and Pluralism in Africa*. Boulder, CO: Lynne Rienner Publishers.

Diamond, Larry. 1987. "Class Formation in the Swollen African State," *Journal of Modern African Studies*, vol. 25, no. 4 (December), pp. 567–596.

————. 1988. *Class, Ethnicity and Democracy in Nigeria: The Failure of the First Republic*. London, UK: MacMillan.

————. 1989a. "Beyond Authoritarianism and Totalitarianism: Strategies for Democratization." *Washington Quarterly*, vol. 12, no. 1 (December), pp. 141–163.

————. 1989b. "Beyond Autocracy: Prospects for Democracy in Africa." In Carter Center, ed. *Beyond Autocracy in Africa*. Atlanta, GA: Emory University.

Diamond, Larry. 1992. "Economic Development and Democracy Reconsidered." *American Behavioral Scientist*, no. 35, pp. 450–499.

———, ed. 1992. *The Democratic Revolution: Struggles for Freedom and Pluralism in the Developing World*. New York, NY: Freedom House.

———, ed. 1993. *Political Culture and Democracy in Developing Countries*. Boulder, CO: Lynne Rienner Publishers.

———. 1994a. "Towards Democratic Consolidation." *Journal of Democracy*, vol. 5, no. 3, pp. 4–17.

———. 1994b. "Introduction: Political Culture and Democracy." In Larry Diamond, ed. *Political Culture and Democracy in Developing Countries*. Boulder, CO: Lynne Rienner Publishers.

———. 1996. "Is the Third Wave over?" *Journal of Democracy*, vol. 7, no. 3, pp. 20–37.

———. 1997. *Prospects for Democratic Development in Africa*. Stanford, CA: Hoover Institute, Stanford University.

———. 1998. "Africa: The Second Wind of Change." In Peter Lewis, ed. *Africa: Dilemmas of Development and Change*. Boulder, CO: Westview Press.

Diamond, Larry and Marc F. Plattner, eds. 1993. *The Global Resurgence of Democracy*. Baltimore, MD: John Hopkins University Press.

———, eds. 1996. *Civil-Military and Democracy*. Baltimore, MD: John Hopkins University Press.

———, eds. 1999. *Democratization in Africa*. Baltimore, MD: Johns Hopkins University Press.

Diamond, Larry, Marc F. Plattner, Juan Linz, and Seymour M. Lipset. 1988. *Democracy in Developing Countries: Vol. 2: Africa*. Boulder, CO: Lynne Rienner Publishers.

Diop, Cheikh Anta. 1974. *The African Origin of Civilization*. Westport, CT: Lawrence Hill & Company.

———. 1987. *Pre-Colonial Black Africa*. Westport, CT: Lawrence Hill & Company.

Dodge, Dorothy. 1966. *African Politics in Perspective*. New York, NY: D. van Nostrand Co., Inc.

Doig, Alan and Robin Theobald. 1999. "Introduction: Why Corruption." *Commonwealth and Comparative Politics*, vol. 37, no. 1 (March), pp. 1–12.

Dowden, Richard. 1993. "Reflections on Democracy in Africa." *African Affairs*, vol. 92, pp. 607–613.

Downs, Anthony. 1957. *An Economic Theory of Democracy*. New York, NY: Harper & Row.

———. 1987. "The Evolution of Democracy: How its Axioms and Institutional Forms Have Been Adapted to Changing Social Forces." *Daedalus* vol. 116, no. 3, pp. 119–148.

Doyle, Michael W. 1983. "Kant, Liberal Legacies and Foreign Affairs, Part I & II." *Philosophy and Public Affairs*, vol. 12, pp. 205–235 and 323–353.

———. 1986. "Liberalism and World Politics." *American Political Science Review*, vol. 80, no. 4, pp. 1151–1169.

Du Bois, W. E. Burghardt. 1965. *The World and Africa*, New York, NY: International Publishers.

Duignan, Peter and Robert H. Jackson, eds. 1986. *Politics and Government in African States, 1960–1985*. London, UK: Croom Helm.

Dumont, René. 1962. *L'Afrique Noire est Mal Partie*. Paris: Éditions du Seuil.

Dunn, John, ed. 1978. *West African States: Failure and Promise*. Cambridge, UK: Cambridge University Press.

————, ed. 1992. *Democracy: The Unfinished Journey*. Oxford, UK: Oxford University Press.

Duvall, Raymond and John R. Freeman. 1981. "The State and Dependent Capitalism." *International Studies Quarterly*, vol. 25, no. 1, pp. 99–118.

Easton, David. 1981. "The Political System Besieged by the State." *Political Theory*, vol. 9, no. 3, pp. 303–325.

Easton, Stewart C. 1964. *The Rise and Fall of Western Colonialism*, New York, NY: Praeger.

Eckert, Paul, ed. 1991. "Sub-Saharan Africa in the 1990s: Continent in Transition." Special Issue, *Fletcher Forum*, vol. 15 (Winter), pp. 1–81.

Eckstein, Harry. 1988. "A Culturalist Theory of Political Change." *American Political Science Review*, vol. 82, no. 3, pp. 789–804.

Edevbaro, Daniel O. 1998. *The Political Economy of Corruption and Underdevelopment in Nigeria*. Helsinki, Finland: University of Helsinki, Department of Political Science.

Ekeh, Peter. 1992. "The Constitution of Civil Society in African History and Politics." In B. Caron, A. Gboyega, and E. Osaghae, eds. *Democratic Transition in Africa*. Ibadan: CREDU.

Ekins, Paul. 1992. *A New World Order: Grassroots Movements for Global Change*. London, UK: Routledge.

Eleazu, Uma O. 1973. "The Role of the Army in African Politics: A Reconsideration of Existing Theories and Practices." *Journal of Developing Areas*, vol. 7, no. 2 (April), pp. 265–286.

Ellis, Stephen. 1995. *Democracy in Sub-Saharan Africa: Where Did It Come From? Can It Be Supported?* ECDPM Working Paper, no. 6. The Hague, The Netherlands: European Center for Development Policy Management, September 7.

————. 1996. *Africa Now: People, Policies and Institutions*. London, UK: James Currey.

Emerson, Rupert. 1960. *From Empire to Nation; the Rise to Self-Assertion of Asian and African Peoples*, Cambridge, MA: Harvard University Press.

Ergas, Zakis, ed. 1987. *The African State in Transition*. New York, NY: St. Martin's Press.

Ethier, Diane, ed. 1990. *Democratic Transition and Consolidation in Southern Europe, Latin America and Southeast Asia*. London, UK: MacMillan Press.

European Center for Development Policy. 1992. *Democratization in Sub-Saharan Africa: The Search for Institutional Renewal*. ECDPM Occasional Paper. Maastricht, The Netherlands: EDCPM, July.

Fage, John D. 1995. *A History of Africa*, 3rd Edition. New York, NY: Routledge.

Falk, Richard. 1995. *On Humane Governance: Toward a New Global Politics.* University Park, PA: The Pennsylvania State University Press.

Falola, Toyin. 1996. "Africa in Perspective." In Stephen Ellis, ed. *Africa Now: Peoples, Policies, Institutions.* Portsmouth, UK: Heinemann and Currey.

Fanon, Frantz. 1966. *The Wretched of the Earth*, translated by Constance Farrington. New York, 1966.

———. 1968. *Les Damnés de la Terre*. Paris: Éditions Maspero.

Fatton, Jr., Robert. 1990. "Liberal Democracy in Africa." *Political Science Quarterly*, vol. 105, no. 3, pp. 455–473.

———. 1991. "Democracy and Civil Society in Africa." *Mediterranean Quarterly*, vol. 2, no. 4, pp. 83–95.

———. 1992. *Predatory Rule: The State and Civil Society in Africa*. Boulder, CO: Lynne Rienner Publishers.

———. 1995. "Africa in the Age of Democratization: The Civic Limitations of Civil Society." *African Studies Review*, vol. 38, no. 2, pp. 67–99.

Faure, Yves. 1993. "Democracy and Realism: Reflections on the Case of Côte d'Ivoire." *Africa*, vol. 63, no. 3, pp. 313–329.

Feaver, Peter D. 1996. "The Civil-Military Problematique: Huntington, Janowitz, and the Question of Civilian Control," *Armed Forces and Society*, vol. 23, no. 2, pp. 149–178.

Feit, Edward. 1968. "Military Coups and Political Development." *World Politics*, vol. 20, no. 2 (January), pp. 179–193.

Fieldhouse, David K. 1999. *The West and the Third World*. Oxford, UK: Blackwell.

Fierlbeck, Katherine. 1998. *Globalizing Democracy: Power, Legitimacy and the Interpretation of Democratic Ideas.* Manchester, UK: Manchester University Press.

Finer, Samuel E. 1962. *The Man on Horseback: The Role of the Military in Politics.* London, UK: Penguin Books Ltd.

———. 1967. "The One Party Regimes in Africa: Reconsiderations." *Government and Opposition*, no. 2 (July–October), pp. 491–508.

———. 1969. "Political Regimes in Tropical Africa." *Government and Opposition*, vol. 4, no. 1 (Winter), pp. 11–27.

First, Ruth. 1970. *Power in Africa*. New York, NY: Pantheon Books.

Foltz, William J. 1993. "Democracy: Officers and Politicians." *Africa Report*, vol. 38, no. 3, pp. 65–67.

Forrest, Joshua. 1988. "The Quest for State 'Hardness' in Africa," *Comparative Politics*, vol. 20, no. 4, pp. 423–442.

Fortman, Bas de Gaay. 1994. "Conceptualizing Democracy in an African Context." *Quest*, vol. 8, no. 1, pp. 31–47.

Frazer, Jendayi. 1995. "Conceptualizing Civil-Military Relations during Democratic Transition." *Africa Today*, vol. 42, nos. 1–2, pp. 39–48.

Freund, Bill. 1998. *The Making of Contemporary Africa: The Development of African Society since 1800*, 2nd Edition. Boulder, CO: Lynne Rienner Publishers.

Friedman, Steve. 1999. "Agreeing to Differ: African Democracy, its Obstacles and Prospects," *Social Research*, vol. 66, pp. 823–841.

Frimpong-Ansah, Jonathan H. 1992. *The Vampire State in Africa: The Political Economy of Decline in Ghana*. Trenton, NJ: Africa World Press.

Fukuyama, Francis. 1992. *The End of History and the Last Man*. London, UK: Penguin Books.

———. 1995. *Trust: The Social Virtues and the Creation of Prosperity*. New York, NY: Free Press.

Gaetner, Gilles. 1992. L'Argent Facile : Dictionnaire de la Corruption en France, Paris : Éditions Stock.

Gaile, Charles M. 1970. "The Military in Developing System: A Brief Overview." In Monte Palmer, ed. *The Human Factor in Political Development*. Waltham, MA: Ginn and Co.

Gallie, W. B. 1956. "Essentially Contested Concepts." *Aristotelian Society*, no. 56, pp. 167–198.

Geisler, Gisela. 1993. "Fair? What Has Fair Got to Do with It: Vagaries of Election Observations and Democratic Standards." *Journal of Modern African Studies*, vol. 31, no. 4, pp. 613–637.

Geertz, Clifford. 1973. *The Interpretation of Cultures: Selected Essays*. New York, NY: Basic Books.

Gibbon, Peter, Yusuf Bangura, and Arve Ofstad. 1992. *Authoritarianism, Democracy and Adjustment*. Uppsala, Sweden: Nordiska Afrika Institutet.

Gifford, Paul, ed. 1995. *The Christian Churches and the Democratisation of Africa*. Leiden: E. J. Brill.

Gifford, Posser and Roger L. William, eds. 1982. *The Transfer of Power in Africa*. New Haven, CT: Yale University Press.

Girling, John. 1997. *Corruption, Capitalism and Democracy*, London, UK: Routledge.

Gleditsch, Nils P. 1995. "Geography, Democratic, and Peace." *International Interactions*, vol. 20, no. 4, p. 318.

Glickman, Harvey. 1988. "Frontiers of Liberal and Non-Liberal Democracy in Tropical Africa." *Journal of Asian and African Studies*, vol. 23, nos. 3–4, pp. 234–254.

———, ed. 1991. "Challenges to and Transitions from Authoritarianism in Africa: Issue on Political Liberalization." *Issue: A Journal of Opinion*, vol. 20, no. 1, pp. 5–53.

———, ed. 1995. *Ethnic Conflict and Democratization in Africa*. Atlanta, GA: ASA Press.

Global Witness. 1999. "A Crude Awakening: The Role of the Oil and Banking Industries in Angola's Civil War and the Plunder of State Assets." London, UK, December.

———. 2004. *Time for Transparency*. London, UK: Global Witness Ltd.

Glossop, Ronald J. 1997. "Democratic Politics: Alternative to War within Nation-States and for Planet Earth." *Peace Research*, vol. 29, no. 3 (August), pp. 21–35.

Godin, Francine. 1986. *Bénin 1972–1982: La Logique de l'État Africain*. Paris: L'Harmattan.

Goldsworthy, David. 1981. "Civilian Control of the Military in Black Africa." *African Affairs*, vol. 80, no. 8, pp. 49–74.

Gonidec, Pierre-François. 1978. *Les Systèmes Politiques Africains*. Paris: Librairie Générale de Droit et de Jurisprudence.

Good, Kenneth. 1994. "Corruption and Mismanagement in Botswana— A Best-Case Example?" *Journal of Modern African Studies*, vol. 32, no. 3, pp. 499–521.

———. 1997. "Development and Democracies: Liberal versus Popular." *Africa Insight*, vol. 27, no. 4, pp. 253–257.

Gordon, Donald L. 1996. "African Politics." In April A. and Donald L. Gordon, eds. *Understanding Contemporary Africa*. Boulder, CO: Lynne Rienner Publishers.

Gourevitch, Philippe. 1998. We Wish to Inform You that Tomorrow We Will Be Killed with Our Families. New York, NY: Farrar, Straus, and Giroux.

Gramsci, Antonio. 1971. *Selections from the Prison Notebooks*. Edited and Translated by Quintin Hoare and Geoffrey N. Smith. London, UK: Lawrence and Wishart.

Griffiths, Ieuan Ll. 1995. *The African Inheritance*. New York, NY: Routledge.

Gros, Jean-Germain, ed. 1998. *Democratization in Late Twentieth-Century Africa: Coping with Uncertainty*. Westport, CT: Greenwood Press.

Guie, Honore Koffi. 1993. "Organizing Africa's Democrats." *Journal of Democracy*, vol. 4, no. 2, pp. 119–129.

Gupta, Dipak K. 1990. *The Economics of Political Violence: The Effects of Political Instability on Economic Growth*, New York, NY: Praeger.

Gutteridge, William F. 1969. *The Military in African Politics*. London, UK: Methuen.

———. 1975a. *Africa's Military Rulers*. London, UK: Institute for the Study of Conflict.

———. 1975b. *Military Regimes in Africa*. London, UK: Methuen.

———. 1985. "Undoing Military Coups in Africa." *Third World Quarterly*, vol. 7, no. 1, pp. 121–146.

Gyimah-Boadi, E. 1998. "The Rebirth of African Liberalism." *Journal of Democracy*, vol. 9, no. 2, pp. 18–31.

———, ed. 2004. *Democratic Reform in Africa: The Quality of Progress*. Boulder, CO: Lynne Rienner Publishers.

Habermas, Jurgen. 1989. *The Structural Transformation of the Public Sphere*. Cambridge, UK: Polity.

Hadenius, Axel. 1992. *Democracy and Development*. Cambridge, UK: Cambridge University Press.

——— and Fredrik Uggla. 1996. "Making Civil Society Work, Promoting Democratic Development: What Can States and Donors Do?" *World Development*, vol. 24, no. 10, pp. 1621–1639.

Hadjor, Kofi B. 1987. *On Transforming Africa: Discourse with Africa's Leaders*. Trenton, NJ: Africa World Press, Inc.

Haggard, Stephen and Robert R. Kaufman. 1995. *The Political Economy of Democratic Transition*. Princeton, NJ: Princeton University Press.

Hameso, Seyoum. 2002. "Issues and Dilemmas of Multiparty Democracy in Africa." *West Africa Review*, vol. 3, no. 2, pp. 10–25.

Hampton, Mark P. 1996. "Where Current Meets: The Offshore Interface between Corruption, Offshore Finance Centres and Economic Development." *IDS Bulletin*, vol. 27, no. 2 (April), pp. 78–87.

Hanneman, Robert A. 1985. "The Military's Role in Political Regimes." *Armed Forces and Society*, vol. 12, no. 1, pp. 29–51.

Harbeson, John, Donald Rothchild, and Naomi Chazan. 1994. eds. *Civil Society and the State in Africa*. Boulder, CO: Lynne Rienner Publishers.

Harrington, M. 1992. "What Exactly is Wrong with the Liberal State as an Agent of Change?" In M. Petersons, ed. *Gendered States Feminist Re/Visions of International Relations Theory*. Boulder, CO: Lynne Rienner Publishers.

Harris, Joseph E. 1998. *Africans and Their History*. New York, NY: Penguin.

Harrison, Graham. 2002. *Issues in the Contemporary Politics of Sub-Saharan Africa: The Dynamics of Struggle and Resistance*, New York, NY: Palgrave MacMillan.

Harsch, Ernest. 1993. "Accumulators and Democrats: Challenging State Corruption in Africa." *Journal of Modern African Studies*, vol. 31, no. 1, pp. 31–48.

Hatch, John. 1974. *Africa Emergent: Africa's Problems since Independence*, London, UK: Secker & Warburg.

Hangerud, Angelique. 1995. *The Culture of Politics in Modern Kenya*. Cambridge, UK: Cambridge University Press.

Hauss, Charles. 1997. *Comparative Politics: Domestic Responses to Global Challenges*, 2nd ed. New York, NY: West Publishing Company.

Haynes, Jeff. 1991. "The State, Governance, and Democracy in Sub-Saharan Africa." *Journal of Modern African Studies*, vol. 31, no. 3, pp. 535–539.

Hayward, Fred. 1987. *Elections in Independent Africa*. Boulder, CO: Westview Press.

Healey, John and Mark Robinson. 1992. *Democracy, Governance, and Economic Policy: Sub-Saharan Africa in Comparative Perspective*. London, UK: Overseas Development Institute.

Hegel, George W. F. 1942. *Philosophy of Right*. Oxford, UK: Oxford University Press.

Heidenheimer, Arnold J. 1996. "The Topography of Corruption: Explorations in a Comparative Perspective." *International Social Science Journal*, vol. 48, no. 3 (September), pp. 338–347.

Heilbrunn, John R. 1993. "Social Origins of National Conferences in Benin and Togo." *Journal of Modern African Studies*, vol. 31, no. 2, pp. 277–299.

———. 1997. "Togo: The National Conference and Stalled Reform." In John F. Clark and David E. Gardiner, eds. *Political Reform in Francophone Africa*. Boulder, CO: Westview Press.

Held, David. 1987. *Models of Democracy*. Stanford: Stanford University Press.

———. 1991. "Democracy and Globalization." *Alternatives*, vol. 16, pp. 201–208.

Held, David. 1993. *Prospects for Democracy.* Cambridge, UK: Polity Press.

————. 1995. *Democracy and the Global Order.* Cambridge, UK: Polity Press.

Helman, Gerald B. and Steven R. Ratner. 1992–1993. "Saving Failed States." *Foreign Policy*, vol. 89, pp. 3–20.

Herskovits, Melville J. 1958. *The Human Factor in Changing Africa.* New York, NY: Vintage Books.

Heywood, Paul, ed. 1997. *Political Corruption.* Oxford, UK: Blackwell Publishers.

Hicks, John F. 1992. "Supporting Democracy in Africa." *TransAfrica Forum*, vol. 9, no. 2, pp. 69–77.

Higley, John and Michael G. Burton. 1989. "The Élite Variable in Democratic Transitions and Breakdowns." *American Sociological Review*, vol. 54, pp. 17–32.

Hirsch, John L. 2001. *Sierra Leone: Diamonds and the Struggle for Democracy.* Boulder, CO: Lynne Rienner Publishers.

Hirschman, Albert O. 1994. "Social Conflicts as Pillars of Democratic Markets Society." *Political Theory*, vol. 22, no. 2, pp. 203–218.

Hirst, Paul Q. 1996. "Democracy and Civil Society." In Paul Q. Hirst and Sunil Khilnani, eds. *Reinventing Democracy.* London, UK: Blackwell.

Hitchcock, Peter. 1997. "Postcolonial Africa? Problems of Theory." *Women's Studies Quarterly*, nos. 3 and 4, pp. 233–244.

Hobbes, Thomas. 1950. *Leviathan,* New York, NY: E. P. Dutton & Cie, Inc.

Hoffman, J. 1988. *Power, State and Democracy.* Sussex, UK: Wheatsheaf.

Holm, John D. and Patrick P. Molutsi. 1990. "Developing Democracy when Civil Society is Weak: The Case of Botswana." *African Affairs*, vol. 89, pp. 323–340.

Hope, Sr., Kempe Ronald. 2002. *From Crisis to Renewal: Development Policy and Management in Africa,* Leiden: Brill Academic Publishers.

————. 2002. "From Crisis to Renewal: Towards A Successful Implementation of the New Partnership for Africa's Development." *African Affairs*, vol. 101, no. 404, pp. 387–402.

———— and Bornwell C. Chikulu, eds. 2000. *Corruption and Development in Africa: Lessons From Country Experiences.* London, UK: MacMillan Press.

Hopkins, Richard L. 1992. "An Education to Fit a Changing World: A Challenge for African Cultures." *Africa Insight*, vol. 22, no. 3, pp. 199–205.

Horowitz, Donald L. 1993. "Democracy in Divided Societies." *Journal of Democracy*, vol. 4, no. 4, pp. 18–38.

Houngnikpo, Mathurin C. 1999. "Peaceful Democracies on Trial in Africa." *Peace Research: The Canadian Journal of Peace Studies*, vol. 31, no. 4 (November), pp. 33–43.

————. 2000. "The Military and Democratization in Africa: A Comparative Study of Benin and Togo." *Journal of Political and Military Sociology*, vol. 29, no. 2 (Winter), pp. 210–229.

————. 2000. "Stuck at the Runway: Africa's Distress Call." *Africa Insight*, vol. 30, no. 1 (May), pp. 5–12.

————. 2001. *Determinants of Democratization in Africa: A Comparative Study of Benin and Togo.* Lanham, MD: University Press of America.

———. 2001. *Contemporary Problems Facing Africa and Viable Strategies for Redress* (with H. Kyambalesa). Lewiston, NY: Edwin Mellen Press.

———. 2001. *L'Afrique au Passé Recomposé*. Paris: l'Harmattan.

———. 2001. "Democratization in Africa: Double Standards in Benin and Togo." *The Fletcher Forum of World Affairs*, vol. 25, no. 2 (Summer), pp. 51–65.

———. 2002. "Africa's Political Renaissance: Myth or Reality?" *Black Renaissance Noire*, vol. 4, no. 1 (Spring), pp. 137–144.

———. 2003. "*Pax Democratica*: The Gospel According to St. Democracy." *Australian Journal of Politics and History*, vol. 49, no. 2 (June), pp. 197–210.

———. 2004. *L'Illusion Démocratique en Afrique*, Paris: l'Harmattan.

———. 2004. *Des Mots pour les Maux de l'Afrique*, Paris: l'Harmattan.

Howbsbawm, Eric. 1994. *The Age of Extremes: The Short Twentieth Century 1914–1991*. London, UK: Penguin.

———. 1996. "The Future of the State." *Development and Change*, vol. 27, no. 2, pp. 267–278.

Hull, Richard W. 1980. *Modern Africa: Change and Continuity*. Englewood Cliffs, NJ: Prentice-Hall, Inc.

Hunter, Guy. 1967. *The Best of Both Worlds? A Challenge on Development Policies in Africa*, Oxford, UK: Oxford University Press.

Huntington, Samuel P. 1956. "Civilian Control of the Military: A Theoretical Statement." In Eldersveld S. Eulau and Morris Janowitz, eds. *Political Behavior: A Reader in Theory and Research*. Glencoe, IL: Free Press.

———. 1957. *The Soldier and the State: The Theory and Politics of Civil–Military Relations*. Cambridge, MA: Belknap.

———. 1968. *Political Order in Changing Societies*. New Haven, CT: Yale University Press.

———. 1984. "Will More Countries Become Democratic?" *Political Science Quarterly* (Spring): 193–218.

———. 1991. *The Third Wave: Democratization in the Late Twentieth Century*. Norman, OK: University of Oklahoma Press.

———. 1992. "How Countries Democratize." *Political Science Quarterly*, vol. 106, pp. 4–17.

———. 1995. "Reforming Civil–Military Relations." *Journal of Democracy*, vol. 6, pp. 9–17.

———. 1996. "Democracy for the Long Haul." *Journal of Democracy*, vol. 7, no. 2, pp. 3–13.

———. 1997. "After Twenty Years: The Future of the Third Wave." *Journal of Democracy*, vol. 8, no. 4, pp. 3–12.

Hutchful, Eboe. 1997. "Militarism and Problems of Democratic Transition." In Marina Ottaway, ed. *Democracy in Africa: The Hard Road Ahead*. Boulder, CO: Lynne Rienner Publishers.

Hyden, Goran. 1997. "Foreign Aid and Democratization in Africa." *Africa Insight*, vol. 27, no. 4, pp. 233–239.

———. 1999. "Governance and the Reconstitution of Political Order." In Richard Joseph, ed. *State, Conflict, and Democracy in Africa*. Boulder, CO: Lynne Rienner Publishers.

Hyden, Goran and Michael Bratton, eds. 1992. *Governance and Politics in Africa*. Boulder, CO: Lynne Rienner Publishers.

Iheduru, Obiama M. 1999. *The Politics of Economic Restructuring and Democracy in Africa*. Westport, CT: Greenwood Press.

Ihonvbere, Julius O. 1996. "On the Threshold of Another False Start? A Critical Evaluation of Pro-Democracy Movements in Africa." *Journal of African and Asian Studies*, vol. 31, nos. 1–2, pp. 125–142.

———. 1997. "Democratization in Africa: Challenges and Prospects." In George A. Agbango, ed. *Issues and Trends in Contemporary African Politics*. New York, NY: Peter Lang, pp. 287–320.

———. 1998. "Where Is the Third Wave? A Critical Evaluation of Africa's Non-Transition to Democracy." In John M. Mbaku and Julius O. Ihonvbere, eds. *Multiparty Democracy and Political Change*. Brookfield, VT: Ashgate.

Ikenberry, G. John and Charles A. Kupchan. 1990. "Socialization and Hegemonic Power," *International Organization*, vol. 44, no. 3, pp. 283–315.

Imam, Ayesha. 1992. "Democratization Processes in Africa: Problems and Prospects." *Review of African Political Economy*, no. 54, pp. 102–105.

Index on Censorship. May 1987.

Jackson, Robert. 1978. "The Predictability of African Coups d'État." *American Political Science Review*, vol. 72, no. 4, pp. 1262–1275.

———. 1986. "Explaining African Coups d'État." *American Political Science Review*, vol. 80, no. 1, pp. 225–232.

———. 1990. *Quasi-States: Sovereignty, International Relations, and the Third World*, New York, NY: Cambridge University Press.

Jackson, Robert H. and Carl G. Rosberg. 1982a. *Personal Rule in Black Africa: Prince, Autocrat, Prophet, Tyrant*. Berkeley, CA: University of California Press.

———. 1982b. "Why Africa's Weak States Persist." *World Politics*, vol. 35, pp. 1–24.

———. 1984. "Personal Rule Theory and Practice in Africa." *Comparative Politics*, vol. 16, no. 4 (July), pp. 421–442.

———. 1985. "Democracy in Tropical Africa: Democracy versus Autocracy in African Politics." *Journal of International Affairs*, vol. 38, no. 2, pp. 293–306.

———. 1994. "The Political Economy of African Personal Rule." In David E. Apter and Carl G. Rosberg, eds. *Political Development and the New Realism in Sub-Saharan Africa*. Charlottesville, VA: University Press of Virginia.

Jain, Arvind K., ed. 1998. *Economics of Corruption*, Norwell, MA: Kluwer Academic Publishers.

Janowitz, Morris. 1964. *The Military in the Political Development of New nations*. Chicago, IL: University of Chicago Press.

Jeffries, Richard. 1993. "The State, Structural Adjustment and Good Governance in Africa." *Journal of Commonwealth and Comparative Politics*, vol. 31, no. 1, pp. 20–35.

Jenkins, J. Craig and Augustine J. Kposowa. 1992. "The Political Origins of African Military Coups: Ethnic Competition, Military Centrality, and the Struggle over the Postcolonial State." *International Studies Quarterly*, vol. 36, pp. 271–291.

Johnson, John J., ed. 1962. *The Role of the Military in Underdeveloped Countries.* Princeton, NJ: Princeton University Press.

Johnson, Thomas H., R. O. Slater, and Patrick McGowan. 1984. "Explaining African Military Coups d'État, 1960–1982." *American Political Science Review*, vol. 78, no. 3, pp. 622–640.

Johnston, Harry H. 1899. *A History of the Colonization of Africa by Alien Races.* Cambridge, UK: Cambridge University Press.

Joseph, Richard. 1983. "Class, State and Prebendal Politics in Nigeria." *The Journal of Commonwealth and Comparative Politics*, vol. 21, no. 3, pp. 21–38.

———. 1987. *Democracy and Prebendal Politics in Nigeria: The Rise and Fall of the Second Republic.* Cambridge, UK: Cambridge University Press.

———, ed. 1989. *Beyond Autocracy in Africa.* Working Papers from Inaugural Seminar of the African Governance Program, February 17–18. Atlanta, GA: Carter Center.

———, ed. 1990. *African Governance in the 1990s.* Working Papers from the Second Annual Seminar of the African Governance Program, March 23–25. Atlanta, GA: The Carter Center.

———. 1991. "Africa: The Rebirth of Political Freedom." *Journal of Democracy*, vol. 2, no. 4, pp. 11–24.

———, ed. 1994. *The Democratic Challenge in Africa.* Atlanta, GA: The Carter Center.

———. 1998. "Africa, 1990–1997: From *Abertura* to Closure." *Journal of Democracy*, vol. 9, no. 2, pp. 3–17.

Kaba, Lansiné. 1986. "Power and Democracy in African Tradition: The Case of Songhay." In Dov Ronen, ed. *Democracy and Pluralism in Africa.* Boulder, CO: Lynne Rienner Publishers.

Kabou, Axelle. 1991. *Et Si l'Afrique Refusait le Développement.* Paris: l'Harmattan.

Kabwit, Ghislain C. 1979. "Zaire: The Roots of the Continuing Crisis." *Journal of Modern African Studies*, vol. 17, no. 3, pp. 381–407.

Kant, Immanuel. 1795. *Perpetual Peace.* New York, NY: MacMillan.

Karsten, Peter. 1998. *Civil–Military Relations.* New York, NY: Garland Publishers.

Karunaratne, Niel D. 1982. "Growth Euphoria, Academia and the Development Paradigm," *Third World Quarterly*, vol. 4, no. 2 (April), pp. 268–284.

Kasfir, Nelson. 1983. "Designs and Dilemmas: An Overview." In K. Nelson, ed. *Local Government in the Third World: The Experience of Tropical Africa.* New York, NY: John Wiley.

———. 1992. "Popular Sovereignty and Popular Participation: Mixed Constitutional Democracy in the Third World." *Third World Quarterly*, vol. 13, no. 4, pp. 587–605.

Kasfir, Nelson. 1998. "The Conventional Notion of Civil Society: A Critique." In K. Nelson, ed. *Civil Society and Democracy in Africa: Critical Perspectives.* London, UK: Frank Cass.

———, ed. 1998. *Civil Society and Democracy in Africa: Critical Perspectives.* London, UK: Frank Cass.

Kaufmann, Daniel. 1997. "Corruption: the Facts." *Foreign Policy,* no. 107 (Summer), pp. 114–131.

Kaunda, J. M. 1998. "The State and Society in Malawi," *Journal of Commonwealth & Comparative Politics,* vol. 36, no. 1, pp. 48–67.

Keller, Edmond J. 1993. "Towards a New African Order." *African Studies Review,* vol. 36, no. 2, pp. 1–10.

———. 1995. "Liberalization, Democratization and Democracy in Africa: Comparative Perspectives." *Africa Insight,* vol. 25, no. 4, pp. 224–230.

——— and Donald Rothchild, eds. 1987. *Afro-Marxist Regimes: Ideology and Public Policy.* Boulder, CO: Lynne Rienner Publishers.

Kemp, Kenneth W. and Charles Hudlin. 1992. "Civil Supremacy over the Military: Its Nature and Limits." *Armed Forces and Society,* vol. 19, no. 1, pp. 7–26.

Khagram, Sanjeev. 1993. "Democracy and Democratization in Africa: A Plea for Pragmatic Possibilism." *Africa Today,* vol. 40, no. 4, pp. 55–72.

Khan, Mushtaq H. 1996. "A Typology of Corrupt Transactions in Developing Countries," *IDS Bulletin,* vol. 27, no. 2, pp. 12–21.

Kholi, Atul. 1993. "Democratic Transitions in the Developing Countries." *Politica Internazionale,* vol. 21, no. 2, pp. 19–34.

Khun, Thomas. 1970. *The Structure of Scientific Revolution,* Chicago, IL: University of Chicago Press.

Kibwana, Kivutha, Smokin Wanjala, and Okeh-Owuti. 1996. *The Anatomy of Corruption in Kenya: Legal, Political and Socio-Economic Perspectives.* Nairobi, Kenya: Claripress Ltd.

Kim, Young C. 1964. "The Concept of Political Culture in Comparative Politics." *Journal of Politics,* vol. 26, pp. 313–364.

Kimenyi, Mwangi S. 1989. "Interest Groups, Transfer Seeking, and Democratization: Competition for the Benefits of Governmental Power May Explain African Political Instability." *American Journal of Economics and Sociology,* vol. 48, no. 3, pp. 339–349.

———. 1997. *Ethnic Diversity, Liberty and the State: The African Dilemma.* Cheltenham, UK: Edward Elgar.

Kisangani, N. F. Emizet. 2000. "Explaining the Rise and Fall of Military Regimes: Civil–Military Relations in the Congo." *Armed Forces and Society,* vol. 26, no. 2, pp. 203–227.

Klein, Martin A. 1992. "Back to Democracy: Presidential Address to the 1991 Meeting of the African Studies Association." *African Studies Review,* vol. 35, no. 3, pp. 1–12.

Klitgaard, Robert. 1988. *Controlling Corruption,* Berkeley, CA: University of California Press.

———. 1999. "International Cooperation Against Corruption." Paper presented at the International Conference "*Democracy, Market Economy and Development*," 26–27 February, Seoul, South Korea.

Kofele-Kale, Ndiva. 1995. "Partimonicide: The International Economic Crime of Indigenous Spoliation." *Vanderbilt Journal of Transnational Law*, vol. 28, no. 45, pp. 45–118.

Kohn, Richard H. 1997. "How Democracies Control the Military." *Journal of Democracy*, vol. 8, no. 4, pp. 140–153.

Kpundeh, Sahr John. 1992. ed. *Democratization in Africa: African Views, African Voices*. Summary of Three Workshops organized by the National Academy of Science. Washington, DC: National Academy Press.

———. 1997. "Political Will in Fighting Corruption." *Corruption & Integrity Improvement Initiatives in Developing Countries*, Seminar Paper, UNDP. New York, NY: UN, October.

——— and Stephen P. Riley. 1992. "Political Choice and the New Democratic Politics in Africa." *The Round Table*, no. 323, pp. 263–271.

Kraus, Jon. 1991. "Building Democracy in Africa." *Current History*, vol. 90, no. 553, pp. 209–212.

Krieger, Winfried Jung Silke, ed. 1994. *Culture and Democracy in Africa South of the Sahara*. Mainz, Germany: V. Hase and Koehler Verlag.

Krueger, Anne O. 1974. "The Political Economy of the Rent-Seeking Society." *American Economic Review*, vol. 3, no. 64 (June), pp. 291–303.

Kunz, Franz A. 1991. "Liberalization in Africa: Some Preliminary Reflections." *African Affairs*, vol. 90, no. 359, pp. 223–235.

———. 1995. "Civil Society in Africa." *Journal of Modern African Studies*, vol. 33, no. 1, pp. 181–187.

Kurer, Oskar. 1996. "The Political Foundations of Economic Development Policies." *Journal of Development Studies*, vol. 32, no. 5, pp. 645–668.

Kuznets, Simon. 1995. "Economic Growth and Income Inequality," *American Economic Review*, vol. 45, no. 1 (March), pp. 1–28.

Lake, David A. 1992. "Powerful Pacifists: Democratic States and War." *American Political Science Review*, vol. 86, no. 1 (March), pp. 24–37.

Lancaster, Carol. 1991/1992. "Democracy in Africa." *Foreign Policy*, vol. 85, pp. 148–165.

———. 1993. "Democratisation in Sub-Saharan Africa." *Survival*, vol. 35, no. 3, pp. 38–50.

Landell-Mills, Pierre. 1992. "Governance, Cultural Change, and Empowerment." *Journal of Modern African Studies*, vol. 30, no. 4, pp. 543–567.

Lawson, Stephanie. 1993. "Conceptual Issues in the Comparative Study of Regime Change and Democratization." *Comparative Politics*, vol. 25, no. 2, pp. 183–205.

Lee, J. M. 1969. *African Armies and Civil Order*. New York, NY: Praeger.

Leftwich, Adrian. 1994. "States of Underdevelopment: The Third World State in Theoretical Perspective." *Journal of Theoretical Politics*, vol. 6, no. 1, pp. 55–74.

Legum, Colin. 1986. "Democracy in Africa: Hopes and Trends." In Dov Ronen ed. *Democracy and Pluralism in Africa*, Boulder, CO: Lynne Rienner Publishers.

———. 1990. "The Coming of Africa's Second Independence." *Washington Quarterly*, vol. 13, no. 1 (Winter), pp. 129–140.

———. 1999. *Africa since Independence*. Bloomington: Indiana University Press.

Leite, Carlos and Jens Weidmann. 1999. "Does Mother Nature Corrupt? Natural Resources, Corruption, and Economic Growth." *IMF Working Paper*, WP vol. 99, no. 85 (July), pp. 23–54.

Lemarchand, René. 1968. "Dahomey: Coup within a Coup." *Africa Report*, vol. 13, no. 6, pp. 46–54.

———. 1972. "Political Clientelism and Ethnicity in Tropical Africa: Competing Solidarities in Nation-Building." *American Political Science Review*, vol. 64, no. 1 (March), pp. 86–99.

———. 1976. "African Armies in Historical and Contemporary Perspectives: The Search for Connections." *Journal of Political and Military Sociology*, vol. 4, no. 2, pp. 261–275.

———. 1990. "Uncivil States and Civil Societies: How Illusion Became Reality." *Journal of Modern African Studies*, vol. 30, no. 2, pp. 177–191.

———. 1992a. "African Transitions to Democracy: An Interim (and Mostly Pessimistic) Assessment." *Africa Insight*, vol. 22, no. 3, pp. 178–185.

———. 1992b. "Africa's Troubled Transitions." *Journal of Democracy*, vol. 3, no. 4, pp. 98–109.

———. 1994. "Managing Transition Anarchies." *Journal of Modern African Studies*, vol. 32, no. 4, pp. 581–604.

Leonard, David K. and Scott Strauss. 2003. *Africa's Stalled Development*. Boulder, CO: Lynne Rienner Publishers.

Levine, Daniel. 1988. "Paradigm Lost: Dependence to Democracy." *World Politics*, vol. 40, pp. 377–394.

LeVine, Victor T. 1967. *Political Leadership in Africa*. Stanford, CA: Stanford University Press.

———. 1980. "African Patrimonial Regimes in Comparative Perspective." *Journal of Modern African Studies*, vol. 18, no. 4, pp. 657–673.

———. 1987. "Military Rule in the People's Republic of Congo." In *The Military in African Politics*, ed. John W. Harbeson. Westport, CT: Praeger.

———. 2004. *Politics in Francophone Africa*. Boulder, CO: Lynne Rienner Publishers.

Levy, Jack. 1989. "Domestic Politics and War." In Robert I. Rotberg and Theodore K. Rabb, eds. *The Origin and Prevention of Major Wars*, Cambridge, UK: Cambridge University Press.

Lewis, Arthur W. 1965. *Politics in West Africa*. Oxford, UK: Oxford University Press.

Lewis, Peter. 1992. "Political Transition and the Dilemma of Civil Society in Africa." *Journal of International Affairs*, vol. 27, no. 1 (Summer), pp. 31–54.

———. 1998. "Political Transition and the Dilemma of Civil Society in Africa." In Peter Lewis, ed. *Africa: Dilemmas of Development and Change*. Boulder, CO: Westview Press.

Leymarie, Philippe. 1995. "Une Afrique Appauvrie dans la Spirale des Conflits." In *Manière de Voir*, no. 25, *Le Monde Diplomatique*, Février.

Leys, Colin. 1965. "What is the Problem About Corruption?" *Journal of Modern African Studies*, vol. 2, no. 3, pp. 215–230.

———. 1982. "Economic Development in Theory and Practice." *Daedalus*, vol. 111, no. 2, pp. 56–72.

Lijphart, Arendt. 1969. "Consociational Democracy." *World Politics*, vol. 21, no. 2 (January), pp. 207–225.

———. 1977. *Democracy in Plural Societies*. New Haven, CT: Yale University Press.

———. 1984. *Democracies*. New Haven, CT: Yale University Press.

Linton, Ralph. 1945. *The Cultural Background of Personality*. New York, NY: Appleton-Century.

Linz, Juan J. 1978. *The Breakdown of Democratic Regimes: Crisis, Breakdown and Reequilibration*. Baltimore, MD: Johns Hopkins University Press.

———. 1990. "Transitions to Democracy." *Washington Quarterly* (Summer), pp. 143–164.

Lipset, Seymour M. 1959. "Some Social Requisites of Democracy." *American Political Science Review*, vol. 53, no. 1 (March), pp. 69–105.

———. 1960. *Political Man: The Social Basis of Politics*. New York, NY: Doubleday.

———. 1990. "The Centrality of Political Culture." *Journal of Democracy*, vol. 1, no. 4, pp. 80–83.

———. 1995. "Economic Development." *The Encyclopedia of Democracy*, vol. II. Washington, DC: Congressional Quarterly Inc.

Lipsey, Richard G. and C. Bekar. 1995. "A Structuralist View of Technical Change and Economic Growth." *Bell Canada Papers on Economic and Public Policy*, vol. 3, Proceedings of the Bell Canada Conference at Queen's University. Kingston: John Deutsch Institute, pp. 9–75.

Lofchie, Michael F. 1968. "Political Theory and African Politics." *Journal of Modern African Studies*, vol. 6, no. 1, pp. 3–15.

Londregan, John and Keith Poole. 1990. "Poverty, the Coup Trap and the Seizure of Executive Power." *World Politics*, vol. 42, pp. 151–183.

Longman, Timothy. 1999. "State, Civil Society, and Genocide in Rwanda." In Richard Joseph, ed. *State, Conflict, and Democracy in Africa*. Boulder, CO: Lynne Rienner Publishers.

Lonsdale, John. 1981. "States and Social Processes in Africa: An Historiographical Survey." *African Studies Review*, vol. 24, no. 3, pp. 139–225.

———. 1986. "Political Accountability in African History." In Patrick Chabal, ed. *Political Domination in Africa: Reflections on the Limits of Power*. Cambridge, UK: Cambridge University Press, pp. 126–157.

Loong, Wong. 1991. "Authoritarianism and Transition to Democracy in a Third World State." *Critical Sociology*, vol. 18, no. 2 (Summer), pp. 77–102.

Luckham, Robin A. 1971. "A Comparative Typology of Civil–Military Relations." *Government and Opposition*, vol. 6, no. 1, pp. 5–35.

———. 1975. *Politicians and Soldiers in Ghana, 1966–1972*. London, UK: Frank Cass.

———. 1982. "French Militarism in Africa." *Review of African Political Economy*, no. 24, pp. 55–84.

———. 1994. "The Military, Militarization, and Democratization in Africa: A Survey of Literature and Issues." *African Studies Review*, vol. 37, no. 2 (September), pp. 13–76.

———. 1995. "Dilemmas of Military Disengagement and Democratization in Africa." *IDS Bulletin*, no. 26, pp. 49–61.

———. 1996. "Democracy and the Military: An Epitaph for Frankenstein's Monster? *Democratization*, vol. 3, no. 2, pp. 1–16.

——— and Gordon White, eds. 1996. *Democratization in the South: The Jagged Wave*. Manchester, UK: Manchester University Press.

Luttwak, Edward. 1968. *Coup d'État: A Practical Handbook*. London, UK: Allen Lane.

Lutz, James. 1989. "The Diffusion of Political Phenomena in Sub-Saharan Africa." *Journal of Political and Military Sociology*, vol. 17, no. 1, pp. 99–104.

Macgaffey, Wyatt. 1966. "Concepts of Race in the Historiography of Northeast Africa." *Journal of African History*, vol. 7, no. 1, pp. 1–2.

Madsen, Wayne. 1999. *Genocide and Covert Operations in Africa, 1993–1999*. Lewiston, NY: The Edwin Mellen Press.

Magang, David. 1992. "A New Beginning: The Process of Democratization in Africa." *The Parliamentarian*, no. 4, pp. 235–239.

Mair, Lucy. 1958. "African Chiefs Today: The Lugard Memorial Lecture for 1958." *African Affairs*, vol. 28, no. 3 (July), pp. 195–206.

———. 1977. *African Kingdoms*. Oxford, UK: Oxford University Press.

Makumbe, John Mw. 1998. "Is there a Civil Society in Africa?" *International Affairs*, vol. 74, no. 2, pp. 305–317.

Mamdani, Mahmood. 1986. "Peasants and Democracy in Africa." *New Left Review*, no. 156 (March–April), pp. 37–49.

———. 1990. "The Social Basis of Constitutionalism in Africa." *Journal of Modern African Studies*, vol. 28, no. 3, pp. 359–374.

———. 1992. "Democratic Theory and Democratic Struggles in Africa." *Dissent*, vol. 39, no. 3 (Summer), pp. 312–318.

———. 1995. "A Critique of the State and Civil Society Paradigm in Africanist Studies." In Mahmood Mamdani and Ernest Wamba-Dia-Wamba, eds. *African Studies in Social Movements and Democracy*. Dakar, Senegal: CODESRIA.

———. 1999. "Indirect Rule, Civil Society, and Ethnicity: The African Dilemma." In William G. Martin and Michael O. West, eds. *Out of One, Many Africas: Reconstructing the Study and Meaning of Africa*. Chicago, IL: University of Illinois Press.

Mamdani, Mahmood and Ernest Wamba-dia-Wamba, eds. 1995. *African Studies in Social Movements and Democracy*. Dakar, Senegal: CODESRIA.

Marchal, Roland. 1998. "France and Africa: The Emergence of Essential Reforms?" *International Affairs*, vol. 74, no. 2, pp. 355–372.

Marenin, Otwin. 1987. "The Managerial State in Africa: A Conflict Coalition Perspective." In Zaki Ergas, ed. *The African State in Transition*. New York, NY: St. Martin's Press.

Markakis, John and Michael Waller. 1986. *Military Marxist Regimes in Africa*. London, UK: Frank Cass.

Markovitz, Irving L. 1977. *Power and Class in Africa: An Introduction to Change and Conflict in African Politics*. Englewood Cliffs, NJ: Prentice-Hall, Inc., 1977.

Marks, Gary and Larry Diamond, eds. 1992. *Reexamining Democracy: Essays in Honour of Seymour Martin Lipset*. London, UK: Sage.

Martin, Guy. 1995. "Continuity and Change in Franco-African Relations." *Journal of Modern African Studies*, vol. 33, no. 1, pp. 1–20.

———. 1998. "Reflections on Democracy and Development in Africa: The Intellectual Legacy of Claude Ake." *Ufahamu*, vol. 26, no. 1 (Winter), pp. 102–109.

———. 2002. *Africa in World Politics: A Pan-African Perspective*. Trenton, NJ: Africa World Press, Inc.

Martin, Michel-Louis. 1986. "The Rise and 'Thermidorization' of Radical Praetorianism in Benin." In Markakis, John and Michael Waller, eds. *Military Marxist Regimes in Africa*. London, UK: Frank Cass.

———. 1990. *Le Soldat Africain et le Politique: Essai sur le Militarisme et l'État Prétorien au Sud du Sahara*. Toulouse, France: Presses de l'Institut d'Études Politiques.

———. 1995. "Armies and Politics: The 'Lifecycle' of Military Rule in Sub-Saharan Francophone Africa." In Anthony Kirk-Greene and Daniel Bach, eds. *State and Society in Francophone Africa since Independence*. London, UK: St. Martin's Press.

———. 1997. "Operational Weakness and Political Activism: The Military in Sub-Saharan Africa." In John P. Lovell and David E. Albright, eds. *To Sheathe the Sword: Civil–Military Relations in the Quest for Democracy*. Westport, CT: Greenwood Press.

Marx, Karl. 1843. "Towards a Critique of Hegel's Philosophy of Right. Introduction." In A. W. Wood, ed. *Marx Selections*, (1988). London, UK: MacMillan.

Matthews, Sally and Hussein Solomon. 2002. "Ethnic Conflict Management in Nigeria." *Africa Insight*, vol. 32, no. 2, pp. 10–17.

Mauck, Gerardo L. 1994. "Democratic Transitions in Comparative Perspective." *World Politics* (April), pp. 355–375.

Mauro, Paolo. 1997. "Why Worry About Corruption?" *Economic Issues Series*, no. 6. Washington, DC: International Monetary Fund.

May, John D. 1978. "Defining Democracy: A Bid for Coherence and Consensus." *Political Studies*, vol. 26, no. 1, pp. 1–14.

Mazrui, Ali A. 1986. *The Africans: A Triple Heritage*. London, UK: BBC Publications.

Mbachu, Ozoemenam 1994. "Democracy in Africa: A Theoretical Overview." *Coexistence*, vol. 31, no. 2, pp. 147–157.

Mbaku, John Mukum. 1992. "Political Democracy and the Prospects of Development in Post–Cold War Africa." *Journal of Social, Political and Economic Studies*, vol. 17, nos. 3–4, pp. 345–371.

———. 1993. "Political Democracy, Military Expenditures and Economic Growth in Africa." *Scandinavian Journal of Development Alternatives*, vol. 12, no. 1, pp. 49–64.

———. 1994. "Military Coups as Rent-Seeking Behavior." *Journal of Political and Military Sociology*, vol. 22, no. 2 (Winter), pp. 241–284.

———. 1994. "Africa after More Than Thirty Years of Independence: Still Poor and Deprived." *Journal of Third World Studies*, vol. 11, pp. 13–58.

Mbaku, John Mukum and Julius O. Ihonvbere, eds. 1998. *Multiparty Democracy and Political Change: Constraints to Democratization in Africa*. Brookfield, Vermont: Ashgate.

Mbembe, Achille. 1985. *Les Jeunes et L'Ordre Politique en Afrique Noire*. Paris: L'Harmattan.

———. 1988. *Afriques Indociles*. Paris: Karthala.

———. 1990. "Democratization and Social Movements in Africa." *Africa Demos*, vol. 1, no. 1 (November), pp. 4–18.

McCaskie, Thomas. 1995. *State and Society in Pre-Colonial West Africa*, 2nd ed. Madison, WI: University of Wisconsin Press.

McCullum, Hugh. 1995. *The Angels Have Left Us: The Rwanda Tragedy and the Chruches*. Geneva: WCC Publications.

McFerson, Hazel M. 1992. "Democracy and Development in Africa." *Journal of Peace Research*, vol. 29, no. 3, pp. 241–248.

McGowan, Patrick. 1975. "Predicting Political Instability in Tropical Africa." In *Quantitative Techniques in Foreign Policy Analysis and Forecasting*. New York, NY: Praeger.

McGowan, Patrick and Thomas H. Johnson. 1984. "African Military Coups d'État and Underdevelopment: A Quantitative Historical Analysis." *Journal of Modern African Studies*, vol. 22, no. 4, pp. 847–882.

———. 1986. "Sixty Coups in Thirty Years: Further Evidence Regarding African Military Coups d'État." *Journal of Modern African Studies*, vol. 24, no. 3, pp. 352–371.

McLean, Iain. 1994. "Democratization and Economic Liberalization: Which Is the Chicken and Which Is the Egg?" *Democratization*, vol. 1, no. 1, pp. 27–40.

Médard, Jean-François. 1986. "Public Corruption in Africa: A Comparative Perspective." *Corruption and Reform*, no. 1, pp. 115–131.

———. 1991. "Autoritarismes et Démocraties en Afrique Noire." *Politique Africaine*, no. 43 (Octobre), pp. 92–104.

———. 1994. *États d'Afrique Noire: Formation, Mécanismes et Crises*. Paris: Karthala.

———. 1997. "La corruption internationale et l'Afrique," *Revue Internationale de Politique Comparée*, vol. 4, no. 2, pp. 12–42.

Meillassoux, Claude, ed. 1971. *The Development of Indigenous Trade and Markets in West Africa*. Oxford, UK: Oxford University Press.

Melvern, Linda and Paul Williams. 2004. "Britannia Waived the Rules: The Major Government and the 1994 Rwandan Genocide." *African Affairs*, vol. 103, no. 410, pp. 1–22.

Memmi, Albert. 1967. *The Colonizer and the Colonized*. Boston, MA: Beacon Press.

Meyns, Peter and Dani Wadada Nabudere. 1989. *Democracy and the One-Party State in Africa*. Hamburg, Germany: Institute for African Studies.

Michailof, Serge, ed. 1993. *La France et l'Afrique: Vade-Mecum pour un Nouveau Voyage*, Paris: Karthala.

Miliband, Ralph. 1969. *The State in Capitalist Society*. London, UK: Camelot Press.

Milimo, John T. 1993. "Multiparty Democracy in Africa: Lessons from Zambia." *International Journal of World Peace*, vol. 10, no. 1 (March), pp. 35–42.

Mistry, Percy S. 2000. "Africa's Record of Regional Co-operation and Integration." *African Affairs*, vol. 99, no. 397, pp. 553–573.

Mittelman, James H., ed. 1996. *Globalization: Critical Reflections*. Boulder, CO: Lynne Rienner Publishers.

Mkandawire, Thandika. 1999. "Shifting Commitments and National Cohesion in African Countries." In Lennart Wohlgemuth, *Common Security and Civil Society in Africa*. Uppsalla, Sweden: Nordic Institute of African Studies.

Monga, Célestin. 1994. *Anthropologie de la Colère: Société Civile et Démocratie en Afrique Noire*. Paris: l'Harmattan.

———. 1995. "Civil Society and Democratisation in Francophone Africa." *Journal of Modern African Studies*, vol. 33, no. 3, pp. 359–379.

———. 1996. *The Anthropology of Anger: Civil Society and Democracy in Africa*, trans. Linda L. Fleck and Célestin Monga. Boulder, CO: Lynne Rienner Publishers.

Mookherjee, Dilip and I. P. L. Ping. 1995. "Corruptible Law Enforcers— How Should They Be Compensated?" *Economic Journal*, vol. 105, no. 428, pp. 145–159.

Moore, Jr., Barrington. 1966. *The Social Origins of Dictatorship and Democracy: Lord and Peasant in the Making of the Modern World*. Boston, MA: Beacon Press.

Morgenthau, Ruth S. 1961. "Single-Party Systems in West Africa." *American Political Science Review*, vol. 55, no. 2, pp. 978–993.

Moss, Todd J. 1995. "U.S. Policy and Democratization in Africa: The Limits of Liberal Universalism." *Journal of Modern African Studies*, vol. 33, no. 2, pp. 189–209.

Mowoe, Isaac J. 1980. *The Performance of Soldiers as Governors: African Politics and the African Military*. Washington, DC: University Press of America.

Mshomba, Richard E. 2000. *Africa in the Global Economy*. Boulder, CO: Lynne Rienner Publishers.

Muller, Edward N. 1988. "Democracy, Economic Development, and Income Inequality." *American Sociological Review*, vol. 53, no. 1, pp. 50–68.

Muller, Edward N. and Mitchell A. Seligson. 1994. "Civic Culture and Democracy: The Question of Causal Relationships." *American Political Science Review*, vol. 88, no. 3, pp. 635–652.

Munck, Geraldo. 1994. "Democratic Transitions in Comparative Perspective." *Comparative Politics*, vol. 26, no. 3 (April), pp. 355–375.

Mundt, Robert J. 1997. "Côte d'Ivoire: Continuity and Change in a Semi-Democracy." In John F. Clark and David E. Gardinier, eds. *Political Reform in Francophone Africa*. Boulder, CO: Westview Press.

Munslow, Barry. 1983. "Why Has the Westminster Model Failed in Africa?" *Parliamentary Affairs*, vol. 36, no. 2, pp. 218–228.

———. 1993. "Democratization in Africa." *Parliamentary Affairs*, vol. 46, no. 4, pp. 478–490.

Murdock, George P. 1959. *Africa: Its Peoples and their Cultural History*. New York, NY: McGraw-Hill.

Mwaipaya, Paul A. 1980. *The Importance of Quality Leadership in National Development, with Special Reference to Africa*. New York, NY: Vantage Press.

Naidu, M. V. 1994. " 'Initial Development:' An Attempt at Conceptualization for Comparative Analyses of Models of Development." *Peace Research*, vol. 26, no. 1 (February), pp. 1–9.

———. 1996. *Dimensions of Peace*, Oakville, Ontario, Canada: MITA.

Nannan, Sukhwant Singh. 1992. "Africa: The Move towards Democracy." *Strategic Analysis*, vol. 14, no. 10, pp. 1221–1232.

Ndue, Paul Ntungwe. 1994. "Africa's Turn towards Pluralism." *Journal of Democracy*, vol. 5, no. 1, pp. 45–54.

Nelkin, Dorothy. 1967. "The Economic and Social Setting of Military Takeovers in Africa." *Journal of Asian and African Studies*, vol. 2, nos. 3–4, pp. 230–244.

Neocleous, Mark. 1996. *Administering Civil Society: Towards a Theory of State Power*. London, UK: MacMillan Press.

Nettl, J. P. 1968. "The State as a Conceptual Variable." *World Politics*, vol. 20, no. 4, pp. 509–592.

Newbury, Catharine. 1994. "Introduction: Paradoxes of Democratization in Africa." *African Studies Review*, vol. 37, no. 1, pp. 1–8.

Ninalowo, Bayo. 1990. "On the Structures and Praxis of Domination, Democratic Culture and Social Change: With Inferences from Africa." *Scandinavian Journal of Development Studies*, vol. 9, no. 4, pp. 107–117.

Ninsin, Kwame. 1998. "Three Levels of State Reordering: The Structural Aspects." In Donald Rothchild and Naomi Chazan, eds. *The Precarious Balance: State and Society in Africa*. Boulder, CO: Westview Press, pp. 265–281.

Nkrumah, Kwame. 1961. *Politics Is not for Soldiers*. Accra, Ghana: Government Printers.

———. 1973. *Autobiography of Kwame Nkrumah*. London, UK: Panaf Books Ltd.

Nnoli, Okwudiba. 1986. *Introduction to Politics.* Harlow, UK: Longman.

Nolutshungu, Sam C. 1992. "Africa in a World of Democracies: Interpretation and Retrieval." *Journal of Commonwealth and Comparative Politics,* vol. 30, no. 3, pp. 316–334.

Nordlinger, Eric A. 1970. "Soldiers in Mufti: The Impact of Military Rule upon Economic and Social Change in Non-Western States." *American Political Science Review,* vol. 64, no. 4, pp. 1138–1148.

———. 1972. *Soldiers in Politics: Military Coups and Governments.* Englewood Cliffs, NJ: Prentice-Hall.

Nordlund, Per. 1996. *Organising the Political Agora: Domination and Democratisation in Zambia and Zimbabwe.* Uppsala: Uppsala University Press.

North-South. 1980. *A Programme for Survival. Report of the Independent Commission on International Development Issues ('Brandt Commission').* London, UK: Pan.

Nyang'oro, Julius E. 1994. "Reform Politics and the Democratization Process in Africa." *African Studies Review,* vol. 37, no. 1, pp. 133–150.

———. 1996. "Critical Notes on Political Liberalization in Africa." *Journal of African and Asian Studies,* vol. 31, nos. 1–2, pp. 112–124.

Nye, Jr., Joseph S. 1990. "The Changing Nature of World Power." *Political Science Quarterly,* vol. 105, pp. 186–197.

Nzouankeu, Jacques-Mariel. 1991. "The African Attitude to Democracy." *International Social Science Journal,* vol. 43, no. 2, pp. 373–385.

———. 1993. "The Role of the National Conference in the Transition to Democracy: The Cases of Benin and Mali." *Issue: A Journal of Opinion,* vol. 21, nos. 1–2, pp. 44–50.

———. 1994. "Decentralization and Democracy in Africa." *International Review of Administrative Sciences,* vol. 60, no. 2, pp. 213–227.

OAU. 1981. *Lagos Plan of Action for the Economic Development of Africa.* Geneva: International Institute for Labor Studies.

Obadan, M. K. I. 1998. *The State, Leadership, Governance and Economic Development,* Nigerian Economic Society, Ibadan.

O'Donnell, Guillermo. 1993. "On the State, Democratization and some Conceptual Problems." *World Development,* vol. 21, no. 8, pp. 1355–1369.

———, Philippe C. Schmitter, and Lawrence Whitehead. 1986. *Transitions from Authoritarian Rule.* Baltimore, MD: Johns Hopkins University Press.

OECD. 2002. *African Economic Outlook 2001–2002.* Paris: OECD Publications.

Ofusu-Amaah, W., Raj Soopramanien Paatii, and Kishor Uprety. 1999. *Combating Corruption. A Comparative Review of Selected Legal Aspects of State Practice and Major International Initiatives.* Washington, DC: The World Bank.

Ogot, Bethwell A., ed. 1972. *War and Society in Africa: Ten Studies.* London, UK: Frank Cass.

Ogunjimi, Bayo. 1990. "The Military and Literature in Africa." *Journal of Political and Military Sociology,* vol. 18 (Winter), pp. 327–341.

O'Kane, Rosemary H. T. 1981. "A Probabilistic Approach to the Causes of Coups d'État." *British Journal of Political Science*, vol. 11, no. 3, pp. 287–308.

———. 1987. *The Likelihood of Coups*. Brookfiled, VT: Avebury.

———. 1989. "Military Regimes: Power and Force." *European Journal of Political Research*, vol. 17, pp. 333–350.

Okpaku, Sr., Joseph. 1994. "Creating a desirable 21st Century Africa: The Role of Leadership and Governance." *Futures*, vol. 26, no. 9, pp. 999–1010.

Okumu, Washington A. J. 2002. *The African Renaissance: History, Significance and Strategy*. Trenton, NJ: Africa World Press, Inc.

Oliver, Roland and John. D. Fage. 1962. *A Short History of Africa*. Harmondsworth, UK: Penguin Books Ltd.

Olivier de Sardan, Jean-Pierre. 1996. "L'Économie Morale de la Corruption en Afrique." *Politique Africaine*, no. 63 (Octobre), pp. 97–116.

———. 1999. "A Moral Economy of Corruption in Africa?" *Journal of Modern African Studies*, vol. 37, no. 1, pp. 25–52.

Olowu, Dele and J. S. Wunsch. 1990. "Conclusion: Self-Governance and African Development." In J. S. Wunsch and D. Olowu, eds. *The Failure of the Centralized State: Institutions and Self-Governance in Africa*. Boulder, CO: Westview Press.

Olsen, Gorm R. 1997. "Western Europe's Relations with Africa since the End of the Cold War." *Journal of Modern African Studies*, vol. 35, no. 2, pp. 299–319.

———. 1998. "Europe and The Promotion of Democracy in Post–Cold War Africa: How Serious Is Europe and for What Reason?" *African Affairs*, vol. 97, no. 388, pp. 343–367.

Olson, Mancur. 1993. "Dictatorship, Democracy and Development." *American Political Science Review*, vol. 87, no. 3, pp. 567–576.

Omaar, Rukiya and Alex de Waal. 1995. *Rwanda: Death, Despair and Defiance*. London, UK: African Rights.

Onwumechili, Chuka. 1998. *African Democratization and Military Coups*. Westport, CT: Praeger.

Orkand Corporation. 1983. *Analysis of the Cause of Coups d'État in Sub-Saharan Africa, 1960–1982*. Silver Spring, MD: Orkand Corporation.

Osaghae, Eghosa E. 1998. *Structural Adjustment, Civil Society, and National Cohesion in Africa*. Harare, Zimbabwe: African Association of Political Science.

Ottaway, Marina. 1993. "Should Elections Be the Criterion of Democratization in Africa?" *CSIS Africa Notes*, no. 145, pp. 1–5.

———. 1997. "African Democratisation and the Leninist Option." *Journal of Modern African Studies*, vol. 35, no. 1, pp. 1–15.

———, ed. 1997. *Democracy in Africa: The Hard Road Ahead*. Boulder, CO: Lynne Rienner Publishers.

———. 1999. *Africa's New Leaders: Democracy or State Reconstruction*, Washington, DC: Carnegie Endowment for International Peace.

Ottaway, Marina and David. 1986. *Afrocommunism*, 2nd ed. New York, NY: Africana Publishing.

Ouma, Stephen. 1991. "Corruption in Public Policy and Its Impact on Development: The Case of Uganda since 1979." *Public Administration and Development*, vol. 11, no. 5, pp. 473–489.

Owusu, Maxwell. 1992. "Democracy and Africa—A View from the Village." *Journal of Modern African Studies*, vol. 30, no. 3, pp. 369–396.

———. 1997. "Domesticating Democracy: Culture, Civil Society, and Constitutionalism in Africa." *Comparative Studies in Society and History*, vol. 39, no. 1, pp. 120–152.

PBS Frontline. 1999. *The Triumph of Evil: How the West Ignored the Warnings of the 1994 Rwanda Genocide and Turned its back on the Victims*. Alexandria, VA: PBS.

Palmer, Monte. 1970. "Development: Political, Economic, Social—An Overview." In Monte Palmer, ed. *The Human Factor in Political Development*. Waltham, MA: Ginn & Cie.

Palmer, Robert R. and Joel Colton. 1971. *A History of the Modern World*, 4th ed. New York, NY: Alfred A. Knopf.

Passerin d'Entreves, Alexander. 1967. *The Notion of the State*. Oxford, UK: Clarendon Press.

Pateman, Carole. 1971. "Political Culture, Political Structure, and Political Change." *British Journal of Political Science*, vol. 1, no. 3, pp. 291–305.

———. 1980. *Participation and Democratic Theory*. London. UK: Cambridge University Press.

———. 1996. "Democracy and Democratization." *International Political Science Review*, vol. 17, no. 1, pp. 5–12.

Patterson, Amy S. 1998. "A Reappraisal of Democracy in Civil Society: Evidence from Rural Senegal." *Journal of Modern African Studies*, vol. 36, no. 3, pp. 423–441.

Perlmutter, Amos. 1977. *The Military and Politics in Modern Times*. New Haven, CT: Yale University Press.

Peterson, David L. 1994. "Debunking Ten Myths about Democracy in Africa." *Washington Quarterly*, vol. 17, no. 3, pp. 129–141.

Pfaff, William. 1995. "A New Colonialism? Europe Must Go back into Africa." *Foreign Affairs*, vol. 74, no. 1, pp. 2–6.

Phillips, Ann. 1989. *The Enigma of Colonialism: British Policy in West Africa*. Bloomington, IN: Indiana University Press.

Plattner, Marc. 1991. "The Democratic Revolution." *Journal of Democracy*, vol. 2, no. 1, pp. 35–52.

Poggi, Gianfranco. 1978. *The Development of the Modern State*. Stanford, CA: Stanford University Press.

Pope, J., ed. 1997. *National Integrity Systems: The TI Source Book*, 2nd ed. Washington, DC: Transparency International & EDI/The World Bank.

Post, Ken. 1964. *The New States of West Africa*. Harmondsworth, UK: Penguin Book Limited.

Potholm, Christian P. 1979. *The Theory and Practice of African Politics*. Englewood Cliffs, NJ: Prentice-Hall.

Press, Robert M. 1999. *The New Africa: Dispatches from A Changing Continent*. Gainesville, FL: University Press of Florida.

Price, Robert M. 1971. "Military Officers and Political Leadership: The Ghanaian Case." *Comparative Politics*, vol. 3, no. 3, pp. 361–379.

Przeworski, Adam. 1999. "Minimalist Conception of Democracy: A Defense." In I. Shapiro and C. Hacker-Gordon, eds. *Democracy's Value*. Cambridge, UK: Cambridge University Press.

Przeworski, Adam and Fernando Limongi. 1993. "Political Regimes and Economic Growth." *Journal of Economic Perspectives*, vol. 7, no. 3, pp. 51–69.

Pugh, Michael and Neil Cooper, with Jonathan Goodhand. 2004. *War Economies in a Regional Context: Challenges of Transformation*. Boulder, CO: Lynne Rienner Publishers.

Putnam, Robert D. 1993. *Making Democracy Work: Civic Traditions in Modern Italy*, Princeton, NJ: Princeton University Press, 1993.

Pye, Lucian W. 1962. "Armies in the Process of Political Modernization." In John J. Johnson, ed. *The Role of the Military in Underdeveloped Countries*. Princeton, NJ: Princeton University Press.

Quantin, Patrick, ed. 1994. *L'Afrique Politique, 1994: Vue sur la Démocratisation à Marée Basse*. Paris: Karthala.

Randrianja, Solofo. 1996. "Nationalism, Ethnicity and Democracy." In Stephen Ellis, ed. *Africa Now: Peoples, Policies, Institutions*. Porstmouth, UK: Heinemann.

Rasheed, Sadig. 1995. "The Democratization Process and Popular Participation in Africa: Emerging Realities and the Challenges Ahead." *Development and Change*, vol. 26, no. 2, pp. 333–354.

Redner, Harry. 1990. "Beyond Marx-Weber: A Diversified and International Approach to the State." *Political Studies*, vol. 38, no. 4, pp. 638–653.

Reed, William C. 1995. "The New International Order: State, Society and African International Relations." *Africa Insight*, vol. 25, no. 3, pp. 140–148.

Reno, William. 1995. *Corruption and State Politics in Sierra Leone*. Cambridge, UK: Cambridge University Press.

———. 1998. *Warlord Politics and African States*. Boulder, CO: Lynne Rienner Publishers.

Riddell-Dixon, Elizabeth. 1997. "Individual Leadership and Structural Power." *Canadian Journal of Political Science*, vol. 30, no. 2 (June), pp. 257–280.

Rijnierse, Elly. 1993. "Democratization in Sub-Saharan Africa: Literature Overview." *Third World Quarterly*, vol. 14, no. 3, pp. 147–164.

Riley, Stephen P. 1991. "The Democratic Transition in Africa." *African Demos*, vol. 1, no. 3, pp. 5–8.

———. 1991. *The Democratic Transition in Africa: An End to the One-Party State?* London, UK: Research Institute for the Study of Conflict and Terrorism.

———. 1992. "Political Adjustment or Domestic Pressure: Democratic Politics and Political Choice in Africa." *Third World Quarterly*, vol. 13, no. 3, pp. 539–551.

———. 1993. "Post-Independence Anti-Corruption Strategies and the Contemporary Effects of Democratization." *Corruption and Reform*, vol. 7, no. 3, pp. 249–261.

————. 1998. "The Political Economy of Anti-Corruption Strategies in Africa." *The European Journal of Development Research*, vol.10, no.1, pp. 129–159.

Rimmer, Douglas, ed. 1996. *Africa Thirty Years On: The Record and Outlook after Thirty Years of Independence*. London, UK: James Currey, Ltd.

Robertson, Roland. 1992. *Globalization: Social Theory and Global Culture*. London, UK: Sage Publication.

Robinson, Mark, ed. 1998. *Corruption and Development*. London, UK: Frank Cass.

————. 1999. "Governance and Coherence in Development Co-operation. In Jacques Forster and Olav Stokke, eds. *Policy Coherence in Development Co-operation*. Portland, OR: Frank Cass.

Robinson, Pearl T. 1994a. "The National Conference Phenomenon in Francophone Africa." *Comparative Studies in Society and History*, vol. 36, no. 3, pp. 575–610.

————. 1994b. "Democratization: Understanding the Relationship between Regime Change and the Culture of Politics." *African Studies Review*, vol. 37, no. 1, pp. 39–68.

Rodney, Walter. 1974. *How Europe Underdeveloped Africa*, Washington, DC: Howard University Press.

Ronen, Dov. 1974. "The Colonial Elite in Dahomey." *African Studies Review*, vol. 8, no. 1, pp. 55–74.

————. 1975. *Dahomey: Between Tradition and Modernity*. Ithaca, NY: Cornell University Press.

————. 1980. "Benin: The Role of the Uniformed Leaders." In Isaac J. Mowoe, ed. *The Performance of Soldiers as Governors: African Politics and the African Military*. Washington, DC: University Press of America.

————, ed. 1986. *Democracy and Pluralism in Africa*. Boulder, CO: Lynne Rienner Publishers.

Roniger, Luis. 1994. "Civil Society, Patronage, and Democracy." *International Journal of Comparative Sociology*, vol. 35, nos. 3–4, pp. 207–220.

Rose-Ackerman, Susan. 1996. "Democracy and 'Grand' Corruption." *International Social Science Journal*, no. 149 (September), pp. 365–380.

————. 1997. "Corruption and Development," Paper prepared for the Annual World Bank Conference on Development Economics, Washington, DC, April 30–May 1.

————. 1999. *Corruption and Government: Causes, Consequences, and Reform*, Cambridge, UK: Cambridge University Press.

Ross, Andrew L. 1987. "Dimensions of Militarization in the Third World." *Armed Forces and Society*, vol. 13, no. 4, pp. 561–578.

Rostow, Walt. 1960. *Stages of Economic Growth*, Cambridge, UK: Cambridge University Press.

Rothchild, Donald. 1987. "Hegemony and State Softness." In Zaki Ergas, ed. *The African State in Transition*. New York, NY: St Martin's Press.

Rothchild, Donald and Naomi Chazan, eds. 1988. *The Precarious Balance: State and Society in Africa*. Boulder, CO: Westview Press.

Rothchild, Donald and V. A. Olorunsola, eds. 1982. *State Versus Ethnic Claims: African Policy Dilemmas.* Boulder, CO: Westview Press.

Rousseau, Jean-Jacques. 1762. *The Social Contract.* Harmondsworth, UK: Penguin.

Rummel Rudolph J. 1985. "Libertarian Propositions on Violence within and between nations." *Journal of Conflict Resolution,* vol. 27, pp. 419–455.

———. 1995. "Democracies Are Less Warlike than Other Regimes." *European Journal of International Relations,* vol. 1, no. 4, pp. 457–479.

Ruschmeyer, D., E. Stephens, and J. Stephens. 1992. *Capitalist Development and Democracy,* Oxford, UK: Polity.

Rustow, Dankwart A. 1970. "Transitions to Democracy: Towards a Dynamic Model." *Comparative Politics,* vol. 2, no. 3, pp. 337–364.

Sahn, David E., Paul A. Dorosh, and Stephen D. Younger. 1997. *Structural Adjustment Reconsidered: Economy Policy and Poverty in Africa.* Cambridge, UK: Cambridge University Press.

Sakamoto, Yoshikazu. 1991. "The Global Context of Democratization." *Alternatives,* vol. 16, pp. 119–128.

Sandbrook, Richard. 1985. *The Politics of Africa's Economic Stagnation.* Cambridge, UK: Cambridge University Press.

———. 1987. "Personnalisation du Pouvoir et Stagnation Capitaliste: L'État Africain en Crise." *Politique Africaine,* no. 26 (Juin), pp. 15–37.

———. 1988. "Liberal Democracy in Africa: A Socialist-Revisionist Perspective." *Canadian Journal of African Studies,* vol. 22, no. 2, pp. 337–364.

———. 1990. "Taming the African Leviathan." *World Policy Journal,* vol. 7, no. 4, pp. 673–701.

Sarkesian, Sam C. 1981. "Military Professionalism and Civil–Military Relations in West Africa." *International Political Science Review,* vol. 2, no. 3, p. 291.

Scarritt, James R. 1986. "The Explanation of African Politics and Society: Towards a Synthesis of Approaches." *Journal of African Studies,* vol. 13, no. 3, pp. 85–93.

Schatzberg, Michael G. 1988. *The Dialectics of Oppression in Zaire.* Bloomington, IN: Indiana University Press.

———. 1993. "Power, Legitimacy and 'Democratisation' in Africa." *Africa* vol. 63, no. 4, pp. 445–461.

Schedler, Andreas, Larry Diamond, and Marc F. Plattner, eds. 1999. *The Self-Restraining State. Power and Accountability in New Democracies,* London, UK: Lynne Rienner Publishers.

Schmitter, Philippe. 1994. "Dangers and Dilemmas of Democracy." *Journal of Democracy,* vol. 5, no. 2, pp. 57–74.

Schmitter, Philippe and Terry L. Karl. 1991. "What Democracy Is . . . and Is Not?" *Journal of Democracy,* no. 2 (Summer), pp. 104–110.

Schmitz, Gerald and Eboe Hutchful. 1992. *Democratization and Popular Participation in Africa.* Ottawa: North-South Institute.

Schraeder, Peter J. 1994. "Élites as Facilitators or Impediments to Political Development? Some Lessons from the 'Third Wave' of Democratization in Africa." *Journal of Developing Areas,* vol. 29, no. 1, pp. 69–90.

————. 1997. "France and the Great Game in Africa." *Current History*, vol. 96, no. 610, pp. 206–211.

————. 2000. *African Politics and Society: A Mosaic in Transformation*. New York, NY: Bedford/St. Martin's Press.

Schumpeter, Joseph A. 1942. *Capitalism, Socialism, and Democracy*. London, UK: Allen and Unwin (Reprint in 1976).

Schwabe, Peter. 2001. *Africa: A Continent Self-Destructs*, New York, NY: Palgrave.

Scott, James C. 1972. *Comparative Political Corruption*, Englewood Cliffs, NJ: Prentice-Hall.

Seers, Dudley. 1979. "The New Meaning of Development." In David Lehmann, ed. *Development Theory: Four Critical Studies*, London, UK: Frank Cass.

Seitz, Steven. 1991. "The Military in Black African Politics." *Journal of Asian and African Studies*, vol. 26, nos. 1–2, pp. 61–75.

Sen, Amartya. 1999. "Democracy as a Universal Value." *Journal of Democracy*, vol. 10, no. 3, pp. 3–17.

Shapiro, Ian and Casiano Hacker-Gordon. 1999. "Promises and Disappointments: reconsidering Democracy's Values." In Ian Shapiro and Casiano Hacker-Gordon, eds. *Democracy's Value*. Cambridge, UK: Cambridge University Press.

Share, Donald. 1987. "Transitions to Democracy and Transition through Transaction." *Comparative Political Studies*, vol. 19, no. 4, pp. 525–548.

Shils, Edward. 1962. "The Military in the Political Development of the New States." In John J. Johnson, ed. *The Role of the Military in Underdeveloped Countries*. Princeton: Princeton University Press.

————. 1991. "The Virtue of Civil Society." *Government and Opposition*, vol. 26, no. 1, pp. 3–20.

Shin, Doh Chull. 1994. "On the Third Wave of Democratization: A Synthesis and Evaluation of Recent Theory and Research." *World Politics*, vol. 47, no. 1, pp. 135–170.

Shivji, Issa G., ed. 1991. *State and Constitutionalism: An African Debate on Democracy*. Harare, Zimbabwe: SAPES Trust.

Shleifer, Andrei and Robert W. Vishny. 1993. "Corruption." *Quarterly Journal of Economics*, vol. 58, no. 3 (August), pp. 599–617.

————. 1998. *The Grabbing Hand. Government Pathologies and Their Cures*, Cambridge, MA: Harvard University Press.

Siddiqui, Rukhsana A., ed. 1997. *SubSaharan Africa in the 1990s: Challenges to Democracy and Development*. Westport, CT: Praeger.

Sigelman, Lee. 1974. "Military Intervention: A Methodological Note." *Journal of Political and Military Sociology*, vol. 2, no. 1, pp. 275–281.

Sklar, Richard L. 1983. "Democracy in Africa." *African Studies Review*, vol. 26, nos. 3–4, pp. 11–24.

————. 1986. "Democracy in Africa." In Patrick Chabal, ed. *Political Domination in Africa*. Cambridge: Cambridge University Press.

————. 1987. "Developmental Democracy." *Comparative Studies in Society and History*, vol. 29, no. 4, pp. 686–714.

Sklar, Richard L. 1993. "The African Frontier for Political Science." In Bates, Robert H., Valentin Y. Mudimbe, and Jean O'Barr, eds. *Africa and the Disciplines.* Chicago, IL: University of Chicago Press.

Sklar, Richard L. and C. S. Whitaker. 1991. *African Politics and Problems in Development.* Boulder, CO: Lynne Rienner Publishers.

Sklar, Richard L. and Mark Strege. 1992. "Finding Peace through Democracy in Sahelian Africa." *Current History,* vol. 91, no. 565, pp. 224–229.

Slater, Robert O., Barry M. Schutz, and Steven R. Dorr, eds. 1993. *Global Transformation and the Third World.* Boulder, CO: Lynne Rienner Publishers.

Smith, Adam. 1977. *An Inquiry into the Nature and Causes of the Wealth of Nations.* Dent, UK: Everyman.

Smith, Robert S. 1976. *Warfare and Diplomacy in Pre-Colonial West Africa.* London, UK: Methuen.

Smith, Tony F. 1993. "Making the World Safe for Democracy." *The Washington Quarterly,* vol. 16, pp. 197–214.

Snyder, Richard. 1992. "Explaining Transitions from Neopatrimonial Dictatorships." *Comparative Politics,* vol. 24, no. 2, pp. 379–400.

Somerville, Keith. 1991. "Africa Moves Towards Party Pluralism." *The World Today,* vol. 47, nos. 8–9, pp. 152–155.

———. 1994. "Africa: Is there a Silver Lining?" *The World Today,* vol. 50, no. 11 (November), pp. 215–218.

Sorensen, George. 1993. *Democracy and Democratization: Processes and Prospects in a Changing World.* Boulder, CO: Westview Press.

Spalding, Nancy J. 1996. "State–Society Relations in Africa: An Exploration of the Tanzanian Experience." *Polity,* vol. 29, no. 1, pp. 65–96.

Starr, Harvey. 1991. "Democratic Dominoes: Diffusion Approaches to the Spread of Democratic in the International System." *Journal of Conflict Resolution,* vol. 35, no. 2, pp. 356–381.

Sundhaussen, Ulf. 1998. "The Military: A Threat to Democracy?" *Australian Journal of Politics and History,* vol. 44, no. 3, pp. 329–349.

Svensson, Jakob. 1999. "The Cost of Doing Business: Ugandan Firms' Experiences with Corruption." *Development Research Group.* Washington, DC: The World Bank.

Sylla, Lanciné. 1982. "La Gestion Démocratique du Pluralisme Socio-Politique en Afrique: Démocratie Concurrentielle et Démocratie Consociationelle," *Civilisations,* vol. 33, no. 1, pp. 23–31.

Szeftel, Morris. 1982. "Political Graft and the Spoils System in Zambia—The State as a Resource in Itself." *Review of African Political Economy,* no. 24, pp. 5–21.

———. 1998. "Misunderstanding African Politics: Corruption and the Governance Agenda." *Review of African Political Economy,* no. 76, pp. 221–240.

Tangri, Roger. 1998. "Politics, Capital and the State in Sub-Saharan Africa." In N. Kasfir, ed. *Civil Society and Democracy in Africa: Critical Perspectives.* London, UK: Frank Cass.

Tanzi, Vito. 1998. "Corruption around the World: Causes, Consequences, Scope and Cures." *International Monetary Fund Staff Papers*, vol. 45, no. 4, pp. 559–594.

Thebold, Robin. 1982. "Patrimonialism." *World Politics*, vol. 34, pp. 548–559.

———, ed. 1990. *Corruption, Development and Inequality: Soft touch or Hard Graft?* London, UK: MacMillan Press.

Therborn, G. 1977. "The Rule of Capital and the Rise of Democracy." *New Left Review*, vol. 2, no. 10, pp. 3–41.

Thompson, Alex. 2000. *An Introduction to African Politics*. London, UK: Routledge.

Tilly, Charles, ed. 1975. *The Formation of National States in Western Europe*. Princeton, NJ: Princeton University Press.

Tordoff, William. 1997. *Government and Politics in Africa*, 3rd Edition. Bloomington, IN: Indiana University Press.

———. 2002. *Government and Politics in Africa*, 4th Edition. Bloomington, IN: Indiana University Press.

Toulabor, Comi M. 1995. " 'Paristroika' and the One-Party System." In *State and Society in Francophone Africa since Independence*, eds. Anthony Kirk-Greene and Daniel Bach. London, UK: MacMillan.

Tucker, Robert C. 1995. *Politics as Leadership*. Columbia, MO: University of Missouri Press.

Turok, Ben. 1987. *Africa: What Can Be Done?* London, UK: Zed Books Ltd.

Udogu, Ike E. 1996. "Incomplete Metamorphic Democracy as a Conceptual Framework in the Analysis of African Politics: An Explanatory Investigation." *Journal of African and Asian Studies*, vol. 31, nos. 1–2, pp. 5–20.

UN. 2002. *Millennium Declaration*. New York, NY: UN.

UNAIDS. 2005. *Press Release: AIDS in Africa: Three Scenarios to 2025*. Addis-Ababa.

UNDP. 1997. "Corruption and Good Governance." *Discussion Paper 3*, Management Development and Governance Division. New York, NY: UN, July.

———. 2002. *Human Development Report 2002*. Oxford, UK: Oxford University Press.

UNGA. 1996. *UNGA Declaration*, New York, NY: UN, December.

United Nations, 1998. *United Nations Human Development Report 1998*. New York, NY: Oxford University Press.

United States Agency for International Development (USAID). 1990. *The Democracy Initiative*. Washington, DC: USAID.

Uvin, Peter. 1998. *Aiding Violence: The Development Enterprise in Rwanda*. West Harford, CT: Kumarian Press.

Uzoigwe, G. N. 1975. "Pre-Colonial Military Studies in Africa." *Journal of Modern African Studies*, vol. 13, no. 3, pp. 469–481.

Valenzuela, Arturo. 1985. "The Military and Social Science Theory." *Third World Quarterly*, vol. 7, no. 1, pp. 132–143.

van de Walle, Nicolas. 1994. "Political Liberalization and Economic Reform in Africa." *World Development*, vol. 22, no. 3, pp. 483–500.

van Hoek, F. and J. Bossuyt. 1993. "Democracy in Sub-Saharan Africa: The Search for a New Institutional Set-Up." *African Development Review*, vol. 5, no. 1, pp. 81–93.

Verba, Sydney and Lucien Pye, eds. 1965. *Political Culture and Political Development*. Princeton, NJ: Princeton University Press.

Villalón, Leonardo A. and Phillip A. Huxtable, eds. 1998. *The African State at a Critical Juncture: Between Distinction and Reconfiguration*. Boulder, CO: Lynne Rienner Publishers.

Viotti, Paul R. and Mark V. Kauppi. 1990. *International Relations Theory: Realism, Pluralism, Globalism*. New York, NY: MacMillan.

Volman, Daniel. 1993. "Africa and the New World Order." *Journal of Modern African Studies*, vol. 31, no. 1, pp. 1–30.

VonDoepp, Peter. 1996. "Political Transition and Civil Society: The Cases of Kenya and Zambia." *Studies in Comparative International Development*, vol. 31, pp. 23–36.

Wallerstein, Immanuel. 1979. *The Capitalist World Economy*. Cambridge, UK: Cambridge University Press.

Waltz, Kenneth N. 1979. *Theory of International Politics*. New York, NY: Mcgraw-Hill, Inc.

———. 1991. "Realist Thought and Neorealist Theory." In Robert L. Rothstein, ed. *The Evolution of Theory in International Relations*. Columbia, SC: University of South Carolina Press, pp. 21–37.

Walzer, Michael. 1991. "The Idea of Civil Society." *Dissent*, vol. 38, no. 2 (Spring), pp. 293–304.

Wamala, A. S. 1992. "The Role of Workers in the Struggle towards Multi-Party Democracy: Africa's Colonial and Post-Colonial Experience." *Eastern Africa Social Science Research Review*, vol. 8, no. 1 (January), pp. 46–61.

Ward, Peter M. 1989. *Corruption, Development and Inequality*, London, NY: Routledge.

Webber, Carolyn and Aaron Wildavsky. 1986. *A History of Taxation and Expenditure in the Western World*, New York, NY: Simon and Schuster.

Wedeman, Andrew. 1997. "Looters, Rent-Scrapers, and Dividend-Collectors: The Political Economy of Corruption in Zaire, South Korea, and the Philippines." *The Journal of Developing Areas*, vol. 31, no. 4 (Summer), pp. 457–478.

Weede, Erich. 1984. "Democracy and War Involvement." *Journal of Conflict Resolution*, vol. 28, no. 4, pp. 849–664.

Wei, Shang-Jin. 1999. "Corruption in Economic Development: Beneficial Grease, Minor Annoyance, or Major Obstacle?" *Policy Research Working Paper*, no. 2048. Washington, DC: World Bank.

Welch, Jr., Claude E. 1967. "Soldier and State in Africa." *Journal of Modern African Studies*, vol. 5, no. 3, pp. 305–322.

———, ed. 1970. *Soldier and State in Africa: A Comparative Analysis of Military Intervention and Political Change*. Evanston: Northwestern University Press.

———. 1975. "Continuity and Discontinuity in African Military Organization." *Journal of Modern African Studies*, vol. 13, no. 2, pp. 229–248.

———. 1983. "Military Disengagement from Politics: Lessons from West Africa." *Armed Forces and Society*, vol. 9, no. 4, pp. 541–554.

———. 1985. "Civil–Military Relations: Perspectives from the Third World." *Armed Forces and Society*, vol. 11, no. 2, pp. 183–198.

———. 1986. "From 'Armies of Africans' to 'African Armies': The Evolution of Military Forces in Africa." In Arlinghaus, Bruce E. and Pauline H. Baker, eds. *African Armies: Evolution and Capabilities*. Boulder, CO: Westview Press.

———. 1987. *No Farewell to Arms? Military Disengagement from Politics in Africa and Latin America*. Boulder, CO: Westview Press.

———. 1991. "The Single Party Phenomenon in Africa." *TransAfrica Forum* (Fall), pp. 85–94.

———. 1993. "Changing Civil–Military Relations." In Robert O. Slater, Barry M. Schutz, and Steven R. Dorr, eds. *Global Transformations and the Third World*. Boulder, CO: Lynne Rienner Publishers.

Welch, Stephen. 1993. *The Concept of Political Culture*. New York, NY: St. Martin's Press.

Wells, Alan. 1974. "The Coup d'État in Theory and Practice: Independent Black Africa in the 1960s." *American Journal of Sociology*, vol. 79, no. 4, pp. 871–887.

Wells, Alan and Richard Pollnac. 1988. "The Coup d'État in Sub-Saharan Africa: Changing Patterns from 1956–1984. *Journal of Political and Military Sociology*, vol. 16, no. 1 (Spring), pp. 43–56.

West Africa. 1998. "Africa: What Future for Democracy." January 19–25.

White, Gordon. 1994. "Civil Society, Democratization and Development: Clearing the Analytical Ground." *Democratization*, vol. 1, no. 3, pp. 375–390.

Whitehead, Laurence. 1996. "Concerning International Support for Democracy in the South." In Robin Luckham and Gordon White, eds. *Democratization in the South: The Jagged Wave*. Manchester, UK: Manchester University Press.

Widner, Jennifer A., ed. 1994. *Economic Change and Political Liberalization in Sub-Saharan Africa*. Baltimore, MD: Johns Hopkins University Press.

———. 1994. "Two Leadership Styles and Patterns of Political Liberalization." *African Studies Review*, vol. 37, no. 1, pp. 151–174.

Wiking, C. 1983. *Military Coups in Sub-Saharan Africa: How to Justify Illegal Assumptions of Power*. Uppsala, Sweden: Scandinavian Institute of African Studies.

Wildavsky, Aaron. 1994. "Cultural Pluralism Can both Strengthen and Weaken Democracy." In Frederick D. Weil, ed. *Research on Democracy and Society*, vol. 2: Political Culture and Political Structure—Theoretical and Empirical Studies. Greenwich, CT: JAI Press.

Willame, Jean-Claude. 1992. *L'automne d'un despotisme. Pouvoir, argent et obéissance dans le Zaïre des années quatre-vingt.* Paris: Éditions Karthala.

Williams, Gavin. 2003. "Reforming Africa: Continuities and Changes." In *Europa Encyclopedia*, pp. 3–11.

Wiseman, John A. 1986. "Urban Riots in West Africa, 1977–1985." *Journal of Modern African Studies*, vol. 24, no. 3, pp. 509–518.

———. 1990. *Democracy in Black Africa: Survival and Revival.* New York, NY: Paragon House.

———. 1993a. "Democracy and the New Pluralism in Africa: Causes, Consequences and Significance." *Third World Quarterly*, vol. 14, no. 3, pp. 439–449.

———. 1993b. "Leadership and Personal Danger in African Politics." *Journal of Modern African Studies*, vol. 31, no. 4, pp. 657–680.

———, ed. 1995a. *Democracy and Political Change in Sub-Saharan Africa.* New York, NY: Routledge.

———. 1995b. "Introduction." In John Wiseman, ed. *Democracy and Political Change in Sub-Saharan Africa.* New York, NY: Routledge.

———. 1996. *The New Struggle for Democracy in Africa.* Brookfield, VT: Avebury.

Wohlgemuth, Lennart, Samantha Gibson, Stephan Klasen, and Emma Rothschild, eds. 1999. *Common Security and Civil Society in Africa.* Uppsala, Sweden: Nordic Institute of African Studies.

Wolf, Martin. 1995. "Cooperation or Conflict? The EU Liberal Global Economy." *International Affairs*, vol. 71, no. 2 (April), pp. 325–337.

Wood, E. M. 1995. *Democracy against Capitalism.* Cambridge, UK: Cambridge University Press.

Woods, Dwayne. 1992. "Civil Society in Europe and Africa: Limiting State Power Through a Public Sphere." *African Studies Review*, vol. 35, no. 2, pp. 77–100.

Woodward, Peter. 1994. "Democracy and Economy in Africa: The Optimists and the Pessimists." *Democratization*, vol. 1, no. 1, pp. 116–132.

World Bank. 1989. *Sub-Saharan Africa: From Crisis to Sustainable Growth.* Washington, DC: World Bank.

———. 1992. *Governance and Development.* Washington, DC: World Bank.

Wunsch, James S. 1990. "Beyond the Failure of the Centralized State: Toward Self-Governance and an Alternative Institutional Paradigm." In J. S. Wunsch and D. Olowu, eds. *The Failure of the Centralized State.* Boulder, CO: Westview Press.

Wunsch, James S. and Dele Olowu, eds. 1990. *The Failure of the Centralized State.* Boulder, CO: Westview Press.

Wyatt-Walter, Andrew. 1995. "Regionalism, Globalization, and the World Economic Order." In Louise Fawcett and Andrew Hurrell, eds. *Regionalism in World Politics: Regional Organization and International Order.* Oxford, UK: Oxford University Press.

Young, Crawford. 1982a. *Ideology and Development in Africa.* New Haven: Yale University Press.

————. 1982b. "Patterns of Social Conflict: State, Class and Ethnicity." *Daedalus*, vol. 111, no. 2, pp. 71–98.

————. 1994a. *The African Colonial State in Comparative Perspective*. New Haven, CT: Yale University Press.

————. 1994b. "Democratization in Africa: The Contradictions of a Political Imperative." In Jennifer A. Widner, ed. *Economic Change and Political Liberalization in Sub-Saharan Africa*. Baltimore, MD: Johns Hopkins University Press.

————. 2004. "The End of the Post-Colonial State in Africa? Reflections on Changing African Political Dynamics." *African Affairs*, vol. 103, no. 410, pp. 23–49.

Young, Tom. 1993. "Elections and Electoral Politics in Africa." *Africa*, vol. 63, no. 3, pp. 299–312.

Zartman, William I., ed. 1992. *Europe and Africa: The New Phase*. Boulder, CO: Lynne Rienner Publishers.

————. 1995. *Collapsed States: The Disintegration and Restoration of Legitimate Authority*. Boulder, CO: Lynne Rienner Publishers.

Zecchini, Laurent. 2001. "Le Double Langage de l'Afrique." *Le Monde*, Octobre 23.

Zeleza, Paul T. 1994. "Reflections on the Traditions of Authoritarianism and Democracy in African History." *Afrika Zamani*, new series, no. 2, pp. 223–240.

Zimmerman, Ekkart. 1979. "Toward a Causal Model of Military Coups d'État." *Armed Forces and Society*, vol. 5, no. 3 (Spring), pp. 384–413.

Zolberg, Aristide R. 1966. *Creating Political Order: The Party States of West Africa*. Chicago, IL: Rand McNally & Co.

————. 1992. "The Specter of Anarchy: African States Verging on Dissolution." *Dissent*, vol. 39, no. 3, pp. 303–311.

Zunes, Stephen. 1994. "Unarmed Insurrections against Authoritarian Governments in the Third World: A New Kind of Revolution." *Third World Quarterly*, vol. 15, no. 3, pp. 403–426.

Index

Printed in the United States
88272LV00001B/94/A